Rosemary DeCamp
Tigers in My Lap

Rosemary DeCamp

Tigers in My Lap

Midnight Marquee Press, Inc.
Baltimore, Maryland

Copyright ©2000 Rosemary DeCamp

Cover Design: Susan Svehla

Without limiting the rights under copyright reserved above, no part of this publication may be reproduced, stored in or introduced into a retrieval system, or transmitted, in any form, or by any means (electronic, mechanical, photocopying, recording, or otherwise), without the prior written permission of the copyright owners or the publishers of the book.

ISBN 1-887664-42-4
Library of Congress Catalog Card Number 00-192545
Manufactured in the United States of America
First Printing by Midnight Marquee Press, Inc., October 2000

Acknowledgments: Michael Fitzgerald, Photofest, Linda J. Walter

*This book is dedicated
to the memory of
Judge John Ashton Shidler,
my devoted husband of 56 years;
to each of our daughters;
to Michael Fitzgerald,
who believed in this book and
made it happen;
and to my fans,
without whom there would be no book.*

TABLE OF CONTENTS

9	Foreword
11	Introduction
13	Chapter 1: I Lose My Ranch, and an Enemy
16	Chapter 2: First Movie—First Costume
22	Chapter 3: Moving
30	Chapter 4: What Was it Like?
33	Chapter 5: Thief and Queen—1919
38	Chapter 6: Jerome Before it Died
42	Chapter 7: Mills College '28
47	Chapter 8: The DeCamps and Howard Hughes
52	Chapter 9: The Audition
56	Chapter 10: *The Drunkard*
62	Chapter 11: Learning the Ropes
67	Chapter 12: New York, New York
73	Chapter 13: The Engineer
78	Chapter 14: A Lovely Lull
86	Chapter 15: *Cheers for Miss Bishop*
88	Chapter 16: My Host
94	Chapter 17: Tigers in my Lap
103	Chapter 18: Long May it Wave
111	Chapter 19: Mexico to Canada
118	Chapter 20: "A Pearl is a Palace Built to Pain"—Kahlil Gibran

Page	
125	Chapter 21: Universal Before *The Black Tower*
135	Chapter 22: The Waldorf at MGM
139	Chapter 23: The Projectionist's Montage
146	Chapter 24: Johnny Comes Home
151	Chapter 25: Mommy to Many
156	Chapter 26: Lotsa Lives
177	Chapter 27: Living the Life of Riley
183	Chapter 28: Emmy... What a Beautiful Smile!
186	Chapter 29: Bob Cummings—Himself
196	Chapter 30: Harry's Masquerade
204	Chapter 31: Gotta Be Live!
210	Chapter 32: Wind 'em Up!
213	Chapter 33: Karachi to the Khyber to Bengal
225	Chapter 34: Memories of a Mule
231	Chapter 35: The Faces of Marlo
236	Chapter 36: The Kidnapped Rolls Royce
240	Chapter 37: The Pleasure of Your Company
246	Chapter 38: How Do You Like the Movies Now?
249	Chapter 39: Good-Bye and Don't Cry
255	Chapter 40: Ghosts at Warner Bros.
257	Filmography
258	Index

On Moonlight Bay **(1951) with Doris Day**

FOREWORD

Dear Rosemary,

How could I ever forget you!!! You were the second-best mother I ever had and I will never forget those days as long as I live. Did you know, Rosie, that the films we did are the favorites of my fans? They adored those movies and never stop writing and telling me so. What fun we had! I still can't believe that Mary and Gordon have gone to heaven.

Love you a lot,
Marjorie aka Dodo Day

P.S. You'll be happy to know that I named one of my little doggies Wesley Winfield!

Doris Day
July 1998

INTRODUCTION

My mother's face was melting like wax, her mouth in a downturned smile. Her eyes were closed and from somewhere inside her an awful "oh...oh...oh..." tolled the end of my secure world.

I was seven and had seen her sniff and turn away from me before, but it had been a game. My next move was always, "I'm sorry. I won't do it again." Then she would use her handkerchief or put her hands over her eyes. I would offer another olive branch of remorse, and so on, until the drill concluded with a mild sentence or probation.

This was different.

My father, handsome in his officer's cap and uniform, had boarded the train in Phoenix and departed for World War I, leaving my mother and me with no home and little means.

I whispered, "Don't cry, Mom." But she wasn't listening. Then I knew the fear that comes when Authority crumbles—when there is no one left to DECIDE.

That phrase, "Don't cry, Mom" has marked every high or low point in my private world, as well as in my 50-year career as an actor, and that is odd, because it is a sad phrase. Yet my life has been joyful, and lucky, full of mischief and laughter.

Soon after my first experience in films I became a professional Mother-Weeper—cheerful but ready with tears on cue for my lost son Sabu, lashed and chained to a temple in *Jungle Book*, and grew dewy-eyed over my handsome son, Ronald Reagan, in *This is the Army*. I doubt there was much weeping over son James Cagney in *Yankee Doodle Dandy*. We were all too busy dancing and dubbing and trying to match Jimmy's genius. I wept for son Robert Alda, who played Gershwin so well in *Rhapsody in Blue*, although it was because of our director's cruelty. Often he put Robert through 30 takes and then yelled, "Print One. Hold 29!"

Dwayne Hickman was my favorite son for five-and-a-half years on *The Bob Cummings Show*. He gave us few tears, howls of laughter, and minor exasperation.

The daughters for whom I sighed and cried professionally were beautiful and beloved worldwide—Ann Blyth, June Haver, Doris Day, Marlo Thomas, and Shirley Jones.

As the mother of George Gershwin in *Rhapsody in Blue* (1945)

These were a few of my film children. I'll tell you more about them later.

The casting directors saw me as a Reality and Reality became Mother. What is Mother? She is comforting, dependable, loyal (similar to a Boy Scout), and she becomes misty-eyed, or even sobs aloud over her famous son or daughter who is a) in danger, or b) performing magnificently on the stage, or c) in trouble with the kid next door.

But in the Reality of my own life, I was the Child whispering, "Don't cry, Mom" when my mother prayed me back from death in the flu epidemic of 1918, when I was caught stealing in grammar school, when I left home on my wedding night, or finally when my mother wept silently as she lay dying of cancer.

Then we changed places. I became Mother and came home to find our youngest child had crashed through a glass door. I couldn't move, or lift the bloody sheet that covered her until she said, "Don't cry, Mom."

Before the wedding of our third daughter to her childhood friend, confined to a wheelchair, she hugged me and said, "Now, Mom, you're not going to cry."

When our lovely second daughter got her divorce, she kissed me and said, "Don't cry, Mom. Be happy for me."

Then when our first daughter gave birth to our grandson, she laughed and said, "Cut the tears, Mom. He's beautiful!"

All those times and places, and the famous faces fit the same old phrase, which I suppose just means, "Cheer up! I love you."

CHAPTER 1
I LOSE MY RANCH, AND AN ENEMY

Look out! Look out for my house!

Hey you! Stop!

The two big mules were thundering down on my fence—my house—my trees! The man on the wagon was laughing and whipping the mules. He just kept right on coming and made a big turn so his wheels smashed my cabin flat, tore up my fence, and wheeled off in a big cloud of dust toward the barn.

The little log cabin can was squashed tin. My matchstick fences were all gone. My hollyhock lady was just a dead flower and broken toothpicks.

I ran into the house where Auntie Axford was at the window. It was so nice to cry on her softness. She put her arms around me and laid her cheek on my forehead.

"I saw it, dear. That's too bad. He's an ornery old muleskinner. Now don't be sad. We'll make a new ranch tomorrow. I've got a little cracker box for the house..."

"But the log cabin had a chimney and windows!"

"Don't you fret. We'll get another one when we go to town."

Her cheeks were downy. Her eyes swimmy and blue. Best of all I loved her mouth. It was like a rabbit's... always tucked up sweetly... about to smile.

At noon we had a hot meal because Uncle Axford came back from the mill hungry. Today we had my favorite dish... homegrown butter lettuce wilted with hot vinegar, bacon grease and pepper. While I was slurping it up, Auntie was automatically wiping my chin and telling her husband about the teamster and his whirl around her back yard.

Uncle Axford chewed slowly, looking out the dining room window toward the mill. I'd heard my dad say that "Old Ax" could tell what gauge the ore was being ground by the dust that came up from the bins.

He always ate in his underwear and suspenders to keep his shirt fresh for the afternoon shift. When he had chewed a while he said, "That man's mean. He beats his mules for fun, and he don't get along with his road crew. But he'll be gone in a coupla days. They've about got the culvert in down in the gully."

Auntie sniffed, "The Postmistress at Mayer says he's drunk there 'most every night."

"Ax" patted her hand. "Now, Dottie, don't you believe everything you hear on our 10-party line."

Ahhh, so they didn't like him either!

When it got cooler I went over to the chicken house with my basket to gather up the eggs.

The muleskinner's tent was a canvas lean-to by the barn. His wagon and mules were gone so he must have left for town.

I stuck my head through the flaps and was surprised. Everything was so neat: shirts and overalls folded, boots by the bed. His bed had a smooth canvas cover folded over the pillow.

He must have lain down after he made the bed because there was this little round hollow right in the middle of the pillow. When I saw that, I knew what to do.

The hens were almost friendly because Auntie Axford let me get the eggs every day when I visited her. They squawked and beat their wings a lot, but didn't seem to mind me taking all I could reach. Today there were 15.

I circled around back of the barn so no one would see me go in the tent. It was scary. The place smelled funny... leather and canvas and hay... but sour, too. I kept thinking of his mean eyes and the whip he always carried.

But I pulled back the canvas cover. Ugh! The pillow was dirty and greasy... just ticking, no case. I broke three eggs into that little hollow, then laid the canvas back over them very gently. I didn't know what to do with the shells but his boots were right there so I stuffed 'em down in the toes.

Back in the house I put the other eggs in the cooler. I knew I had to tell Auntie, but she was playing the piano. Every afternoon she played the piano. It was pretty, but sad, because she sat so she could see the pictures of her two little girls on the wall above the old upright.

Maybe they had played, too. My mother said they had died of typhoid years ago, but Auntie never mentioned them at all. I wished she would tell me their names and how old they were.

When she was at the piano I didn't talk or move around because it was like she was visiting with them.

Her hands were beautiful even with all the scrubbing and planting she had to do, but some of the skin was white and some of it coffee colored. When I first came she noticed me staring, and said, "Don't worry about my hands. They really are clean. This is just some kind of nervous thing that makes them spotty."

She finished an old song called "Aura Lee," closed her eyes for a moment and then whirled around on the stool and gave me a nice soft hug.

"Where's you been? Your forehead's all wet, and your eyes are too big!"

I felt hot and guilty. "Auntie, I borrowed three eggs. There's still 12 left."

She waited. I looked away.

"Is it a secret?" I nodded. She laughed. "I love surprises. Do you think I'll be surprised?"

She was so dear to me... her eyes shining that way. But if I told her, she might go clean up the mess and spoil my revenge. I sidled out of the room mumbling that she might know tomorrow.

All evening I dodged her eyes, building card houses and playing in her button bag. Finally I went to bed without being told. She felt my head and threatened castor oil if I didn't cheer up.

In the middle of the night there was a lot of shouting, banging, and swearing. I heard Uncle Alex get up and look out the kitchen window. Then we went back into the bedroom. Pretty soon Auntie said, "On no! Don't! He's just drunk." But Uncle was on his way to the door saying, "I've got to be sure he doesn't set fire to anything."

I lay there with my teeth chattering. He'd taken his old shotgun with him! And fire! What if I caused the whole place to burn up? Why had I done it? My dearest friends, and they were coming to harm because of me!

The yelling stopped. Uncle "Ax" was talking. The teamster was arguing. Then everything got quiet. I heard Uncle come back, put out the light and close his door.

I finally fell asleep with bad dreams of mules and giant chickens and eggs that spilled fire.

At breakfast the next morning I mentioned casually that I had been out for a walk and, by the way, the teamster and his rig were gone.

Uncle "Ax" looked at me gravely. Behind his glasses his eyes were bright. "Is that a fact?"

He took a mouthful of hot cakes and then said, "That fellow had some pretty bad luck." After pausing for his wife's reaction, he continued, "Seems one of our hens laid a little omelet in his bed last night. No wonder he packed up 'n left."

Auntie Axford looked startled, and then at me. She smiled and gave a little throaty chuckle. "Land sakes, yes! That's enough to drive any man away!"

I relaxed. They weren't going to beat this subject to death; they would not moan about childish pranks. I was among civilized people. We were adults together.

Hurray! It was a new day and time to build me a bigger and better ranch.

CHAPTER 2
FIRST MOVIE—
FIRST COSTUME

The first movie I ever saw was a part of a serial starring Art Accord. He wore a coonskin cap and his eyes were very light. They weren't exactly crossed but they didn't always look in the same direction. He was brave and wonderful. After that first matinee, I schemed to go as often as possible.

As I was only five years old, it took a lot of persuading. The Lyric, in the little town of Mayer, Arizona, was the only movie house for 50 miles around.

First I had to get someone to take me to Blue Bell Siding, three miles from Dad's mine, the Blue Bell. Then I had to coax my Aunt and Uncle Axford to get out their buckboard and hitch up old Minnie, the horse, dress for town, pack a lunch, and then plod four miles over rough roads to The Lyric.

If we missed the 1:30 p.m. beginning, it was tough to figure out how Art Accord had gotten out of last week's cliffhanger because there was just one show. But never mind, it was heaven to be sitting on Uncle's lap, holding Minnie's reins and clop-clopping toward high adventure with my pale-eyed hero.

Several times I went to a movie at night with my parents. But it was not as much fun for two reasons.

The audiences consisted of grown-ups and were, therefore, taller, so I couldn't see very well. Also, my father invented a form of censorship I found disgusting.

When the hero and heroine became amorous or even just close-up friendly, he would hold his old Stetson hat over my face.

Four generations: My great-grandmother (left), my mother Margaret Elizabeth Hinman (center), Effie Houck my grandmother, and me

So dumb! I was scared someone I knew would see.

Besides, his hat smelled of leather and sweat. It had a little ring of holes in the middle of the crown, but there was no use trying to see through them. If I squirmed too much, or if the picture bored him, he would take me out to the lobby where there was a soda fountain.

I remember looking back at the movie once when he was pulling me up the aisle. I think the star was Mary Miles Minter. The hero had his arms around her, and they were slowly sinking to the ground. Suddenly the scene switched to two flowers bending toward each other. It looked SO PHONY! Even I could see the flowers were pulled by threads.

As those two flowers nuzzled and smooched, Dad grabbed me firmly by the arm and said, "That stuff is not for you."

How right he was. I already knew you had to have bees; and flowers don't kiss each other.

My family background included fragments of legend concerning Guillaume Francoise Dechamps, a red-bearded giant who crossed over from Quebec to Michigan on the Grande Traverse. Years later in Wisconsin, he "Americanized" his name to DeCamp. He married Sadie Campbell, an Irish girl in Bodie, California, when it was a roaring gold camp. Sadie was still so pretty at 90, I suspect she was a dance hall girl—specious logic perhaps, but what was she doing in Bodie? Later, old Red Beard narrowly missed being hanged by the Mexican Bandit, Pancho Villa.

The Hinmans, my mother's people, were bright and progressive: One was a founder of Northwestern University, and another invented the dial telephone. They later had a daughter who became a vice-president of McGraw Hill. Both sides of my family lacked even normal acquisitiveness and willed my brother and me only curiosity and health.

But the dial phone, Northwestern University, and McGraw-Hill were a long way from the Blue Bell Mine, deep in the mountains of Arizona circa 1915.

My father, Val DeCamp, was Superintendent, head man of the mining camp—population 405.

Everything we ate or used came past our front porch on a tram line in big iron buckets. I remember my mother groaning when she'd see the ice go by, dripping out of its gunny sack cover. If it was a 500-pound cake when it left the railroad siding, it would be 50 pounds when we got it. Then it had to be split with the boarding house next door.

The Sears-Roebuck catalogue was our department store. We ordered all our clothing, utensils, bedding, even furniture from it. The goods came by train to the end of the railroad and then over to us on the tram buckets.

When I was six I longed to be an Indian Chief. In the Sears catalogue there was a complete suit and feather war bonnet, "$7.98 prepaid." The picture was

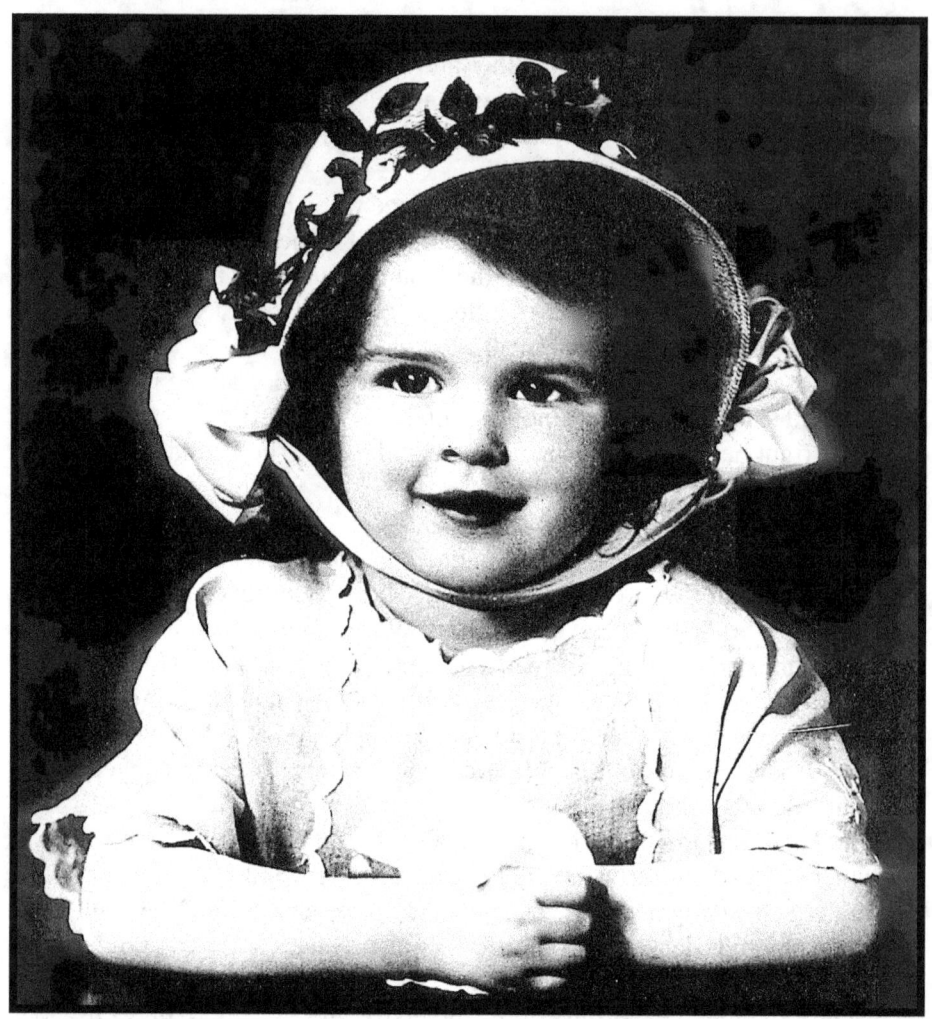

Posing in my bonnet in 1913

beautiful. It looked like the drawings from "Hiawatha." The feathers went around the hat and down the back. Most of the orders were C.O.D., but this costume had to be paid for in advance. They must have feared we'd muss the feathers if we sent it back.

Finally the Indian suit arrived. It was a dream come true, my first costume! The feathers were all colors, and the tacky khaki was embroidered with fake beads. It fit fine, only the pants were long for me; I was short for my age.

As soon as I put it on, I was somebody else. I was a great Chief. A Great Chief in Search of My People!

While mother was absorbed in her packages I skipped out the back door to a trail that led over the mountains away from the tram line. My People wouldn't be near a tram line.

The sun was hot and two or three hours later I felt very lost. Cactus was everywhere, big and little, and under my knees when I stumbled. I had climbed up and down gullies, over rocks, and had seen lizards and snakes and prairie dogs, but none of My People. There didn't seem to be any water, or even any shade. I sat on a rock, too tired to worry about rattlers. The cicadas made a buzzing hum that hurt my head and seemed to bore right into my ears.

When I woke up, there was somebody watching me. It was a real Indian—no feathers. He was sitting on an old white horse. His clothes were beat-up Levis, no shirt, a vest, a necktie, and a greasy black fedora. I looked at him. He smiled, showing brown teeth in a brown face.

"You lost, kid?"

"No... well, a little."

"Yeah... you from the mine. Come on. I take you home."

William "Val" DeCamp in his early 20s, c. 1905

He turned the horse, got off then beckoned to me.

This was embarrassing, but better than stumbling along behind. He put me up on the dirty blanket that covered the horse's back. Then he took the reins and we started for home. I wondered why we couldn't both ride. The horse was very old and bony—maybe it couldn't carry two.

When we arrived at the mine, there had been some concern. In the language of the corral, my mother was "fit to be tied." Dad rewarded the Indian. Mother snatched my suit and hat, all the while wailing and crying, "Don't you ever... ever... ever again!"

It was all really overdone and unfair. After all, I had found My People. No use to make such a flap.

Mother was my only teacher until I was eight, and a good one. At least, she had me reading novels when I was six. After the Indian suit episode, she leaned rather heavily on "What is REAL?" and "What is MAKE BELIEVE?" She was firm about it, and I am grateful, although I must admit I still have philosophical doubts about which is which. I have seen several actresses and actors get caught in the romantic morass of a role, or a series of parts, and never quite make it back to solid ground.

As a mother she gets "A" for not promoting the "Big Santa Claus Myth." She refused to be trapped, and always said, with a twinkle in her electric-blue

My mother, called "JoJo," in her early 20s, c. 1905

eyes, "He is The Spirit of Christmas." She knew that the impact of whatever is read to us in nursery years is greater than we realize. By "we," I mean the reader or readee. My mother seemed to have an inexhaustible supply of Mother Goose, Aesop's Fables and Grimm's Fairy Tales around, and she read well—dramatically.

For me she populated the world with lost children, mysterious forests, and wolves. The Wolf was the big enemy in my fantasies—the one who waylaid Little Red Riding Hood for instance. Also, Aesop had a lot to say about them and none of it good. But the one who was outsmarted by the Third Little Pig made the deepest impression on me. He was so successful and so tricky that only a very diligent and thoughtful little pig could survive. The message was clear: "They are out there. They will GET YOU unless you best them by getting up early, and THINKING AHEAD!"

It took me a lot of years to realize that's why I am not on time, but always EARLY—not optimistic about any project without an uncomfortable amount of planning, and a nag about my appointments and everyone else's.

Mother said these compulsions were inherited from Grandpa DeCamp who packed his lunch and left early just to say "good-bye" at the train station. But I know it's the Wolves out there waiting for me to be late, or make some dumb move.

Meanwhile, another danger lurked for all of us. The day my father got his commission, and orders to report for World War I, any security we had vanished abruptly.

Our phone was a 10-party line, and I can still see his face, young and excited. He jiggled the receiver hook and shouted, "I can't hear! Some of you folks get off the line, will you?? I've got to get this right... Yeah... Phoenix before the 10th... Right... First lieutenant... Engineers... Got it!"

He turned away from the phone, saw my mother's face and wiped his grin. I don't think he had told her he was going. They talked late that night, and once I thought I heard her crying.

It was puzzling. My father was going away but what for? The war didn't mean much to me, except that the Kaiser's picture was on a roll of toilet paper in our bathroom. I knew we were supposed to hate him, which was easy with his spiked helmet and the weird mustache.

Besides, because of him, old mustachio, we were going to have to leave our home, and no one would tell me where we were going.

That paranoid face came back to haunt me years later when I was in Munich in 1930 with a group of students. We attended a dance program called *1918* performed by Martha Graham and her company. They used sirens, gunfire, recorded explosions, and a strange greenish light that wandered over dozens of writhing figures. The ushers wore German helmets and skull masks. I sat through it as long as I could and then stumbled out in the hall, faint and nauseated, feeling gassed by the mustard light. I could smell death in the cordite fumes, but maybe it was a presentiment of horror for the future as well as the past. Munich seemed to be a suppurating sore of war memories—of hate and death, where almost every shop sold tourists the city's official symbol—little silver skulls.

CHAPTER 3
MOVING

We had so few possessions, leaving the Blue Bell Mine just meant putting three boxes in the tram buckets and watching them wing off over the mountains to some vague storage. Our suitcases went into the Oldsmobile, the only thing of value my parents owned.

It was black with a cloth top, yellow wire wheels bracketed by wide running boards. I hated it because I always had to sit in the back behind Mother. Sitting behind Father was out of the question, because he would lean out and spit, and the wind would carry it back to my face. (The wind, indeed! I don't think we averaged 20 miles an hour as the roads were rutty paths, the tires were bicycle size and hard as rocks.)

My father was impatient with any signs of illness. Mother and I were constantly car-sick, and so was our old Pit bulldog, named Beefeater. When we had to stop, and "urp," Mother would hold my head when she was through, then I would hold Beefeater's head while Dad marched up and down muttering. Then he would swing into the driver's seat and squeeze the big rubber horn.

But this ride was quiet. Dad concealed his happy anticipation of army life, while Mother used her handkerchief a lot, and was silent.

She always managed to shed a few tears for each scruffy boarding house, or company cabin, we left. I don't remember having any regrets. We always moved. We had no home. Packing and moving was usual, though this time I knew that Mother was not only sad, but worried. I had heard them talking about "the savings" and selling the car in Phoenix, so this departure was different. It was more final.

When we reached the Blue Bell Siding, Aunt and Uncle Axford were dressed up, and standing on their little wooden porch—a solemn sign, because it was nine in the morning and "Ax" belonged at the mill.

I climbed over the side and ran to Auntie's loving softness. She smelled of lemon verbena, and her eyes were pink from crying. But she laughed and said, "Come on in! I made cinnamon rolls. You've got to stop a minute!"

Dad finally got out of the car and followed Mother. Uncle "Ax" looked at Dad and didn't say much. Maybe he was afraid the owners would not keep him on to run the mill, with Dad gone, or that the mill would close down.

While we wolfed the hot rolls and sweet butter, Auntie Axford pressed a little tissue-wrapped locket into my hand. Then I knew it was "good-bye." It had belonged to her youngest daughter, the one who had died first.

In the dark old parlor, I looked at the girl's picture over the piano, and there was the locket at the little one's throat. Auntie stood in the doorway, a silhouette; a dear, surrogate mother. I wanted to hear her play so much she must have sensed it, because she came toward the old upright and pulled out the stool and swirled it around.

Then Father yelled, "Come on! We're late. Gotta go!" I kissed Auntie quickly and ran.

As we drove off I looked back through the isinglass window in our car. The Axfords were standing like two dolls on their porch growing smaller and smaller until they were hidden by the dust we made.

Beefeater kept licking the tears off my face but I pushed him away and unwrapped my little locket. It was pretty and round with pink flowers on a blue ground. The clasp wouldn't open so I held it in my pocket, warm and comforting, and smelling faintly of lemon verbena.

When we got to Prescott Dad said, "We'll go to the drug store and grab a sandwich. You order for me. I've got to see a man about something."

Mother and I sat down in those funny, curly ice-cream chairs. I could look out the window and was surprised to see Dad taking Beefeater out of the car on a leash. I wondered why—then the lady came to take our order.

When Father came back he was alone. He patted me on the shoulder and said, "Honey, I left that old bulldog with a friend. We couldn't take him where we're going. He's too big and he eats too much."

My throat choked up so I couldn't drink my milkshake. But there wasn't any use making a fuss. Mother was dabbing her eyes and Dad looked grim. Everything was just awful—especially the rest of the day. We drove for hours through the desert to Phoenix and I was lonesome in the backseat without my big slobbering friend.

When we reached Phoenix we drove to a place Mother called "The Governor's Mansion." It was just a big house with lots of cool lawn and trees around it. Mother's best friend was Mrs. Campbell, the Governor's wife.

We stayed there for two happy weeks.

At least it was a happy time for me because I found a new and fabulous companion. His name was Jansen. He was the only certified lunatic I've known and I adored him. He was magic. In the daytime he wore a big blue smock, ballet slippers, and a pointed yellow straw hat. He didn't walk, he skipped. He was gardener, dishwasher, and after dark, "The Butler."

He had come from the state insane asylum one day, carrying a plaster statue of the Holy Mother, knelt at the Campbells' door, and prayed that "the

Governor's Lady" would accept him as her "slave." Mrs. Campbell had a wry sense of humor and no staff to care for the mansion and grounds, so she offered him "temporary quarters." By the time we visited them he must have been there three lively years.

He was fey and gay—in the old as well as the modern sense. His silver curls whirled up into a candy kiss, and only his eyes betrayed the phantoms lurking behind. The pupils were shattered Rorschach blots which changed shape in the sun. I knew about his pupils first hand, because Jansen had taught me to play "Owl-y." You kneel, facing your partner, touch foreheads, match noses, close your eyes, yell "Owl-y!" and open your eyes wide. It's a game best played with someone you like, because when you open your eyes you are almost inside your partner's head.

He was a dramatic friend. Of course I had only Beefeater and Auntie Axford to measure him by. But he always had time for me—time to dance with butterflies—to build flower dolls—to skip rope—roll on the grass or to make up songs.

The adults, I noticed, were not as enthusiastic about Jansen. This was evident the night my father had to catch his train to Camp Humphrey, New Jersey. We all sat around the fireplace in the living room. The floors were waxed and reflected the fire in the polished brass grate. There was a scarlet rug, and everyone was all dressed up. Dad looked tall and handsome in his uniform. I sat on the floor leaning against his knees, wondering how long he would be gone but afraid to ask, because when I asked questions everyone's face changed.

The governor said, "This fire's not going to last. Let's have Jansen bring in some coal." Mrs. Campbell went into the dining room and murmured a few words and returned. Time passed. The fire flickered. Dad fidgeted. The silence lengthened, then suddenly my friend whirled through the kitchen door in his ballet slippers, a red cummerbund, and ruffled shirt, carrying a silver salver high, on which were three lumps of coal. He knelt and in absolute silence placed the coal with ice tongs, a lump at a time, on the fire. Rising, he bowed low and skipped from the room.

I thought the whole act had a lot of style and that they were rude to laugh. They must have been nervous because the stifled whinnies and giggles went on until it was time to take Dad to the depot.

That night I woke up and my mother was crying. The light was on and I had never seen her face like that—all torn up and ugly.

"Mom, Mom!" I touched her shoulder but she didn't hear me, "Please don't cry."

She wouldn't answer. I knew she was worried about my father, but there was more. We had no home and very little money. I put my arms around her and she stopped shaking. We fell asleep with the light on. I dreamed of riding in a car for hours and hours with no one driving—no one behind the wheel.

The next morning I heard her tell Mrs. Campbell that we were going to Los Angeles to stay with some friends. She seemed so cheerful and self-assured I wondered if I'd imagined the night before.

Jansen was tippy-toeing around in the background. Surely he would be devastated at my departure. He beckoned to me to meet him in the kitchen where he whispered, "You're going to Los Angeles! You lucky child! That's where they make movies. You will meet the stars and see all the wonders of the motion picture world!"

He didn't seem to be sad at all—just twinkling and chuckling so happily I wondered if he planned to go with us. Reaching in his smock pocket he took out a little square of pasteboard. "Now I am going to give you my picture of Viola Dana, the loveliest star of all. She sent it to me personally. When you meet her you must tell her about me and give her my love!"

The face on the little card was blurry—probably kissed into oblivion—but the printing was clear, "Good wishes from Viola Dana."

He hugged me. There was a flurry of "thank yous" and packing, until we left on the train bound for California.

The night on the train was dreamy. We had a lower berth with little frosted lights and a green net hammock I wanted to sleep in, but Mother said that was for our shoes and clothes. She propped me up on a fat pillow so I could look out the window. There was nothing to see but mountains and cactus going by in the moonlight. The sound of the wheels on the rails was lulling, "Chucketa, chucketa, chug," then over a cattle guard "Kawonk, kawonk" and back to "Chucketa, chucketa" with once in a while a lonesome "Whooooo, whoooo" on the curves.

In the morning it was foggy with the San Bernardino smell of orange blossoms and celery and wet earth. After the dry heat of Arizona, California was moist balm for the skin and spirit. It all seemed vaguely familiar to me. Mother explained that we had been to California before when I was three. The people we were going to visit, Mr. and Mrs. Alex Mills, were old friends from Huntington Beach.

"Grandma" Mills claimed she had found me in a sandcastle on the beach. She was a homely little lady with a tart tongue and great authority. She and her aristocratic husband, "Daddy Mills," lived in a rambling old house near Westlake Park. They had two grown daughters who were to become lifelong friends.

I wondered about "the movies." Westlake Park seemed a long way from Jansen's world of stars.

Oddly enough it wasn't so far from a darker side of that world.

On a warm, sweet-smelling day in Los Angeles, I was sitting up in a fig tree looking over six or seven back yards, where the flowers were thick and rainbow-colored: big dinner-plate dahlias, roses, hollyhocks, and cerise bougainvillea. The orange trees had orange blossoms and oranges on them at the same time.

My tree had sweet purple figs and I had eaten too many. The ants were getting even by crawling on my sticky hands.

The kid next door was about my age, a scrawny seven or eight, with big dark eyes. But she was snooty—or else shy. Today she sat in an old porch-swing with her back to me.

She knew I was there, though, because I had yelled at some bees flying around the figs.

Finally I said in a loud voice, "Hmmmmm... Well, I guess I better get down."

She stopped swinging and looked around. I gave a kind of half-wave which I could pretend was for the bees if she didn't respond.

She walked over to the fence and looked up at me.

I was very offhand, "Want some figs? Come on up."

Then I really got a surprise. Her face cracked into a big grin. She jumped the fence, grabbed a limb of the fig tree, and swung onto a branch beside me so fast it took my breath away.

"Bet you can't do that."

"No... I guess I can't."

She looked off into space and bit into a fig.

"I used to be with the circus."

I was dazzled. She was so young—and little. Less than my size.

She gave me a cool Gypsy stare. "My family's in pictures now."

"Pictures?"

Her lip curled. "The movies, kid. Where're you from?"

She was too much! The circus. Now movies. Boy, was I a hick!

I got my voice back. "You mean... you are in the movies?"

She was world-weary. "Not yet. But I will be."

"Who is in the movies? I mean at your house?"

For a moment her face was grim. Then she grabbed another fig and said nonchalantly, "My sister. She's a stunt girl."

A stunt girl. What was that? My ignorance was so vast I didn't know what to ask, how least to risk her scorn.

I settled for, "I sure would like to see her."

She shook her head. "No... I tell you what, I'll get some of her 'stills.' Wait right here."

She did some kind of quick flip and was running up her own porch steps.

What were stills? And why couldn't she have asked me over to her house, the way we did at home?

Her porch door banged and she was back with a large envelope, scrootching down beside me, not even out of breath. "Now we have to be very careful of these. Don't get any muck on 'em. And we mustn't bend 'em."

She took out a big glossy black-and-white picture of the most beautiful human being I had ever seen. It was a portrait of a young woman.

The face was misty white, eyes big and dark, with lots of eyelashes. She seemed delicate but strong, like a marble statue. There was a lot of fluffy tulle around her shoulders. The eyes were looking right at me, ready to smile.

"Pretty, huh? That's Rosa."

I just kept looking into those eyes.

"Hey! Don't get it sticky. Here's the other one."

This one was different. She was on top of a train and seemed to be about to jump down. Her body was tense, her eyes glowered. She must have been joking with whoever was taking the picture, because her smile was wide and mischievous. Her arms were up, a coat flung out and the wind blowing against her silk dress molded the lovely body and long legs.

I knew it was time to say something, but I couldn't stop staring. My friend was chewing and spitting out fig skins.

"Y'see, these here are what they call 'stills.' All actors have 'em to get jobs. She's about to do a stunt... gonna jump off a moving train. She can do all kinds of stunts. Jump off buildings, drive over cliffs, fall off horses. She used to be in the circus. She taught me a lot of swings and loops and stuff on the high wire, when I was real little. But then... we quit the circus 'cause somebody discovered her."

My friend looked sideways at me to see if I was getting all this.

I closed my mouth and nodded, not having any idea what "discovered" meant.

A voice from behind her screen door called, "Lena!"

She wiped her hands on her skirt and carefully put the pictures back in the envelope. "Gotta go. See ya tomorrow." She was over the fence, up her back steps and out of sight.

I tried to talk to Grandma Mills about our glamorous neighbors, but she was peeling peaches for dinner and in no mood for gossip. At dinner I waited for grace to be said, Father Mills' assessment of the stock market, Aunt Nita's "How naughty-my-pupils-were-today" story, until finally everyone took a mouthful of food at the same time. Then I plunged:

"Uh...I met the girl next door today. Did you know her sister Rosa's in the movies?"

Grandma Mills sniffed. "Not any more. That poor thing lies up there in a dark room with a crushed spine."

Aunt Nita glanced over at me, and then whispered, "Mother, don't!"

But Grandma Mills went right on, "Well, they've had to cut off one leg already. I doubt she'll ever get downstairs again."

My throat closed. I couldn't swallow, or excuse myself. Those beautiful long legs... that laughing face...

I left the table just in time.

It was several days before I saw Lena again. She came over to the fence one morning when I was picking snails off the dahlias. She was so quiet I was startled and shouted, "Hi! Where've you...?" She whispered, "Don't make any noise. Rosa's very sick. The doctor's there now. I can't play. I have to do dishes. I'll see you tomorrow."

But I didn't see her the next day. The house next door was dark and quiet in the daytime. At night there were lights at all hours. Out front, people were coming and going in carriages and motor cars.

Two days later Lena called to me from the fence. Her eyes were big and sad. "Rosa died. The funeral's this afternoon. You oughta see the flowers the studio sent!"

I couldn't find any words. I just stood there, dumb.

Lena turned and walked toward her back door. I noticed she was all dressed up in white lace with shiny black shoes. She looked different. Older. Maybe because she moved slowly.

The next day my mother came to take me with her. Just before we left, I ran out and climbed up in the fig tree to look at Lena's house. There were no signs of life. The curtains were drawn, no smoke came from the kitchen chimney. I whistled. Pretty soon her back door opened and I waved. She came hurtling over the fence and swung up into the tree.

"Lena, I've got to go with my mother. But I'll be back."

She gave me the faraway Gypsy stare.

"I'm sorry about Rosa."

She turned her head and didn't say anything.

"What happened to her?"

Her back was to me now. She threw a fig at a cat in the next yard. "She died. She just died."

"But I mean before.. How did she get hurt?"

Lena's face was hard. I thought she wasn't going to answer. Then the words tumbled out like sobs. "She... she had to jump from a big building... supposed to be on fire. The first time they did it, it was all right. The rehearsal, you know. Then when they lit the fire... I guess it scared her. She jumped, but... they didn't catch her right."

I waited, but she didn't say any more.

My mother called me from the house. I put my hand on Lena's shoulder. She didn't move, so I climbed down. When I looked back, she was still sitting all hunched up in the tree.

That was the last time I saw her except in my mind. Later, when we returned, her house was all closed up. Grandpa Mills said they had moved.

Many years afterwards when I was sitting on the Screen Actors Guild Board, it all came back, clear and sharp.

One of the stunt men was urging a wage raise for his group. He said something like, "Hell! You oughta see our insurance rates. And most of the time we can't get any. Who wants to bet on the life of a guy jumping out of a burning building?"

We voted for the raise. But I remembered Rosa and thought, "It's never enough."

CHAPTER 4
WHAT WAS IT LIKE?

The Mills Family and my mother held one of those exclusive board meetings to which no minor is ever invited, and decided I must enter a girls' private boarding school. They helped mother enroll in a secretarial school on Flower Street, in downtown Los Angeles, and she found a one-room apartment across the street.

It was time to stop visiting friends, and step out in the world. Mother had been a pianist and music teacher, so I suppose she planned to transfer her digital competence to the typewriter and earn us a living.

This all sounded very practical and wise, except that I was paralyzed with fear. What did I know of other children? What did I know of classes, or manners, or all those other things I knew would be forced upon me? I had never been in a schoolroom in my life. I had never played with a child my own age.

My school was on West Adams—a vast old house with "day" and boarding pupils from five years to 12. The first night at dinner my social fate was sealed.

I sat next to the headmistress, a bony lady with too much smile. There was cocoa and toast and not much else. Feeling sorry for this meager outlay, I was determined to put them at ease. I seized a piece of toast and said, "Oh, toast! Mother says 'Toast is good for kids...'"

There was silence for a few moments and then snickers down the long table. The head said condescendingly, "I'm glad you like it. We don't say 'kids' here, unless we are speaking of baby goats."

From then on I was Baby Goat and lacked any friends except the motherly cook, who often took me to her room to show me pictures of her home and all her relatives in Austria.

It was a bleak time for us. My school work was all right. They put me in the third grade where I could do neat sums. But after the books Mother had allowed me to read, the reading material was asinine. It was a kind of neo-Mother Goose, so I looked out the window and dreamed of freedom, which came rather suddenly one spring day.

At 10 o'clock, during recess, everyone got a slice of brown bread smeared with applesauce. And we had better eat it. Our brave soldiers were fighting and lacked anything this delicious, so eat it up, every crumb! This logic, like the "starving Armenians," was patently false, but by now I had learned to shut up and question nothing.

All of a sudden my head felt burning hot and the grass went round and round. When I fell, my face went flat in the applesauce. I couldn't move.

It was 1918 and the influenza epidemic hurt almost everyone to some degree. I was taken to my mother's apartment. No hospital beds were available, and we couldn't have afforded one anyway. Mother had paid my school tuition, as well as her own, and then taken a year's lease on her tiny one-room-and-kitchen apartment. There must have been very little left to live on.

For me, time was a dream, and fever the illusion of Time and Space reversed. Space ticked off hours, while Time enveloped me in spider's silk.

I had double pneumonia with a high temperature and I can recall only snatches of those weeks. Mother found an elderly doctor nearby. I don't remember seeing his face; I only remember hearing a far off, mumbling voice.

One day Mother said she felt her "little eight-year-old was slipping away." (Her generation loved phrases like that.) She called the doctor to tell him, but the nurse who answered the phone was crying. She said the doctor had died that morning.

Somehow, with prayer and a lot of will power, Mother dragged me back to life. When I became conscious, our little room seemed surprisingly dark. I had been a long way from there, where there was light and endless space. There were times when I would wake up and my mother would be kneeling by my bed fast asleep, her face and hair wet with tears. She remembered that I touched her face and said, "Don't cry, Mom. I'm all right." That may not have been true, but that's the way she always told it. The residue of her story stayed with me the rest of my life—the conviction that prayer can be stronger than death.

Later, when I could sit up, she would look searchingly at me and ask all kinds of questions, principally, "What was it like?" and "What did you see?" I wasn't sure what she meant, but I tried to oblige with some Sunday School fantasies. All I really remembered was light and sound—sound that wasn't exactly music, just pleasant.

Mother enjoyed telling me I was "different now"—probably because she was lonely. She HAD pulled me through a serious illness; also it was more dramatic to believe that I had died, and come back. Maybe she hoped for a docile, "color-it-Angel" type of behavior. Whatever the basis, it was ego-sauce for an id that was already bigger than both of us.

I began to think of myself as "precious," with a kind of spiritual antenna which could pick up extra-sensory data. This must have been sticky at age eight.

Nevertheless, I have a kind of "borrowed time" optimism and I still have days when I know what people will say before they say it. I have attacks of prescience that precede disasters, that tell me what card will be drawn, how to find lost articles, and—something very valuable in raising the young—tells me who did it.

I also believe that every human has potentially the same insights, and that it is simply a discipline of concentration, having nothing to do with "coming back."

As for death, no one in all of literature has summed it up quite as well as Woody Allen who said, "I'm not afraid to die. I just don't want to be there when it happens."

Fortunately for us, as well as the whole world, the war ended and we were on our way to meet Dad in New York.

CHAPTER 5
THIEF AND QUEEN–1919

The spring day when New York's own 49th Division came home from France was cloudless and warm.

We were hurrying along Riverside Drive bound for Fifth Avenue and Washington Square, where the big parade was starting. My mother and father were arguing furiously, which was usual. She looked beautiful to me. Her red hair was glinty and soft. She wore a black satin suit piped in pale green that she had just finished sewing. Dad had on a suit instead of his uniform. I was out of breath because his stride was two-and-a-half times as long as mine. Mom was five paces ahead, hurling jibes at Dad over her shoulder.

Suddenly she stopped and yelled, "Get over by the bushes! I'm going to try something."

My dad was so surprised he obeyed, and we stopped in the shade, panting. My mother, slim and elegant, waved her little gloved hand at a passing car. I was amazed. Did she know those people? I guessed not, because they sailed on by.

Then a big, shiny touring car pulled up at the curb. The driver was a handsome, sporty fellow who smiled at Mom and leaned over to open the door. She turned and beckoned to us. Quick as a wink we were sitting on the red leather seats in back, and she was sitting up in front beside the driver. My dad began to laugh and even our chauffeur smiled grudgingly, and off we went on our way to Washington Square.

That was the first time I ever saw anyone hitchhike. No one explained anything, but inside I had a feeling that something was not quite right about it.

The day of that parade New York went mad. After all, "the 49th" had practically won the war, hadn't it? For the first time in history American troops were returning from a war on European soil, and in that year-and-a-half-long bloodbath they had been victorious. We had not yet learned that no one wins.

Dad held me up on his shoulders, with one arm around a lamp post. The crowd was suffocating to me. Women screamed and pushed. Men yelled and cheered at the troops. One man was swept off a ledge of a building and was trampled by the crowd. I remember a sea of hats and helmets, with torn paper sifting down on them like snow. And over it all, the military drums and the rhythmic pounding of the soldiers' marching feet made a frightening roar.

As I look back on it, I wonder, why did we go to watch that parade? Dad had just gotten out of the army. Perhaps he was grateful for what "the 49th" had done, and at the same time felt guilty because he had never left Camp Humphreys in New Jersey.

In those days we were living in a rented house in an artists' and professors' colony on the New Jersey Palisades. It was a lovely, secret place, where violets and lady's slippers grew in the shadow of oak and birch trees. My father was elated that he could cut his own firewood in sight of Grant's Tomb and the 12th Street ferry.

Mother and Dad were both enrolled at Columbia University. He was a graduate engineer from Golden, Colorado, working on an aqueduct project to bring water to New York City. What mother studied at Columbia is a mystery. She hated housework and loved the city for its concerts, opera, and art galleries. So any course was an excellent excuse.

I was alone a great deal, but being an only child at that time, I was accustomed to loneliness. When we had lived out West, my parents were often away on trips and I had been left with a series of neighbors—"Aunties" and "Uncles" who were unfailingly kind and courteous. Unlike my parents, they LISTENED to me from infancy onward—a rare treat for any child, I now realize. Perhaps this attention gave me an exaggerated sense of the importance of my thoughts. But never mind, it was combat pay for loneliness.

Now in New Jersey, things were very different. The neighbors were polite, but busy. No Western "open house," no "stay with us" policy. They were teachers and artists with few, if any, children, and they regarded my nine-year-old chatter with impatience or suspicion.

Then there was the rather sticky question of my education. Except for the time when we lived in Los Angeles and I had attended a girls' boarding school for a few days before I got so ill, I had never had any regular schooling because we lived in remote mining camps and moved so often. I never had more than a few months with a local teacher. Mother had taught me to read before I was five, then opened up the world of books for me and allowed me to explore. Aside from funny papers, she imposed no censorship, nor did she add very much in supplementary discussion.

I could escape into sets of Kipling or Conan Doyle on the dusty shelves of our various "company" houses, but I had no drill in arithmetic, or even the alphabet. To this day, when looking up words in the dictionary or telephone I have to recite the ABCs.

Being an early riser, I learned to take long walks before anyone was up to forbid it. The Hudson River was wide and mysterious, our small forest misty with fog and perfumed with sweet earthy smells. As I wandered past the little homes tucked away on that lovely hillside, I noticed milk bottles on every doorstep. How pleasant to pinch off the cardboard caps and skim the cream from the top. ("Homogenized" came later.) Moving from one refreshment to another, I pretended I was a cat, licking the rich, cold cream.

Of course, the complaints surfaced, then multiplied, and united. One elderly artist (probably elected by the group), set his trap by asking the milkman to wake him. Then he sat by his kitchen window to catch the thirsty thief. I remember him waving at me—the traitor! He didn't have the heart to confront me personally, but simply reported to my father. Maybe if he had jumped out and yelled, I would have been deterred from continuing my criminal career.

After the cream burglaries, I was enrolled in the Edgewater Grammar School. Since my vocabulary was drawn from Kipling, Washington Irving, and even Nathaniel Hawthorne, I was the darling of the teachers—but not the other pupils. They avoided me, knowing I was not one of them, nor likely to be.

So I was lonelier than ever. Being lonely when alone is less painful than being lonely in a crowd. A child can bear anything except rejection, and I was rejected as I walked to school alone, recessed alone, and worst of all, ate out of my lunch sack, alone.

There was a tiny candy shop a block from school. Inside, a Dutch woman weighed out gumdrops, licorice, mints, candy corn, and little red-hots by the ounce, for a few pennies. My classmates would hang around outside, staring in the window, or drool over the tantalizing displays in the glass cases inside. But this was a poor factory town and children didn't have many pennies to spend.

It occurred to me that here was the solution to my solitude. Bring money. Buy treats. Then they would love me. For a nine-year-old it was not cynicism, just practicality.

Asking for money would require admitting my need. I don't remember analyzing it that way. But now I am certain, no one—least of all a child—could say aloud, "I need friends and recognition. Give me money, so I can buy them."

I didn't ask. The old Early Riser just went through Dad's pockets and Mom's purse.

Now, each day I would casually invite a few friends to "pick out something you'd like" at the candy store. This was amazingly successful. I became the Pied Piper. I no longer ate alone. There were plenty of pals to walk me home, carry my books, and praise my clothes.

It went even further. The election of King and Queen of Edgewater Grammar School was imminent. This splendid melding of monarchy and democracy enthroned the boy and girl. who received the most votes.

I was hard put to get cash for the sweet teeth of those three other grades, as well as my own class, but I managed—progressing from filched change to palmed paper money.

I was duly elected, along with a little Italian boy whose father was grand mucky-muck of a local lodge. He had promised crowns, scepters, and robes for the occasion. So, in a way, we both "bought in" for the throne.

It may have been a good investment for my consort; for me, it was a disaster.

On the day of the coronation I was confronted by both my father and mother and declared "a thief!" I can still see my mother weeping over my fake ermine train that she had made by hand—I wanted to say "Don't cry, Mom—You're wrecking my costume" but it didn't seem appropriate. My father paced up and down and swore. I cried. We all cried. But it was too late, even for remorse and repentance. The crowning was only an hour away.

My shame had faded by the time I marched up the aisle wearing a huge, red velvet crown with glass "rubies." My king sported a green plush crown with golden spikes. We were a couple of handsome midgets, and I forgot all my problems as the squeals and applause followed us up to our cardboard thrones.

The bill for this was presented immediately. First of all, my real Aunt Doris moved in "to keep an eye on me," which she did with skill and imagination, knowing me to be a Gypsy and a thief. But, second and worse, I got LICE from my fancy crown! Lots of lice, of a species immune to tweezers, vinegar, or kerosene.

A week later, the ex-queen went to school with a shaved head, bankrupt, with no money for the votes I had received, and no more freedom walks in the forest.

But all tragedy abates. My hair grew out. My aunt got married, and we moved again, as we had so many times before.

The next stop was a scruffy little smelter town in Arizona called Humboldt. Since Dad was a mining man—and "smelter men" are to "mining men" what sheep men are to cattlemen (natural enemies)—his job must have been a postwar stopgap.

We moved into a "company house" on the edge of town (population 850). There was a lovely old cottonwood tree in the yard where I could hide high up in its branches and ignore all chore calls.

Some doctor had told mother I had a heart murmur as a result of the flu, so I was supposed to walk sedately a quarter mile to the village school. But every day, as soon as I was out of Mother's sight, I ran like the wind. In view of some of the medical advice we now hear about running, it is possible I strengthened my heart for a long life ahead.

Most of the places I knew as a child are associated with pets I had, or longed for. Dad, guessing I suppose that each home was temporary, refused to spring for another dog. In Humboldt he bought me a rabbit—a Belgian hare. We taught him how to hop up and down the piano keys. Since each hop was an approximate octave he accomplished some pleasant runs and trills, with the turn-around a surprising accent. We called him Feet of Melody. He didn't last long but burrowed under his wire cage to join a crowd of delinquent jack rabbits, who had hung around eyeing him, or possibly her, with predatory eyes.

One day I embraced a big shaggy dog in front of the post office. He bit me right through my upper lip making a small window, which healed in a surprisingly short time, leaving a tiny scar that in no way diminished my affection for stray dogs.

There was no flap about rabies or shots. Everyone in town knew the dog and felt that I had invaded his privacy. The doctor who treated me suggested I give up hugging strange dogs.

Dad's next offer was for a "boss job" at the United Verde Copper Mine in Jerome. Once more we packed all our belongings for the almost-annual move. This time they barely fit into an ancient Haynes touring car that Dad had bought third or fourth hand. We made the 50-mile journey over the mountains to a mining camp that has since become a famous ghost town.

CHAPTER 6
JEROME BEFORE IT DIED

Jerome, Arizona, was named for the Indian warrior, Geronimo, or for the millionaire mine investor, Jerome. Take your choice.

The years we spent there remain in my memory as a mosaic of poverty, mine disasters, fires, picnics, wildly beautiful scenery, ugly houses, and strong, willful people.

There were rows instead of streets. You lived on First Row, Second Row, Top Row, or down on The Hogback. There were shaky, wooden sidewalks between rows. Children were NEVER to throw rocks. The town clung to the side of a steep mountain at the "angle of repose." It was obvious that a few rolling rocks could trigger a slide.

A long wooden sidewalk angled up to the mine, its tunnel entrance burrowed into the side of the next mountain. When the men came off shift, you could hear their boots thumping down those knotty old boards.

If there was an accident in the mine, the men would carry the victims down the hill on stretchers. I remember my mother's face—listening. When they were burdened, the rhythm of their footsteps was different, regular and ominous.

The mine, United Verde Copper, had been on fire for 25 years. The consequent build-up of gas resulted in explosions that caused slopes and tunnels to collapse. Dad was Underground Superintendent for several years. When there was trouble, he had to go down and assess the damage, and rescue the victims.

His men loved him because he would never send anyone else in ahead. He would laugh and say, "I'm the boss. I gotta go 'cause you bohunks wouldn't know what to do when you got there."

But they knew that he suffered more than they when some poor "mucker" was buried or half smothered in a cave-in. They also knew how dangerous it was to be the first one in.

There were days when he would rage around the house, drink too much, and look right through me when I spoke to him. Those were the days after a tragedy when he had failed to save some miner who had been with him a long time, and whose family he knew would be destitute.

His anger and despair at the frequent loss of life in the United Verde Mine motivated the single biggest engineering project of his life. A year or so after he became General Superintendent, he decided to end the long years of the fire by taking the top off the mountain that covered it. There were many experts on that operation, but Val DeCamp was the moving force. The excavation was so vast he must have known he was putting his reputation on the line.

Actually, it almost destroyed him, but I think he would have gone ahead, even if he had foreseen how frustrating and cruel both the circumstances and the mine owners were to be.

Moving the mountain was a great affirmative act, one involving thousands of people. The final hole was bigger and deeper than the big Culebra Cut of the Panama Canal. The dirt from the excavation of the mountain was dumped and packed nearby into a baseball diamond.

Dad recruited dozens of bright young engineers from Yale, Carnegie Tech, Michigan, and Golden, Colorado, to work on this project. He tried to choose men who were athletes as well as mining experts. So Jerome in its palmiest days had a champion basketball team and Arizona's leading baseball club.

My brother Jerry in 1930

It also had Tom Mix, who came out to Jerome almost every year. The whole camp was excited when Tom and his company arrived. He always had a big open touring car, brand new and shiny. He would have a new wife, too. Or at least she looked new because her hair was a different color each time. The car was white or yellow, and Tom wore white buckskin suits and a 10-gallon white Stetson hat. I think he was part Indian, and that white really set off his dark skin and black eyes.

They would zip around our mountain roads, dash over to Oak Creek Canyon, or back to Prescott where he kept his horse, Tony, and where the rest of the movie company stayed.

One year Harry Carey came to Jerome and made a picture called *East is East* about a tenderfoot Easterner trying to make it in old Arizona. Everyone in the town felt involved because they used some of the mining camp people in the crowd scenes.

One night my folks bundled me up and took me down to the old mine shaft where the company was shooting. I was pretty young and sleepy, but I'll never forget the dazzling white lights shining down on the leading lady.

She was sitting on a pile of rocks by the mouth of a tunnel. At first I thought she must be an Indian because of all the paint on her face, white and black, and her eyes were rimmed all around with blue. Her mouth was dark red. Her hair was pretty though, kind of fuzzy-blonde and long.

The best part was the accordion music. They had a fellow there playing Gypsy songs. It sounded so lovely in the warm night. My mother explained that the actress had to cry and the music was supposed to bring tears. Well, sure enough, as soon as the camera started grinding, that girl's eyes ran rivulets. Some of the paint ran, too. Then they would stop and mop her face, paint it some more, and do it all again. I finally fell asleep, but years later when I had to weep in front of the camera, I wished for that Gypsy music.

The best part of the Harry Carey episode was the "takeoff" my dad and some of the mine executives put together. It was called "Yeast is Yeast" and was all about a moon shiner and his daughter being chased by the "revenooers." I don't know how it got filmed and processed, but the result was weird. It was all black and white, no grays, and very jerky. My mother said it made her seasick to look at it... kind of like some of the "hand held" jobs we see today.

That was the first "home movie" I ever saw. Unfortunately, it was not the last.

Most of the whirl of activity was around my parents. My own life was separate; not quite that of a mining camp child, because my father was "super"—a boss. But my mother never referred to our status, or allowed me to feel superior. Row 1 and Row 2 played Run-Sheep-Run until twilight through spring and summer. We walked to school and to Sunday school together.

There were two churches on the long diagonal sidewalk. The old Episcopal Church was just below the end of our Row. The brick Catholic Church was right under our front window, about 100 feet away.

I had a perpetual cold during those years, which was later diagnosed as tuberculosis, so I spent a lot of time on that window seat observing the entrance to the Catholic Church. All the meaningful life of Jerome seemed to be centered there: christenings, confirmations, funerals, weddings. It was rather like watching television today, looking down on that busy Catholic doorway. For a child watching alone, it made an indelible picture.

One day I witnessed a jealous woman stab the best man at a wedding as the guests crowded out the narrow door. She killed the wrong man. Her intended victim, the groom, went off with his bride. The woman was left with the police, and the priest giving last rites to the dying boy. Those figures standing calmly by the body, the priest brushing off his robes as he stood up to join the discussion, held a horrible matter-of-factness that never left my memory.

Years later, in a summer course at USC, I wrote a play about that doorway. It was a fair one-act titled *Conchita*. We produced it at USC and later it was published in one of Frederick Koche's anthologies of folk drama.

In 1930, a bad accident triggered the downhill slide of our family fortunes, as well as those of the United Verde Mine.

At night, the big open pit where the fire was being uncovered looked like Dante's Inferno. The levels on which dozens of steam shovels worked wound around and around, and downward thousands of feet to the lowest levels of the mine. The steam from the shovels, and the smoke from the burning sulfides below were turned orange by great searchlights. The operators maneuvered their machines on wide roadways, but one night a driver was drunk or asleep. He drove his steam shovel over the ledge. It rolled all the way to the bottom, taking tons of earth, and several other workers, with him. My father, as Superintendent, had to take full responsibility.

About this time the assay returns on the copper ore went down, so that it cost more to mine and smelt what ore was available. The price of copper was falling, which meant fewer and fewer dividends for stockholders.

Then, to compound the pain, the government sued the United Verde Copper Company for back taxes. My father was forced to testify for weeks at the tax trial in Prescott, 36 miles away over the mountains.

Dad was not the top administrator, and he knew little of the stock operations or financing of the company. His job had always been to get the ore out as efficiently as possible. But, the Board of Directors, the owners, and Bob Talley, Chairman of the Board, threw my father to the government lawyers, saying in effect, "The big steam shovel cut was your project. You had a bad accident. Now you testify on the taxes the way we want you to, and WIN it. That is, if you wish to continue."

He did the best he could but was no match for the tax lawyers. Day after day the testimony on the witness stand wore him down to a raging wreck. Mother had taken me to Piedmont, California, for treatment by a tubercular specialist. Our absence left Dad lonely and discouraged.

My father ended his long service at the United Verde Mine in 1933, ill and despondent. He was unable to foresee that within a year he would be managing an important group of mines in South America.

In 1965 I went back to visit the gloomy little ghost town of Jerome, still clinging to the side of the mountain. I marveled at the great red rocks of Sedona across the Verde Valley, with the white cones of the San Francisco Peaks rising above them. I saw the homes of my friends on my Row, now battered and wrecked with broken windows and doors swinging in the wind.

The Catholic Church was still standing, boarded up, beneath the window of our crumbling house. Part of the sidewalk was still there. The mine had long been closed. No miners came down the hill now.

With closed eyes I could imagine the sound of their boots on the boards, and I could see my mother's face—listening.

CHAPTER 7
MILLS COLLEGE '28

Mother and I walked down a narrow path between giant eucalyptus trees. Their trunks were too big to embrace and their tops waved 40 or 50 feet above us. Fog softened the pink and silver bark and dripped from long aromatic branches

This was Mills College, an exclusive institution for the higher education of women. The cost of the tuition as well as the entrance requirements made it exclusive. Situated in the hills near Oakland, California, it had been founded in 1863 as a young ladies' seminary, then became a college and gradually achieved scholastic standing comparable to Wellesley and Smith.

We were on our way to my room in old Mills Hall. I don't think I ever asked why this school had been chosen for me. Mother was like the weather—so pervasive I never questioned her influence. She decided everything and always had. I was still 17 and numbed by four high schools in as many years, so it was simpler not to rebel.

Never having had a real home, it couldn't be homesickness that clutched my heart and burned behind my eyes.

The assigned room was sunny with an odd, long closet ending in a wash basin. Mother laughed nervously and said, "You'll have to back out carefully as you dry your hands on your wardrobe."

If I had not been so wrapped up in my own misery, I would have realized she was very sad to be leaving me. My brother Jerry was only three years old, my father was busy and, I learned later, less than faithful. She was giving me my best chance to escape the mountain mining camp, though it would leave her lonely.

She dabbed her eyes and trotted us off to the Dean's office to complain about the room.

Dean Helen Moreland's dear, light-filled face beamed in amusement, "Why, Rosemary, we gave you one of the best rooms in Mills Hall because you are rather young and from out of state. I think after you have seen the other accommodation you'll be very happy there."

Her voice was so warm she even hypnotized Mother; and it was as though she programmed me for four fine years—willing me to be content, and to succeed.

The Mills years were the best times of my youth—full of learning and mischief—three or four great friends—three great teachers—innumerable dramatic productions—a tour of Europe—and finally two degrees, a BA in Speech and Drama, and a Masters in Speech with a Psychology minor. These facts have little to do with what happened inside of me. First came the shattering realization that I was nobody.

There were several beautiful, wealthy girls living in neighboring rooms—heiresses to Texas oil, to Hollywood fame, even to Hong Kong rice fortunes. They flitted from room to room, by-passing mine, as their phonographs played "Ain't She Sweet!" Their clothes were fabulous. They had cars secretly garaged off campus. They talked of dates at "The Frantic" (meaning The St. Francis Hotel where The Rhythm Boys were featured—Bing Crosby being one of them). They had charge accounts at Ransohoff's and sweethearts at Stanford or "Cal."

I listened and watched, appalled at my fall from Adored-Only-Daughter-of-the-Big-Boss-of-the-Mine to this eavesdropping nonentity. My hunger for recognition was a fox gnawing in my vitals.

I tried Hall politics and was elected Assistant Fire Chief. Mills Hall was built entirely of wood in the '60s (not the 19th century but the 18th)—a huge Victorian pile with elephantine charm. Understandably the weekly surprise fire drill was important, with loud bells, marching, shouting, hose pulling, and roll calling. But when you long for social acceptance, a fire drill in a too-small red helmet is merely pitiful.

Dorothy Stauffer, my classmate from Phoenix, was in my hall. A graceful aristocrat with no social compulsions, she was comfortable and soothed my own aggressions. We listened together to all the competitive maneuvering on our floor. Her perspective made the whole scene bearable.

She arranged our first date, and it was a curious disaster. It seemed there was a Stauffer cousin who would "borrow his auntie's car, and bring a friend" for me. We were so naïve that this sounded fine, since we had not left the campus for a month. Neither of us had ever had a blind date before. I had rarely been allowed out of the house without a chaperone and Dot had gone steady with Cub Fahlen, a man whom she eventually married.

It was pouring rain on the appointed Saturday evening when we were called by two bleeps on the buzzer, meaning "come to the lobby for guests." We were dressed in our best with tiny little hats, heels, and fur coats.

Dot recognized her cousin—a pallid, bespectacled fellow of a reasonable height. This left me with the remainder, a chubby quince of a boy, inches shorter than my five feet two inches.

But all self-consciousness vanished when we saw the ancient conveyance awaiting us at the front door. It was 10 feet high with a ragged cloth top, celluloid curtains, and carbide lanterns fore and aft. I wondered why they had unhitched the horse.

The rain came through the roof in several places, dripping down to form pools on the hard leather seats. An hour later, we stopped in Oakland for a Sunday paper to caulk the leaks and cover our heads. When we drove onto the San Francisco Ferry and wobbled into place, a deck hand ran over, pointed at our lights and screamed, "Blow 'em out for Chrissakes! Ya wanna set the ship on fire!?"

Dot's cousin and my little endomorph hopped out and doused the lamps while everyone in the surrounding cars giggled and pointed. With grave dignity we folded our wet newspapers and climbed down out of the puddles. Upstairs in the lounge it was dry and warm, with a beautiful view of the bay and the lights of San Francisco.

When the ferry drew into its slip we remounted the old classic and waited for our dates' search for matches to light the lanterns. Then the engine had to be cranked while those behind us honked and yelled. We finally bumped off to Market Street and headed for the St. Francis Hotel. Once there, the doorman seemed to be having some kind of seizure. He danced and whistled and pointed, apparently wanting us far from his premises. As there was no attendant capable of driving the buggy, Dot and I de-trained and watched the flickering tail lamps fade off down Powell Street.

We spent a long time and a lot of towels in the marble gilt of the ladies room, and more time in the lobby waiting for our coachmen. We found them at last under a palm tree, wringing out their overcoats.

Inside the big ballroom it was magic. The lights were soft and pink, the orchestra smooth and saxaphony. Phil Harris was singing "When I Take My Sugar to Tea" with titillating overtones. The maitre d' gave us a tiny table near the pantry, but nevermind, we could dance right up close to the bandstand and watch Phil's teeth and rolling blue eyes. My date wasn't too skillful a dancer and smelled of wet wool, but he was an enthusiastic drinker. We ordered ginger ale and he produced a flask of some awful liquid that ruined the ginger ale.

The bill for this night on the town was considerable: a three-hour trip home in the covered wagon, bad colds, campussed for a month for getting in late, plus the sneers of the In Crowd, who must have seen us performing on the ferry. But the experience gave us a protective cynicism concerning future blind dates.

Registration Day opened and closed several doors for me. By the time you reach college you are supposed to have some idea of what you want to BE (as if you weren't already IT by the time you are five).

Like every young female, I had thought of being an actress. There had been some success in two high school plays, and innumerable elocution lessons, but I had also dreamed of being a writer or a painter. The theater and motion pictures were wonderful and exciting but I really didn't know very much about them, nor did anyone in our family. Mother took me to an occasional matinee but complained that I became so emotionally involved with the play or the movie that I often had to be led away sobbing; or, if it was a comedy then she had to put up with my aping the actors long after it was over.

When I signed the registration form for Speech and Drama, Miss Adams, Dean of Curriculum, said firmly that those courses were filled. "O.K.," I replied, "Then put me down as an Art Major." When she started a hard sell on zoology I came close to quitting.

I had squeaked through Chemistry because the professor had spilled some sulfuric acid on my leg and I had been rather generous about it. Physics was a fog that never cleared, and I barely passed biology by getting a boy friend to do the autopsies or whatever they call that nasty carving. So—I was not going to get trapped in any labs for this abrasive Dean-lady.

We finally settled on a mild four units of geography, Design I, and a lot of required English and French. Registered at last, I gave a sigh of exhaustion only mildly regretful at giving up a career in the theater.

However, in December "all freshman interested" were called to try out for the Christ Miracle Play. Mrs. Stebbins, a glamorous but formidable woman who headed the Drama Department, sat on a throne as we tripped or stumbled past her. She tagged me for The Virgin probably because of my looks, as the part demanded little except the ability to sit still.

My pudding-faced performance elicited snorts from the Social Leaders. But at least I was no longer Nobody. I was the Virgin Nobody.

That winter and spring meant long hours for me in the old Arts building under Roy Partridge's jutting eyebrows. He was more of a personality than a teacher, given to flares of temper and scathing criticism. Being married to Imogene Cunningham, who was becoming a world-famous photographer, probably played havoc with his ego.

My work was less than mediocre. My charcoal copies of Greek heads and columns were smears. My Mondrian design patterns were wobbly and lacked invention. Finally Roy said, "Rosemary, you aren't hacking it here. There must be some other department that will accept your major."

My ego was only slightly bruised because Mrs. Stebbins had just asked me to play Beatrice in *Much Ado About Nothing*. The outdoor theater in the Eucalyptus Grove was misty and beautiful and I was waking up to the music and color of Shakespeare's lines. So my major was changed, leaving a faint scar that still itches and burns when I see a lovely painting or a piece of sculpture.

Marion Stebbins had studied with Yvette Guilbert in Paris. What that meant none of us was certain, but she certainly had great presence and high standards of voice and diction, consequently her classes were crowded and stimulating. She was big on contra-casting—assigning us roles that were different from our physical selves. Playing Mosca one week and Perdita the next, or Juliet's nurse followed by Oedipus gave us all a range and understanding we would never have experienced in a coed drama class.

I learned to project my voice outdoors—"to speak poniards and every word stab" for Beatrice. Then the next fall I was given Mercutio to play in the same romantic grove. That summer my family and I had a rather surprising brush with the Hollywood which had always seemed so remote.

CHAPTER 8
THE DECAMPS AND HOWARD HUGHES

No modern memoir of an actress should fail to include a Howard Hughes story.

The Hughes brush with our family was at first amusing, then it became an ugly accident. For me it had overtones of a kind of metaphysical revenge, but I have a tendency to fantasize so perhaps it was just coincidental.

Carmel, California in the early '30s was a secret mystical village facing a brilliant blue bay surrounded with twisted black and silver cypress, and peopled with painters, sculptors, and poets.

Robinson Jeffers hid in a hand-built stone castle on one headland, facing a more modest half-castle owned by Robert Kuster and his family. He was the owner and director of the Carmel Community Theater. Mrs. Stebbins knew him and persuaded him to offer me a summer's work if I could live nearby.

Mother, delighted to get away from Jerome, brought my little brother Jerry to Carmel and rented a lovely house near the bay. It was built around a big patio with some fine old trees and a grape arbor.

The first play was Elmer Rice's *See Naples and Die*. I had a kind of "other woman" part in this dramatic meringue. I was young and good-looking for the femme fatale type I imagined myself to be, with too-white skin, lots of eye shadow, and dark auburn hair.

One Saturday night at the theater word went 'round backstage that Howard Hughes was out front. I had never heard of him, but the rest of the cast was fluttery.

After the curtain calls, a chauffeur came backstage with a scrawled note inviting the whole group for cocktails the following afternoon on the Hughes yacht, which was anchored offshore in the placid Carmel Bay. We were to be picked up at such and such a dock and launched out.

There didn't seem to be any "Yes" or "No, thank you" indicated, but we all agreed to go. I knew I still had to ask my mother's permission and toyed with the idea of taking her along, but I couldn't very well include my little brother Jerry. She said she hoped I could swim, and urged me please not to be out late. That's how square we were in the '30s.

The yacht was a monster, 175 feet long, and crowded with people. Most of them were "Hollywood hangers-on," though I didn't know that then. I simply marveled at their elaborate clothing.

I remember being startled, and sort of angry, at the way Hughes' guests would talk about him when his back was turned. Such remarks as, "When's this bastard going to feed us?" or, "God, I'm sick of this boat! When do we go ashore?" All this was said within two or three feet of our host.

A gray-haired man standing next to me saw my shocked expression. He smiled, "Don't worry. Howard's deaf. He can't hear 'em." Somehow that seemed even worse, and I felt a wave of sympathy for the skinny, sad-eyed Hughes. The man turned out to be Micky Neiulan, one of the millionaire's cronies. I didn't know anything about Hollywood then, but apparently he had been a famous dancer.

Mother was amused at my account of the afternoon. Then later in the week a note came from Mr. Hughes asking me to go out to the yacht for "supper after the show."

Ah ha! Here we go, I thought. Here comes the millionaire and the chorus girl bit.

Mother said, "Oh, go if you want, but don't do anything stupid, and don't go alone."

There had been so many people on the boat; it never occurred to me we would be alone. Sure enough, however, everyone melted away, even Mr. Neiulan, and we dined "a deux."

I'll never forget that meal in the huge yacht dining room. Hughes at the end, sitting beneath a large mounted fish, and me at his left a few feet away. I was nervous because he said very little and I come from a long line of talkers. The DeCamps are not known for their pauses. Hughes had a strange, hungry way of looking at you that was disconcerting. Most people, I suppose, thought he was infatuated with them. Actually he was just reading lips. I already knew he was deaf, but the whole scene was like a *New Yorker* cartoon. I kept looking up at the fish to see if it was rolling its big glass eye.

Also there was the possibility of a "pass." But no! No hand-holding, no physical contact of any kind, just that intense hungry stare. I ate like a horse; he nibbled. No drinks, just plain meat and potatoes. After the ice cream, he said the car would take me home from the dock. Then, as an afterthought, he asked if he could call on my mother.

I 'llowed as how he could, or why not? And that was the end of the evening.

The next day he arrived with some flowers and met Mother. I was busy with costume fittings for another play, but I remember Howard Hughes and Mother sitting stiffly in the patio watching my little brother bouncing a ball. It was then I realized that Mr. Hughes was NOT a lot of fun.

He seemed fond of my brother and returned several afternoons to "play ball" with Jerry. My brother was a bright, agreeable child of three or four and looked like a chubby, gold angel. He adored people, pets, and games, not always in the same order. Howard would throw the ball and my brother would trot off and retrieve it endlessly. Jerry was polite, but obviously bored, and our guest didn't seem to know any variations on this game.

Finally my mother said, "The next time that man calls, tell him not to come any more. He makes me nervous."

That was hard to do because I felt sorry for Howard, but I explained as gently as possible that Mother wasn't well and that we were leaving soon.

Howard was quiet for longer than was comfortable. Then he got up and left, with the usual dark stare.

The next time Howard Hughes came into our lives was in Beverly Hills 15 years later, July 7, 1946. He literally dropped in, piloting a huge experimental plane. He crashed through my brother's bedroom, left a landing light on the bed and part of one engine in the bathroom.

The odd thing about that disaster was that my brother had just returned the day before from the army in Germany. He and his bride, Elizabeth, had moved their bed from the southwest corner to the opposite side of the room because the morning light was too bright.

Just six hours later, at dusk, Hughes came barreling over the living room at 805 North Linden Drive and into Jerry's room. My brother was standing by the bed on which his wife was sitting. Mother had just closed the garage doors when that plane tore the roof off and crashed into the house across the alley.

Amazingly, no one was hurt except Howard Hughes himself. He was pulled out of the burning plane by a neighbor of ours. My brother had a scratch on his nose. Mother, who had always been an insurance salesman's pigeon, had so many policies that her house was repaired in a few months, even the damage done by sightseers who trampled the place for days.

The crash happened two weeks before the birth of my second child, so the news came by phone from 30 miles away.

Later this all came back to my mind when I read that "Howard Hughes had been addicted to drugs since his severe injuries from the plane crash of '46."

Howard Hughes is dead now and all this is long gone. But I still get a nervous twinge when I think how close he came to killing the little boy he had played ball with so long ago....

My senior year at Mills was so complicated it made a good rehearsal for the rest of my life.

There were endless night rehearsals in the Greek Theater. Mrs. Stebbins had cast me as Clytemnestra in *Agamemnon*, a role beyond any actress under 40. As you may remember, she is the Greek queen who murders her husband in his bath when he returns from a 10-year war with Troy. Aeschylus made her his most human tragic character—full of hate for a husband who has made a bloody sacrifice of their daughter on an altar in Taurus just for good luck in his campaign against the Trojans.

That production gave me a glimpse of how much I had yet to learn about voice, command, and perception.

The old anxiety about social acceptance or recognition no longer concerned me. I had my own close friends and was a familiar figure on campus because of all the plays I had been in. But now I had no time for dates, or trips to the city. There was always a rehearsal, or evenings dyeing costume fabrics, or hours with carpenters building sets. My classmates were getting engaged, dating, planning to be married after graduation, all of which seemed very remote to me. I lived in a practical world, but one dedicated to make-believe—of lighting, lines to learn, characterizations, scripts to write, music to select.

The real world was out there beyond the Mills gates suffering from a profound financial depression. I wouldn't meet it until its problems had worsened a year later. Graduation was exhausting for me and several classmates. The Physical Education Department was either deliberately malicious or kept sloppy books. Four days before the diploma ceremony we were notified of the hours we lacked to graduate.

Two close friends, Ruth Fennessy and Madge Baylis, had to tread water for five minutes, having failed to do this when they were sophomores. Some of us were minus five to 10 hours of hockey, or fencing. I lacked eight hours of jumping and dressage at the college stables.

Old Col. Kress, a Teutonic cavalryman, guided me through four consecutive days of agonizing horsemanship. I jumped, low—high—and broad. I was thrown, I fell off, I slid off. Every night while the other seniors were dancing and dressing and partying, I lay in a tub of hot Epsom salts.

When it came time to stagger across the stage for my diploma, my legs were so bowed and stiff I walked like Quasimodo.

The good news was a generous scholarship for the following year requiring nine hours of teaching a required speech course, and 15 graduate units to acquire a Master of Arts. I was grateful and humble, too, as there were better students competing who had greater financial need.

That fifth year became a blur of teaching young ladies to relinquish their hard Midwestern R's and aiding those who had serious defects. Some of them were older than I, and loath to change their speech.

The remedial work with stammerers and stutterers was rewarding, and unusual. The psychology staff and I had become enamored of the Knight-Dunlap theory, which was based on the premise that involuntary habits, such as "tics" and stuttering could be eliminated by making them voluntary. In other words, practice the mistake until you could control it. This theory also laid claim to curing alcoholism and masturbation. Happily there was no talk of working in those areas.

I was assigned several stutterers and "tic-types" for private tutoring. They would come to my room at all hours and we would repeat over and over the consonants and vowels which were troublesome. The tics and twitches were not technically speech-oriented but we worked on those with some success, although I had a horrid suspicion that we were trading my speech for theirs, my steady face, or head, or arms for their spasms.

June came at last with a paper on Diction for the Deaf for Louise Stephens, a survey of the work in Remedial Speech, a two-hour oral and a four-hour written exam. After that, school was out! I had secured my MA.

Was I educated? No, not noticeably, but Mills had given me a few clues and keys to the world of learning which I could use or not. Twenty years out of school I found a quotation by Joseph Addison in the late 18th century that defines education in a rich and classic manner: "Education is a companion which no misfortune can depress, no crime destroy, no enemy can alienate, no despotism can enslave. At home a friend, abroad an introduction; in solitude a solace and in society an ornament. It chastens vice, it guides virtue, it gives at once grace and government to genius. Without it what is man? A splendid slave, a reasoning savage."

CHAPTER 9
THE AUDITION

Every young girl from Petaluma to Algonquit, from El Paso to Toronto, was supposed to cherish the dream of Hollywood stardom in those halcyon days. At least the publicists for the film factories told the world that was The Dream. But when I emerged from Mills with my two degrees, certain that I must be a classical actress or nothing, I was already a little long in the tooth for the ingenue trip, being a know-it-all of 23.

Dad, Mother, and my brother, Jerry, had moved from Jerome and we were all living in a rented house on Hyde Street in San Francisco. It was just above the old Ghirardelli's factory (now the Square) and the odor of chocolate was so heavy we all lost our appetites. The house was a skinny, three-story job with a garage so narrow it had a turntable to get the car out.

Jerry and I spent many happy afternoons crab-netting off a pier near Fisherman's Wharf. Finally my mother grew weary of the constant odor of crabs boiling in the kitchen. (It did not blend well with the chocolate fumes.) So she told my brother he would have to get out of the house, find a paper route, or whatever job was open to a nine-year-old.

Then she and Father closed in on me for a "little talk" wherein they mentioned the astounding cost of my education and the fact of my father's unemployment; then they asked me what I intended to "do."

I blithely replied, "Oh, if you need help, I'll just run down to KGO and try radio."

My optimism was insufferable, particularly as it was 1933 and soup kitchen lines were clearly visible for those with eyes to see, and even Ph.D.s were selling apples at street corners.

When I arrived at radio station KGO, there was a general audition in progress. At least 80 people stood, sat, or squatted in the tiny lobby. I added my name to a long list and after two hours of observing those who went through the big STUDIO 4, KEEP OUT door, I knew no more than I had before. I noticed when leaving, each one handed a tattered mimeo sheet to the handsome dark-eyed man at the entrance.

When my turn came, he ushered me through the three-foot padded door into a 10-by-10 padded cell. It had a big glass window that looked like a fish tank—unlighted. They could see me, but I could not see them. Occasionally a shadow would swim behind the glass.

I was handed a worn paper and led to a microphone. Then a big voice from the fish tank boomed, "Just read what's there, please."

To my horror, the purple ink on the mimeographed sheet was blurry and almost illegible. The fuzzy words proclaimed the dreamy excellence of Meredith Wilson's Chiffon Jazz, a program I had never heard of.

My voice must have saved me because I had no idea what I was reading. Since childhood I had had a perpetual cold and it had given me rather mellow, furry head tones. I had been teaching speech in college, so the diction was passable.

I stumbled out of the fish tank and someone murmured, "Thank you. Leave your name and number at the desk. Next... " The only reward was the smile of the dark-eyed man at the door. I had no way of knowing he was Mike Raffetto, one of the most famous voices in radio of that period. He played Paul in *One Man's Family*, a weekly program that was loved from coast to coast.

Several days went by during which I signed up with the Carmel Little Theater to do sound and light production on Lincoln Steffens' production of *Amoco*.

Lincoln Steffens was famous for his muckraking stories and had just been acclaimed for a recently published autobiography. I was thrilled to be working anywhere near that radical pixie. He and his wife were said to be wild socialists, or perhaps even Communists.

In my last two years at Mills I had realized that this was not the best of all possible worlds. I spent my senior year running down to UXA headquarters in San Leandro. This was a kind of pseudo-commune where my friends and I volunteered to haul produce, gasoline, and people who were unemployed in a giant barter network that extended from Berkeley to San Jose.

It was this operation that had given me a glimpse of the realities in Steffens' articles. I could see close-up the poverty and despair of families whose breadwinners stood in line to trade hours of work for a sack of beans or a pound of flour.

Then the call came. I had gotten the job, Mother informed me. What job? She was so happy she was dancing. "You have a part in *One Man's Family*! Rehearsal tomorrow. Twenty-five dollars a show."

That salary certainly was not commensurate with my opinion of my talents—but Hi Ho! And O.K.!

The rehearsal of the radio script went well, I suppose. I only remember the writer, Carlton Morse: plump, bald, and wearing a fringed granny-shawl. He had cool little eyes, rimless glasses, and a pinched, timorous way of speaking. But it was evident that he was The Boss. Even Mike Raffetto did exactly as Morse suggested.

When the show was over, I was patted on the back and told my check would be mailed and that I'd be informed of my next appearance by phone.

It did not sound too imminent, so I neglected to mention that I was off to Carmel.

The Carmel Little Theater was a very different scene—thrilling and alive. The play, *Amoco*, was a stridently anti-capitalistic piece. I was in charge of rattling chains, triggering the sounds of explosions, strike breakers' riots, and gun shots. I dimmed the lights, pulled the curtains, and ran sound turntables. I was a Boss.

My stage set for Synge's *Deidre of the Sorrows* had won a Theater Arts monthly prize the year before; consequently, I thought of myself as God's all-around gift to the theater.

When the call came to return to *One Man's Family* for "rehearsal on Tuesday, show on Wednesday," I calmly wired back, "Can't make rehearsal. Will be there for the show," unaware that I had just signed my own "black-ball" in radio and was headed for long months of job hunting.

Back in San Francisco, I noticed everyone was rather starchy at the pre-show run-through. Carlton Morse's little eyes were frosty, Mike was perfunctory. I couldn't see why they were miffed, because my part was so small I could have "phoned it in." The fact that he had probably cut the part when I had not come to the rehearsal didn't penetrate my ego. No one explained that I had broken the rules. They just let me finish, then wrote the part out.

After a few weeks, I called and asked about the show but I was never able to reach anyone who would discuss it. I took to haunting the station and received the calm brush-off of the employed for the one who is "at liberty."

At last, a kind man and good actor, Bart Yarbrough, took me aside and said, "Don't hang around here. Carlton will never use you again. If you really need work, meet me tomorrow and I'll see if I can't get you cast in some cheap records we make in a studio down on Mission."

I felt hollow. Suddenly, I was OUT, my self-importance dissolving. The record offer sounded so sub-rosa...so illicit. But I had no choice.

I met Bart and got a job playing two or three parts PER PLATTER, for five dollars a day. Only they didn't say how many records you did in a day. It was grisly. Sometimes choking yourself—playing killer and victim in two different dialects in the same scene. All of us had a collection of phony accents. Mine could only be described as Middle-European Poor, Middle-European Rich, and Deep South (Arizona).

I have heard some of these little jewels through the years, usually emanating from out-of-the-way stations, or pulled from a nostalgia buff's locker. They are certainly period pieces and the kindest adjective one can apply is "implausible."

Perhaps that experience had some value under the "You-have-to-begin-somewhere" label; like the old supernumeraries of the opera and musicals, or the cruel tours of the second, third, and fourth companies, who traveled all over the United States before films and television.

I am sure I gained a great deal of facility and self-confidence, but I had already proven I had too much of the latter, and facility can often be equated with superficiality.

There simply wasn't time to delve very deeply into "character" while one was playing both Snow White and the Wicked Witch, with a 10-minute run-through before recording. During the '30s, in radio, FACILITY meant that you worked often. The Stanislavsky Method might get you one big, sweaty role in six months.

You see how much I changed? I came out of college as Clytemnestra, and eventually a few years later I became Judy Price, Dr. Christian's nurse, on a weekly radio program. So much for pragmatism and survival in The Great Depression.

CHAPTER 10
THE DRUNKARD

In 1934 I heard that Galt Bell was putting together a road company of *The Drunkard*. This old melodrama had played successfully at The Theater Mart in Los Angeles for years. There the audience sat at little tables, drank beer, hissed the villain, sang with the cast, and threw peanuts at the actors.

Galt had produced the Carmel plays I had done two years before, so I went to L.A., begged a try, and won Mad Agnes, a dopey Ophelia-like part, in a play where everyone was a stylized cut-out.

Kathleen Fitzpatrick, Tom DeGrafenreid, Bob Bixby, Jack Wagner, Frank Ferguson, several "supers," and I left on a Greyhound bus in July to travel across country to the Schroeder Hotel in Milwaukee where we were to play in the big hotel dining room.

The next six months are a blur of incredible discomfort and confusion. We played in hotels where the patrons threw ice cubes and hard buns, then we went into five-shows-a-day movie houses, ending up broke and worn out in South Bend, Indiana.

The theater laws in most states do not permit a child to work in public after 9 p.m., so we carried a midget for the child's role in *The Drunkard*. She became my responsibility because I was too inexperienced to protest. I shall just call her "Mousie," though often I called her other names. A two-and-a-half foot alcoholic can really gum things up, but she was affectionate and had spells of good will and high resolve. Somehow we muddled through and stayed out of jail.

The original dream of playing in hotel dining rooms ended in Chicago. The expected diners were all out at the Fair. It was '34 and the Midway was booming. With the last-ditch philosophy of "in for a penny, in for a pound," our producer spent thousands of dollars for theatrical scenery so that we could play in movie-vaudeville houses. We opened at the Oriental Theater just off State Street in the heart of Chicago. We entered the theater at 10 a.m. and left at 11 p.m., after doing five one-hour shows, sandwiched in between whatever movie was showing, plus several other vaudeville acts—tumblers, magicians, and jugglers. Most vaudeville acts at that time ran less than eight minutes. We were exhausted after doing five hours a day on stage, and six more hanging around in make-up.

NBC portrait taken in 1934

That was grim, but it got worse as we were booked by Balaban and Katz to do four-a-day one-night stands throughout Illinois and Indiana. No wonder vaudeville died. This kind of scheduling helped kill it.

That tour gave me an intense, crash course in crummy hotels, tank towns, mean managers, and how to watch a movie while lying on the stage, looking up. But it also gave me a resiliency for the future. No matter how bad working conditions became, I had *The Drunkard* background to make them appear bearable.

As Mad Agnes in *The Drunkard* (1934)

During the last performance of *The Drunkard* in South Bend, Indiana, some happy Notre Dame warrior threw a pop bottle from the balcony and felled me with a glancing blow to the head. I was playing Mad Agnes, and though the audience had been encouraged to hiss and boo the villain and even throw peanuts and pennies, I thought throwing that bottle was overdoing audience participation. Anyway (I told myself and relatives), it was really aimed at the villain.

Memories of getting paid off, saying good-bye to the company, or even why I boarded a bus for New York, are blanked out. I remember that the trip took 36 hours, and every time I woke up, we were just pulling away from a food stop.

New York City at midnight in a winter drizzle looked shabby and discouraged from all its 1934 ills. And there was I, wobbly in the knees, with an empty stomach, $3.00, and an uncashed check for $50.00 in my pocket. We were a good match, the city and I.

When I was a child, New York had been the 125th Street Ferry building... cobblestone streets... fish markets... a Russian movie... *The Rose and the Ring* at Tony Sarg's jewel of a marionette theater. We sat in little velvet boxes. Everyone in the audience looked like dolls watching other dolls. There was opera—Galli-Curci from the highest balcony where garlic fumes were a visible haze, and people held musical scores and hummed the arias. There had been battleships on the Hudson with lights and flags and music, and people dancing on the decks in bright-colored dresses and navy whites. The big Aquarium down at the Battery had monsters swimming in glass tanks of yellow-green light. There were legless beggars on little roller-skate platforms. Hawkers of mechanical toys on the sidewalks screamed like auctioneers. The smells of Mott and Delancey Street were spicy, and as foreign to me as the bazaars of Karachi years later.

I got off the bus from South Bend, hungry and with a slight concussion, and realized that both the city and I had changed since 1919—and not for the better.

After a few days of sleep in a drab little theatrical hotel on 49th Street, my mother wired me money from California, with terse instructions: "Live at Barbizon Plaza. Go see Sam Harris."

The Barbizon Plaza was clean and modern. It had two advantages: Breakfast came through a little trap door in your room every morning, and consisted of rolls, butter, and a thermos of coffee, all included in the rent of $17.00 a week. There were weekly professional performances in a little theater off the lobby. Shirley Booth appeared there once, and she was so wonderful I tried to imitate her for months. Offsetting these items were the disadvantages: No men were allowed above the lobby, the rooms were the size of closets, and its reputation as an address was comparable to that of the YWCA.

Central Park was around the corner and I could go there and sit in the sun, or go to the zoo and look at the animals, or wander around the lake and watch the remarkable collection of exotic humans who frequented its paths and benches.

All this, of course, was putting off the visit to Sam Harris. He was a Broadway legend and I was scared of it, and of him. A year on the road playing "five-a-day" in dingy movie houses and one-night stands in little towns had developed a belated humility in me.

The connection with Sam Harris was tenuous and unrelated to the theater. My father was running a mine in California for a group of investors, among whom were Max Gordon, Sam Harris, and two of the Marx brothers. They all must have been gamblers at heart, for what could be more risky than a small gold mine in the Sierras thousands of miles away? Especially as none of them knew a stope from a shaft. An example of their light-hearted attitude occurred a week or so before I met Mr. Harris.

Dad had telegraphed them: "Mill burned down last night. Wire instructions." Their joint reply, recounted later with glee, was "Love the title. Get new script."

However, I was ignorant of this exchange when I reported to Sam's Music Box Theater on 45th Street. Here was his kingdom; here was the man who had produced more hits than anyone else in Broadway's history. He had given half the great names of musical comedy and stage their start. He was reported to be the only man in New York with whom no written contract was needed. His word had always been his bond.

It was one of Broadway's worst seasons. *Victoria Regina*, *Petrified Forest*, and the Music Box production of George Kaufman's *Merrily We Roll Along* were the only shows running. The Shuberts and the Theater Guild had closed and the WPA productions were not yet on the boards.

So there were a lot of actors waiting in the hall off the Music Box lobby. Max Siegel, the theater manager and Sam's factotum, told us all that there was "nothing today and Mr. Harris is very busy." Most of us waited anyway. Max disappeared and after about a half-hour the paneled door at the end of the hall opened and a tiny man came out. He wore an exquisite gray suit that blended with his silver hair. He had big blue eyes and a soft whisper voice, "I'm Sam Harris. Does anyone wish to see me?"

His appearance was such a surprise. He was so wistful and friendly, I had to fight off the urge to run over and comfort him. But the legend was big enough to keep me on the bench until called.

His office was fine. I have unconsciously used it as a gauge for the offices of famous and successful people, and not one that I have seen has measured up. It was comfort, rich wood and leather, portraits and photographs of beloved friends, a great stone fireplace burning bright and cozy, with real logs. It was taste, and elegance without a fashionable note. I was there often in the next three years, and that room never failed to welcome and warm me.

During that period Sam introduced me to many celebrities: Edna Ferber, George Kaufman, Bill Liebling, Harold Clurman, Ina Claire, and many editors, writers, and newspaper publishers whose names meant little if anything to me.

Ferber and Kaufman were both big people—steel graying hair, dressed in expensive dark wools, and always discussing some deal. It was as though they were business partners and not much else. I knew very little about him, except the wonderful lunacy of *Once in a Lifetime*, and later the personal glimpses in *Merrily We Roll Along*, but I worshipped her for her novel, *So Big*.

They all came and talked in Sam's office, occasionally asking advice. I think it comforted them to be with him. He was real and sane. They had all lost a lot of money in '29 and '32, and I got the impression that they had become more cautious than they had been in the past. I don't really know, as I was only a fly on the wall, allowed to sit quietly and watch the big names mill around, jockeying for Sam's advice.

That first time I sat in Sam's office he inquired kindly about my experience, my living quarters, and what I wanted to do. My answers were probably callow and trite, but he nodded gravely. Then, with happy chortles, he told me about the telegrams. When he asked me about the mine, all I could do was describe the scenery; four-foot foxgloves, rushing water, lupine, and ferns and the snowy Sierra. It seemed to be enough, since neither of us understood blasting, or ore samples.

He suggested that I get a pass to see *Merrily We Roll Along* from Mr. Siegel, and then promised they would "find a spot for me in the company." He also said it would pay very little, but that I would be learning the ropes.

CHAPTER 11
LEARNING THE ROPES

I wonder about that phrase. Did it come from boxers bouncing off ropes? Or from backstage where the curtain man learns which ropes belong to which pieces of scenery to raise and lower? Or is it for sailors and ships? Or maybe the hangman? No matter, I followed instructions and set out to learn the ropes.

The job paid $16.50 a week, so even if I didn't eat anything but the trapdoor breakfast, I was still 50 cents short. Never mind bus fare; I could walk from 59th to 45th Street if the snow wasn't too deep. It really made me mad though, to walk along Sixth Avenue in the rain and see ladies walking their little dogs wearing raincoats and rubbers. I mean the DOGS did! There was a little money from home. I could get a lunch at the automat for 25 cents that would take me through till morning. But it was difficult to pass those little glass windows with the lemon cream pies looking out.

Those five months were hard. Sort of split-level poor. Six nights and two matinees I reported to a tiny dressing room with three other extras. There were 45 non-speaking parts in that play. *Merrily We Roll Along* was not a comedy. It was probably the only autobiographical play George Kaufman ever wrote. It had one glaring defect—it ran backwards.

Starting with a hectic cocktail party, the audience sees the leading figure is a writer on a downhill road with few options remaining save bankruptcy or suicide.

In the following scenes the author grows younger, more hopeful and successful until the last act. There he stands in cap and gown before a stained glass window delivering a valedictorian address: "To thine own self be true, and it must follow as the night the day..."

In the '30s, New York audiences thought it smart to arrive late and full of cocktails, so they really could not figure out what was going on.

Merrily We Roll Along stopped rolling after six months. The week the show closed, I had worked up to a part with four lines. Now I had no rent money and very little experience to point to; there was no casting, only vague gossip about summer stock. I was sorry, too, because in his play George Kaufman had tried to say something about values and perhaps about his own life.

The ugly postscript to the play came a few months later when Mary Astor's diary was published in every big newspaper in the country. In this syndicated slop, she described graphically her intimacies with Kaufman and dozens of famous men. Miss Astor didn't sleep around with just anybody. Her text even stated that she and Kaufman were doing IT in the balcony during a performance of *Merrily...*!

Our last cast scattered with some grim good-byes. It was meaner than most "closings," because we had been scheduled to open in Philadelphia with a possible cross-country tour ahead.

Kenneth McKenna, Jessie Royce Landis, and Sophie Tucker went off to Hollywood, but the rest of us faced a rough summer. Unemployment insurance did not exist. Roosevelt was struggling with the Supreme Court and NRA [National Recovery Administration]. Hoover's dictum, "You cannot legislate against poverty," was still gospel.

I missed the girls I had dressed with, too. They had been garrulous and coarse. And they had found me very square and delighted in shocking my country morality. One, named Elsie, always talked about her "Daddy," where they dined, and what he had bought her, the apartment he had rented for her. I thought he was her father until she showed us, one night after the curtain, what "Daddy" liked her to wear for "midnight supper." With make-up she made eyes of her nipples, a nose on her navel, and a mouth above her pubic hair. Then she put a man's hat over her face, her hands behind her back, and undulated around the room in her stockings.

The other girls with boyfriends were paying their own way, and were frankly envious of Elsie. When the show closed we all said "Good-bye... We'll have to have lunch," and all the things people say daily in New York. Just as one says, "How do you do?" and never listens for the answer.

The stage manager let me keep the silver slippers that had belonged to Marilyn Miller. I wore a four-and-a-half B and they were the only ones in the wardrobe that fit. Elsie said that I would be lucky like Marilyn, who had made her big hit in *Sunny* at the Music Box. But one of the other girls said, "Forget it. She was a beautiful lush and died a drunk."

I put the shoes away and never wore them. At the automat silver pumps with huge rhinestone buckles would have probably gotten me arrested for soliciting.

Elsie told me of a nine-dollar-a-week place on East 56th Street that sounded like my pocketbook.

It was a sort of club-hotel with dual suites containing two tiny bedrooms, a shared hall, phone, and bath. Men and women were relegated to separate floors and everyone had swimming privileges in the basement "plunge." There was a five-table restaurant where residents could get a 35-cent breakfast of orange juice, coffee, and toast.

This proved to be a remarkable bargain if you could survive the distance from the subway along three slummy blocks.

The inhabitants of those tenements between Third and First Avenues lacked any recreational programs other than spitting gum, or throwing garbage down on passing pedestrians.

My half-suite was on the fifth floor. It was dark and small, but newly painted and possessed a window on 56th Street. I had no idea who lived behind the closed door in the hall.

In those days I "maintained" my hair a ruddy gold with applications of henna and peroxide. It was long and thick and wound around my head in a crown braid, rather effective. By using very little make-up, I achieved the wan, romantic air I fancied.

I mention the hair coloring only because it made the first phone call in my new quarters confusing.

When the ring came, I jumped to answer, hoping it was a job. A rich Latin voice crooned, "Rosemary! How wonderful, you are in!"

My heart leapt. In what? "Thank you. Who is this?"

When he replied, "Ah, darling, beautiful redhead, you know who this is..."

Phooey! It was no job. "As the caterpillar said to Alice, 'Whooooooo are youuuuuuuuu?'"

At that point the other door opened and a beautiful, tall girl with red hair came toward me. We looked at each other coolly and she said, "I think that is for me," and took the phone.

Later we became friends—the two red-haired Rosemarys in 530. She was a model at Bergdorf-Goodman and in love with a professional fencer. That seemed the ultimate in glamour to me, and so did she. Her clothes were fabulous but she made very little money, and, being a high fashion model, she ate hard boiled eggs, lettuce leaves, and cottage cheese. She had all kinds of dates who came in big fancy cars. I knew because I hung out the window like everyone else on 56th East. But she stayed true to the fencer, after her fashion, and eventually married him.

Years later I saw her at "21." She was still beautiful, still a model, and accompanied by a fleshy fellow in cashmere. I forbore asking after the swordsman, having a feeling he might not have survived in his line of work.

When I took fencing at Mills, those little corks kept popping off the epees.

She offered me blind dates during that year: double dates, rich-and-ugly, handsome-and-poor, even rich-and-handsome, and poor-and-ugly. I never accepted. Elsie's "Daddy" lurked in my memory and I had a country girl's suspicion of one-nighters who seemed so available.

All that period and the following months of job hunting were made bearable by the sweetness and wisdom of Sam Harris. He was my tiny Jewish genius godfather. He often took me out to dinner, probably guessing it would be my meal-of-the-day.

He shared memories of departed fighters, actresses, and dancers. He spoke lovingly of his dead wife who had been George M. Cohan's sister. He frequently asked me how I was getting along, but he never offered me money and I never asked.

He had a beautiful apartment, all done in misty gray velvet and broadloom, with a grand piano and many long windows. It was usually enlivened by a crowd of racing bugs, or a theater crowd—pleasant, rather rough wits, who drank his liquor, played his piano, and also played lots of practical jokes.

When the phone rang and the butler announced, "It's the Coast, Mr. Harris," there would be a rush for the extensions in various rooms. It was fun to hear them shouting and laughing at each other. Often they would forget who was calling and finally drift back into the living room disgusted because so-and-so had hung up.

It was all a happy game. They would rather talk to each other than sell some play, or horse, or song. The phone was just a great chance to jibe at one another, practice their newest one-liners, as well as show their contempt for Hollywood.

One of the men I met through Sam was Henricci, *nom de guerre* for a millionaire restaurant owner from Chicago. I doubt his millions came from serving food, however excellent, but in those days no one said "rum-runner" or "bootlegger" right out loud. Dutch Schultz might be sitting next to you in disguise.

Henricci was quiet and small and seemed old to me, with Sam's kind of realistic irony. We talked at length about Life—Literature—Death—and Humanity, but it was always at a party, or gathering, in some crowded living room. One night he gravely proposed that I marry him. It would have been more honest to say "No" then, but I delayed answering. He was rich and powerful, and apparently gentle. I was not working, trying to eat on one dollar a day, and my shoes were getting thin. I was ashamed, too, of begging money from my father.

I asked Sam about Henricci. What did he think? He looked out the window for a few minutes and then said, "Visit his apartment some day, unexpectedly. See what you think of the way he lives."

The Essex House was just around the corner from the Barbizon Plaza, but it was a long social jump. I was surprised to find Henricci's menage was a whole top floor with several wrestler-type doormen. Soon after I arrived three young, sultry-looking girls were shooed out by the doorman. I couldn't help noticing that they were putting on their shoes and buttoning their blouses.

Henricci was an unembarrassed sultan, affectionate and apparently unaware anything was amiss. He renewed his offer to make me Queen of Chicago. I was tongue-tied and evasive, getting out as soon as possible and saluting Sam's intuition.

The whole incident was as predictable as a gangster film. I have wondered since if gangster films were a reflection of that period, or were we, the public, imitating the films? The experience was corny, but those were corny years—extravagant, gambler times, with gangland growing in power and insolence, while old values were being sold short on a declining market.

One Sunday morning I was invited to Sam's for brunch and came too early. I didn't know "brunch" meant closer to noon than breakfast. Mr. Harris' "man" (butler, cook, valet, housekeeper, ad answering service) let me in. It is likely he was an ex-fighter because his ears were rumpled, but his manners were fine and no matter what happened, his face stayed blank. He said, "Mr. Harris is reading." I sat in the living room and wondered if I should leave. He came back and said, "Mr. Harris will see you now." I followed him into the largest bedroom I'd ever seen. The room wasn't big—just the bed. I had never seen "king size," but this must have been one-and-one-half king size.

Against a stack of pillows, tiny Sam sat reading play scripts. The bed was covered with them; green, gray, red, black folders. There must have been 15 or 20.

Sam didn't say anything. The "man" brought me scrambled eggs and I ate in silence. Finally Sam slapped a script shut and growled, "Why don't you write? Anybody can act."

There didn't seem to be any place to go from there, but I tried because I knew how much he wanted a good play.

"With all these, can't you find one you like?"

He snorted.

I wanted to say something fancy, like "What are your criteria?" But Sam didn't care for that kind of language so I tried, "What do you want, Sam? What do you look for?"

He took off his glasses and rubbed his eyes like a sleepy child. "I gotta have somebody I can go along with. You've seen all those bound volumes of my hits..." and he gestured toward the living room. "I gotta CARE about the people. I gotta care what happens to 'em. If I don't care, how the hell will the audience?"

I never forgot that. It was basic. Though how to achieve it apparently isn't simple. It's not technique, or structure, or language. It's an emotional key. How do you build CARING?

CHAPTER 12
NEW YORK, NEW YORK

From the bow of a boat, New York, a mirage of gold and silver towers, rises from green water. It grows misty, then smaller, and finally sinks into memory. It's a Promise, a lie, a preposterous fabrication. Millions of us have been caught in the mirage. Like flies in honey, millions have never escaped. Some of us know about the honey... the comb that conceals it... the creatures that guard it. It is a Tolkien land. To pass safely through the mirage, you must abandon memory. See only what is before you. Accept only the finite—so many blocks... so many floors... this number... so many dollars for this. Don't grovel for friendship. Don't whine for courtesy. Attend to your business and leave—if you can.

Sam sent me to every theatrical office that was casting on Broadway. I dutifully dressed in my best and went, although with less and less confidence.

There were dingy stairs to climb, and when you reached a waiting room it was always dark and shabby. The reception desk was usually presided over by the producer's wife or mother-in-law. They were, almost without exception, Medusa heads, tough and rude and noncommittal. If you managed to wait, or con your way past them, the office within was worse. There was either a lone, shirt-sleeved boss on the phone, or a group of cigar-smoking pals who had come to ogle the girl candidates for whatever parts were available.

What was there to say? They only looked at my legs, or asked me to take off my coat and turn around. "Sam sent me" would get me through the door, but then what? I did not want to work for them, or with them, and I'm sure they guessed how I felt.

Radio offices, on the other hand, were clean, modern, and comfortably furnished. The producers, or casting people, were educated and pleasant and did not put their feet on their desks.

Like many radio actors in those years, I spent endless hours on the red leather benches at NBC's eighth floor. I waited to read for auditions, to see producers or directors, and sometimes just because I was tired and that big lobby was thickly carpeted and quiet.

It was there that The Engineer marked me for a pigeon.

He was short with a young, snub-nosed face and a distinguished head of gray hair.

He stood beside me and smoothly lighted my cigarette. Then with grave courtesy he asked, "Are you waiting for an audition?"

When I shook my head and went back to my novel, he said, "Because there are none scheduled for this afternoon. Are you waiting to see someone?"

Oh, all right. Maybe you have orders to clear the lobby. Maybe you are a janitor. Maybe you are Sarnoff himself. I grudgingly replied that I had been told to see Paul Stewart on this floor.

He grinned engagingly, "Now, that I can arrange. He is in my studio now talking to Goodman Ace. Come alone, I'll introduce you."

From then on it was simple—for him. Or perhaps it was I who was simple.

Looking back on the long episode that followed, I can only plead that my lack of insight was shared by dozens of intelligent people.

Yet even at the end, most of us were still laughing at his practical jokes, still re-telling some of his outrageous pranks. He was funny and he was fun, and as tricky as they come!

In the '30s, radio was still young enough to have few caste barriers, but an engineer who controlled the microphones in the studio and plugged them in for transmission had a little prestige. He could foul up your voice, your volume, and your "tone" either by inadvertence or malice; but since engineers were always company men, few pieces of deliberate sabotage occurred, although mistakes were plentiful.

So my engineer was a factor in the success of the programs he monitored, but not a large one. However, he knew everyone, and managed to work only the well-known shows, convincing each producer that he alone could give them the clarity, tone, and "pick-up" to make them outstanding.

He had quite a system—he would ask me to sit in the booth with him, where I was inevitably introduced as a visiting actress. Then, somehow, there would be an audition, and Presto! I would have a part in the show.

Before our first date, he told me a heartbreaking story of his wealthy wife, who had thrown him out of his home, who seldom allowed him to see his children, who had forced him into a lonely life living with his father on Long Island, and whose divorce settlement left him penniless.

All very, very sincere and quietly heartbroken. He had recognized at once my vulnerability, my staid morality and naïveté, and overcame them all with one artistic lie. From then on he moved further and further into my private life.

When I told Sam Harris about the Engineer and radio jobs, he nodded and said, "Well, that may be the way to go. Broadway is having a rough time now." Another time he said, "Tell me about this guy at NBC. You seeing a lot of him?"

On *The Bakers*, NBC, May 15, 1935

I told him a little about the Engineer's circumstances and admitted we had "gone out quite a bit."

He was quiet for a while, then suddenly looked at me and growled, "You loan him any money?"

I was startled and stammered, "Uh, no. I don't have much, Sam. We usually go Dutch."

He snorted, "Listen, Kid. Any man who will take money from a woman will finally take everything she's got. I've seen it over and over. Now you remember that. Get one that will take care of YOU. You can't afford a bum."

That was the beginning of a drift away from Sam. He was still kind and solicitous, but I had left his world of the theater and gone on to radio. I'm sure he knew I did not take his advice about the Engineer.

Thanks to Paul Stewart (and the Engineer), my first broadcast in New York was *Easy Aces* written by Goodman Ace, featuring his wife, Jane, himself, and "Marge," and an occasional writer. Goodman Ace was a wise and witty intellectual. His *Saturday Review* page kept that magazine a delight for many years.

The show was tops in the East, but I had never heard it. Luckily I did not mention "bridge" or "poker" because, although they worked around a card table with a microphone in the middle, *Easy Aces* had little to do with cards. It was based on Jane's malapropisms and manic misconceptions of accepted social practices. She was similar to Gracie Allen, with a distinctive New York drawl, while he, Goodman Ace, was a calm repairer of the damage she wrought.

After that first break, I worked most of the regular shows broadcast from Radio City, though there are few names worth remembering. *The Helen Hayes Show*, Walter Winchell, who used some dramatized stories and commercials, and *Eno's Crime Clues* were current, with an occasional musical. I remember meeting Ruth Etting there once with The Gimp, dour and persistent by her side.

Gradually I became well known enough to branch out to 485 Madison, the CBS Studio, where I fared well. As yet there was no AFTRA organization so our fees were stingy. A daytime spot would pay $10 to $15. If you ran from Rockefeller Center (NBC) to CBS on Madison Avenue and made the traffic lights just right, it was possible to do three shows in one hour. However, if you did not arrive on time, the producer of whatever show you were scheduled for would simply reach out in the hall and grab another actress.

WOR was the third network, poorer and further downtown, but it offered several mystery shows. I remember meeting Orson Welles on a *Shadow* episode. He was a tweedy suburbanite then, with pipe and commuter problems.

Agnes Moorehead, Mark Smith, Walter Tetley and I were regulars, along with Alice Frost and many other well-known radio voices, on *The Sunday Morning Funnies*. This meant arriving at NBC at 7 a.m. to get the mimeographed scripts written after the Sunday edition of the night before.

Most of us did the show for fun, because it paid only $15 and took at least two hours; but here we had freedom and could do fantastic "doubles" and accents. There was Earthquake McGoon, Li'l Orphan Annie, Harold Teen and Lambie Pie, Mutt and Jeff, and Maggie, and so on and on. NBC had a stopwatch man there for timing but the lid was off on interpretation, burlesque, or raw farce. For actors, it was like going to the gym to flex your muscles and exercise the imagination. We would be out of the plaza by nine, have breakfast and then a long walk down Fifth Avenue to Washington Square, in sunshine or rain. It was lovely to ride back on a double-decker bus, tired and happy. New York was beautiful, clean, and empty on those Sunday mornings.

Bob Hope's first continuing radio show was a mess called the *Atlantic Family*, done by N.W. Ayers for Atlantic Petroleum. I was some kind of nonentity female in the "family" part of the show which grew smaller every week. Hope knew that we had to go, and that his show should be just jokes and music. We departed after five or six shows. Then he and "Honeychile" (Patricia Wilder) finished the 13 weeks. It was certainly not "socko" entertainment, but he was fun and I was impressed with his lovely wife, Dolores, who attended most of the rehearsals and was always calm and gracious.

Now Bob Hope is an American phenomenon. He is apple pie, the Fourth of July, and the American Flag. Whether his decision to become a stand-up comedian was gradual or occurred about this time, I don't know; but it was wise. As an actor, he lacks reality. Even in the *Road* pictures, when he listened, it was for the cue followed by the punch line—the turnaround—the sell-out. This kind of comedy is very hard to keep fresh and alive, because it has such a predictable rhythm. Bob is superbly skillful in the timeliness of his material and his own electric energy. But he could never be a believable underdog, or the guy you pulled for, in a contest. His self-confidence needs no boost.

I have a feeling the Vietnam War was Hope's personal tragedy, because those grueling tours he made into the war zones really reached his heart. In the WW II trips he did not seem as emotionally involved. But he cared deeply for the boys in "Nam." His greatest moments came when he talked to, or about, them. The anti-war activists, and the whole attitude of this country must have hardened his cynicism which perhaps began as a defense years ago, when he realized his kind of comedy must never depend on heart, or sympathy.

For me the best part of the tentative *Atlantic Family* experiment was meeting Stephen Longstreet, who wrote the family episodes. He is an exuberant, witty man, as well as a delightful novelist.

By now the Engineer was my only "after hours" companion. His biggest assignment was a program called *Let's Dance*. It was conceived and produced by an almost legendary woman named Dorothy Barstow. She had found the then-unknown Benny Goodman and was featuring him in this enormous, national format, involving famous bands across the country, "cut in" live from Chicago, San Francisco, New Orleans, and Los Angeles. It doesn't sound remarkable now, but then it was a big, original departure in material and scope. She ran the whole show with a firm fist.

She was a startling figure. I sat mesmerized in the control booth one night, awed by her appearance and manner. She was slim, dressed in silver sequins to the floor, banded with blue fox. Her hair was cloudy white. He face was young, but covered with shocking acne, lumpy and red. She had no time for socializing, or even the amenities. She clicked the stopwatch and barked orders over the intercom, icy and imperturbable.

She was said to be the long-time mistress of H.K. McCann, President of McCann-Erickson, the largest advertising agency in the world, and had complete control of its radio division. She had produced many successful shows, one of which was the perennial *Death Valley Days*.

I wanted to meet her. I wanted to work for her. For days I sat on benches at McCann's and never received even an interview or an audition. She represented to me the ultimate position a woman could reach in New York City.

Years later, when we were friends, I admired a beautiful white peau-de-soie gown she was wearing. Her blue eyes brightened and she laughed. "You know why I bought this outrageously expensive thing? I got it because it helps me remember how poor we were. Did I ever tell you that my mother made my graduation dress out of an old linen sheet?"

One night in 1952 in her penthouse on 72nd Street we watched the lights come on in the great towers and form the bright lines of the bridges. She said, "This is my city. I worked hard and I won it." She had won it, too, in a way. She was then a powerful and respected woman, now married to Harry McCann, wealthy in both money and achievements. I was proud of her friendship. She had planned several radio and television campaigns around my children and me for *Death Valley Days*. We worked on them for many years, even after her death in 1961.

It was strange that the city she claimed was hers, finally took her life. She and "Boss," as she called Mr. McCann, went to a party at the McCann-Erickson office a night or so before Christmas. He, with customary generosity, had told his chauffeur to go on home to his family. Then he must have had a stroke, or fallen asleep at the wheel, because they smashed into an abutment approaching the 59th Street bridge and they were both killed instantly.

But that was all to come. Now, in New York in 1935, she would not even say, "How do you do?"

CHAPTER 13
THE ENGINEER

That fall my mother came for a visit, and like many new to 56th Street East, she failed to dodge a sack of garbage thrown from an upstairs window. Mother was not one to stand around and wring her hands. Within a week she had me out of the club-hotel and installed in a furnished apartment on 46th Street, around the corner from Lexington, with a doorman, and a year's lease. It was sunny luxury. I even had a tiny kitchen and could look out on a little garden restaurant below.

The cost was nominal, especially as Mother had paid the first and last months' rent, and I was doing enough shows now to live modestly.

During this period Sam Harris sent me to the management of *The Morning Telegraph* for a second string critic's job. The Telegraph was a 10-cent stapled racing sheet, but it had a lot of theater news. Whitney Bolton was the Drama Editor, and as Broadway was slowly coming to life, there were occasionally two openings to be reviewed the same night. They hired me for $25 a show and a press pass, saying I'd be notified when needed.

A second string critic is not likely to draw any jewels to review. The first play where I had "two on the aisle" could be termed outstanding only by its parent. It had a lot to do with outhouses, getting there on time, and sharing them.

To a city dweller, this theme could conceivably be hilarious; to me, from the back country in Arizona, outhouses were not all that much fun.

My review was unnecessarily cruel, especially for the hungry actors trapped in the play's vulgarity. I should have found some thoughtful, affirmative words, but I was young and impatient.

The paper got a few protest letters from the cast which didn't dent my ego. After three more smart-ass efforts, I had the temerity to ask Whitney Bolton not to "cut my copy." That did it. I was fired, and a good thing, too, for *The Morning Telegraph* and for the theater.

The Engineer absorbed almost all of my free time. He would write "scripts" for me which seemed flattering, though they were never sold, and probably not even considered by the producers he took them to. He seemed devoted to me, but in retrospect, his pranks eclipsed any romantic possibility in our relationship. Perhaps, as would become my type, I played The Mother and he was less The Lover than an errant Child.

On *The Atlantic Family*, CBS, October 19, 1936

His real charm for me lay in his wild and elaborate pranks. He was fearlessly creative and I was the perfect audience to applaud each mischievous scenario.

One day he smuggled a beautifully framed cartoon into the Metropolitan Museum and hung it when the guard left the room. He would sometimes fake an epileptic seizure to avoid paying a check. On another occasion he freed some owls from the Bronx Zoo with wire clippers. He would heat pennies and toss them onto the rumps of mounted policemen's horses. Then he would run, with nauseating solicitude, to help the cop up off the street, where he was often thrown. He was an expert on fancy "sound" games, hooking up recordings of "night noises" or "locomotives" into symphony rehearsals. He gave the great Toscanini a shock one afternoon in studio 8E by piping a train wreck into the middle of Debussy's "Les Nuages." The first violin was through the exit before order was restored. Walter Winchell was understandably furious when giant frogs croaked over his newscast.

This was fun at first, but soon I wearied of his awful lying to get out of the mischief. I became wary, too, wondering how long I would have to pick up dinner checks or cook meals for this adolescent gray-haired clown.

He had gradually cut me off from any other social life or companions. If I went out with anyone else, he would find us and join the party, taking over the conversation and itinerary.

Work was far from stimulating. Most of the "dramatic" shows were performed in small, stuffy studios that were inadequately lighted for reading endless scripts printed in blurry purple ink. Mama or Daughter or Sister were stereotype cutouts decrying, approving, or reproaching some predictable hero or villain.

The Goldbergs was the only exception. Molly Berg's warmth and vitality helped everyone search for real characters and original rhythms of speech. Just the way you cleared your throat on her program became a delicious punctuation.

But most of my work was cemented into a repetitive pattern of run, speak the piece, run, get food, run, catch a bus or cab—run, get home, run, get dinner—clean up, get enough sleep to start all over again.

Montaigne lauds Homer's line, "Treacherous ashes hide the fires through which you stride." I was living on a thin crust of such ashes. But in New York the surface is so complex and bewildering there seems to be no time, or way, to get beneath that layer to find a warm hollow in the earth for quiet, for thinking, or just being. I am also certain there is not enough oxygen in those canyons to support sanity.

I was an atom in a cyclotron, bouncing off walls or other atoms, emitting sparks of energy, but losing, losing, growing less and yet unable to stop, unable to recharge.

Then, in a few hours everything changed.

I was sitting in a lavatory booth and overheard two actresses gossiping at the washstand.

"...Oh, he never lets her out of his sight around here."

"What about his wife? She's a nice little thing—lives next door to my folks in East Orange."

"I thought he was divorced?"

"Oh, no. He lives at home. He often drives his youngest girl to school."

"Does you-know-who know?"

One of them laughed. "The redhead? Maybe she doesn't care."

They left and I heard the outer door close.

The day blurred, dissolved, and re-focused, until I could lock my apartment door and take the phone off the hook. Most re-evaluations are gradual; mine came swift and sharp in one afternoon. I spent a long time sitting in my only good chair staring at the past two years. I could hear the phone clicking.

The switchboard operator disapproved of "receivers off." You were supposed to ask her not to put any calls through, but she was chatty and I didn't want to talk to her.

It was almost dusk when some young woman several floors above me evidently reached the end of her will to live. There was an odd rustling sound—I looked up and saw her go past my window—a blur of arms and legs and some trailing robe. The crash, four floors down, sounded soft but final. It took me a long time to move. I couldn't go near the window.

When I reached the phone, there was no response. My door buzzer sounded. I heard a key in the lock and then the manager was standing there with tears running down her face.

She said, "Oh! I thought it was you," and turned away.

The hours, even days, that followed were a confusion of anger, for all the wrong reasons; a search for victims to blame, loneliness, and a final confrontation with the sole architect of my little personal hell—me.

There was no real information about the woman's suicide. She had been a transient visitor in a "vacant" apartment. The tight faces and noncommittal answers from the staff added to my bewilderment. I began to wonder if they were humoring me. Had I imagined her death? Was she only a projection of my mind—me, watching me end my life?

It took less than a week to pack my things and reserve a flight to the West Coast. I had refused all calls, but the confrontation with the Engineer was inevitable.

He stood in my apartment door, his wide-brimmed gangster hat dripping rainwater on his shoulders.

"You're a liar... a pathological liar! I don't think you even know when you're lying. You're sick!"

"Will you just listen a moment...?"

"And take off your hat."

"Are you going to let me in? Or do we talk this over in the hall where everybody can hear?"

He came in. Then he had to put his wet coat in the shower. Now he was installed for the Talk-It-Out game he had so often won.

I always attacked first, like a fool—marched right out over the drawbridge leaving my rear unguarded.

"Get out of my life. You have lied from the first day I met you!"

"Rosemary, in a way you are right. But you are my whole life now. I've given up everything and everyone for you!"

"Put down your violin. I'm packing and going home. I don't want to see you... at all... ever again!"

I tried to think back to when he had first befriended me. I must have cared about him. He looked like a little boy, with unruly hair, snub nose, and laughing mouth.

Always when someone threatened me, or was unkind, I had played a game of Turn-Them-Into-Children. Could I see him, or her, when they were five years old? What kind of little girl was she? Shy? Was he a misfit? Lonely? Punished? Abused? A tattletale? Did he lie because he was afraid? Or because the lie was more exciting than the truth?

The Engineer was a perfect subject for the regression game. The little child came through so clearly—trying to oblige—appease—make the adult laugh. I had failed to see that he had never grown up. He was a classic case of arrested development.

When I had let him into my world to play, it was as though I were an absentminded mother, thinking of other things, allowing a disturbed child warmth and comfort, without being emotionally involved at all.

I sat. He stood uneasily.

So I look at you, you 35-year-old deceitful child. And I am bored with you; your tricks and your lies. I am weary of you, and I am dumping you.

"Now, Rosemary—listen."

"Get out of my life!"

He left, giving a dignified performance of the wronged lover. His sweet backward glance failed to remind me that I had forgotten to ask for his key to my apartment.

The return to my family in California meant quiet and sunlight, affection and belonging; although I was momentarily startled by my mother's cheerful announcement that she had sub-let my apartment to "that nice young engineer."

I was too weary and embarrassed to enlighten her, marveling to myself that he had consummated the deal during the time I was airborne. But I felt sure his first check would bounce, and that would be the end of it. Of course, I had also forgotten that the phone was still registered in my name.

CHAPTER 14
A LOVELY LULL

The summer of '37 was a lull for most of the world, according to the press. The exception was Amelia Earhart's doomed flight. Hitler and Tojo were planning their own disasters, but most of us were unaware, and were still struggling with the Depression.

The little apartment where Mother and Jerry lived on Durant Street in Beverly Hills had a small garden that was dear to me after the cacophony of 46th and Lexington in New York City. I planted a squash there that grew so big it moved the garage an inch off its foundation. Jerry finally took an ax to it, suspecting it had more than mere vegetable hostility. I wish I had saved the seeds; there must be a use for that kind of force.

I made a few attempts to find work—an agent, and a radio show. Agents pointed out that I was over 25 and had a bumpy nose, advising me to "stick to radio." The radio and advertising offices assured me they had plenty of competent actresses. Since I had no car, the bus trip to and from Hollywood took a whole day to harvest several rejections.

My mother and father had lived on different continents for three years. He was high in the Andes running silver and tin mines for Mauricio Hochscheild. She did not discuss their marital status. I assumed it was friendly, though distant.

One spring day he sent passage money for the three of us to come to South Amer-

My father, age 50, in 1935

ica. We were to go by Grace Line to Valparaiso and then by train to Santiago for three months. My brother would join Father in Potosi and Oruro for a few weeks, then we would all meet in Santiago with my aunt, Doris Ward, whose husband, Jack, was an engineer with my father.

Those three months were a happy dream. The end of our summer is the beginning of spring in Central Chile. That place and time is closer to Heaven than most places on Earth. The Andes rise white and cruel above green foothills covered with almond and peach trees in bloom. The farmers on their little fincas were plowing and lambing. The sound of cowbells, roosters, and sheep wove a daytime lullaby that erased memories of home.

Me, Jerry, and our mother visit our dad in Chile in 1937.

We rode fine horses for miles every day through mountain meadows. We drank Chilean wine and danced at night in Santiago's Cantinas, awakening at noon the next day to see pear blossoms fall in the Plaza when the bells of Santa Lucia tolled.

My father came down to Santiago for five days, bringing my brother, and crates of silver, furs, and film he had accumulated during his three years on the Alto Plano.

I now realize that my parents probably concluded the terms of a divorce settlement at that time, although there was no verbal indication of their forthcoming separation.

The week we had to leave to catch our boat in Argentina, there were several violent spring storms. We had to "weigh-in" at dawn every morning to be ready for the flight over the Andes to Buenos Aires. After five days of this, the sun came out, the skies were blue-white and clear and we were notified we would fly at 9 a.m. in two tri-motor Ford planes. They each seated 10 passengers and looked very fragile sitting on the tarmac facing the Andes wall, dead ahead.

Jerry wanted to go in the second plane with Dad's souvenirs and the film, a lot of which he himself had exposed, but at the last moment he was sent with us in the lead plane.

The flight was unforgettable. We flew over the Christ of the Andes, almost lost in the snow. Then our wing tips almost seemed to scrape the grim face of 23,000-foot Aconcagua. On the eastern side we could look down on a boiling storm a mile below. Badly buffeted, we landed safely at Mendosa on the Argentine side of the Andes.

The second plane was struck by lightning and burned with everyone and everything lost.

Since we had only the winter clothing on our backs, the 27-day voyage by freighter to New Orleans was an uncomfortable ordeal, but we survived and were a boon to the crew of our little coffee boat. In those days every merchant seaman took his prized photographs down to Rio to get them framed in galloping blue butterfly wings. Having no luggage, we carried a lot of quaint portraits through customs for our seaman friends.

Back in Beverly Hills there were stacks of mail, not all of it affirmative. The Engineer had officially left his family and was now employed at CBS Hollywood. The bill for his phone calls to Santiago, Chile, was also waiting payment. Those calls had been billed to my apartment in New York. If I had realized I was to pay so dearly for the privilege of not talking to him, I certainly would have been more available.

There was also a notice to appear immediately for an audition by McCann-Erickson, CBS, at 10 a.m. next day. I had returned in the nick of time "for an important change in life," as the astrological forecasts say.

I dressed as "New York" as I dared for a hot September day—white gloves, purse and, that California rarity, a hat—caught the bus, arriving too early, as usual. In the glass booth of the studio I got an occasional glimpse of Jean Hersholt and the legendary, white-haired Dorothy Barstow, whom I had unsuccessfully tried to meet in New York.

Jean Hersholt was a great actor and a sweet man with a kissy mouth, rosy cheeks, and twinkling blue eyes. His charming Danish accent had withstood 25 years in Hollywood when I met him. He had become world-famous as the country doctor in the Dionne Quintuplet pictures. McCann-Erickson wisely decided a radio show about him in the same kind of role would make a popular series. In classical films he will always be remembered for his work in *Greed* and *Grand Hotel*.

The audition went on for three days. About halfway through the first session Jean Hersholt was called to the phone, leaving me seated and alone in the studio. The door opened and the Engineer walked in. I gave him a cool stare and went back to reading the script. He leaned over and whispered, "Did you get my letter? I am out here permanently now."

"Yes, I got your letter and the phone bills. I hope you took care of the rent. I can't afford that, too."

As nurse Judy Price with Jean Hersholt as *Dr. Christian* in 1940

"Rosemary, trust me. I will, of course, take care of all bills. I just need a little time. I don't get my first CBS salary check until Monday."

"Will you please just leave!"

Instead of leaving he marched into the booth, shook hands with the engineer, and Dorothy Barstow, whom he knew from her *Let's Dance* program in New York. Then just to show off, he fiddled with some of the equipment panels behind the console.

I ground my teeth, knowing he had now made CBS Hollywood his territory and put me in the position of an outside contender, again dependent on his assumption of authority.

I managed to outstay everyone for the three days of auditioning. It meant brown-bag lunches, buses, and skirting contact with the Engineer, but I finally won the continuing part of the nurse "Judy Price" opposite Jean Hersholt's *Dr. Christian*. If I could have foreseen that the show and my part would continue

The cast of *Dr. Christian*, where I worked for 17 years, Art Gilmore is between me and Jean Hersholt.

every week for 17 years—through two wars, marriage, and four children—I might have opted for a quick return to Chile. But I was prescient enough to know I had won a big one.

The only problem now was to avoid my friend from New York. He had little or no money and I heard that he had even begun borrowing from some of the CBS staff. My only hope of staying clear was his lack of mobility, because he did not have a car. But I was sure it wouldn't be long before he would con some unsuspecting victim into selling him one on credit.

His social skill at insinuating himself wherever he wished made Dorothy, as well as my mother, easy targets. He managed to convey the lie that he and I were a "duo," and to imply to Mother that he had arranged for me to win the audition. There did not seem to be much use of protesting. He was amusing and earned a certain tolerance for all sorts of services: "I'll take care of your transportation," "I'll see to our reservations," "You must have a nicer dressing room," "I'll see that your guests are seated," and so on and so forth. Mother and Dorothy found him indispensable.

I was caught in the middle; weary of him, weary or protesting that he did not belong to me, that I had not asked him to come to the coast, weary, too, of

Dick Powell, me, Victor Moore, and Harold Lloyd in a radio rehearsal

never being allowed more than 10 minutes alone with any other male. If I had a coffee break at Brittingham's with fellow actors, he would join us. If I rode home in someone else's car, he would borrow a car and follow.

When I tried to convince my mother he was cutting me off from any social life, she said, "Why you ought to be ashamed! He is devoting his life to you."

There was nothing to do but work, and to work well enough to earn my freedom. I bought a car, a Plymouth coupe for $750. It was a little gray louse of a car that was a marvel of dependability and anonymity. (I sold it six years later for $750.) I took to wearing weird hats and dark glasses, managing to fool my shadow at least part of the time.

Radio was booming. There was *Hollywood Hotel*, *Lux Radio Theater*, *Hedda Hopper's Show*, *I Love a Mystery*, *Arch Obler's Theater*, *The Jack Benny Program*, *Calling All Cars*, and dozens of others. Russ Johnson at CBS built a morning soap for me, called *Sally of the Star* which lasted a season. There was so much work that any actress with a drawer full of accents could make a good living.

A year after *Dr. Christian* was launched, Dorothy Barstow and Mr. McCann were married. The change in her was startling. Her acne disap-

Jean Hersholt, me, and Dorothy Lovett in *Dr. Christian*, c. 1939

peared. She smiled and chattered like a young bride, referring to her husband as "Boss" constantly and lovingly, a hand on his shoulder, soliciting his opinion. (She had never before been known to solicit anyone's opinion publicly.)

She invited me to accompany them on a "little honeymoon" to Palm Springs. Since they had been living together for at least 10 years, this was not as odd as it seemed. I knew she had few friends so I was flattered to become one of her intimates.

She was a kind of legendary "tycoon" at a time when women rarely made it to the policy-making level. Her physical appearance was formidable—snow-white hair worn like a George Washington wig and tied with a black velvet ribbon in the back. Sometimes she would tint her hair green, or apricot, or violet to match a special gown. Her body was slender and flat, with good legs and arched feet usually shod in elegant Capezio slippers. She walked quickly, with a kind of controlled precision, like a fighter or a dancer. Her rigid New England upbringing may have caused some inner revulsion during the years she was Mr. McCann's mistress. Perhaps the acne was an outer sign of guilt. In any event, it was now replaced by a roseate glow that was very becoming.

Dorothy made the *Dr. Christian* show a milestone in radio history. First, because it ran almost as long as her other success, *Death Valley Days*. Both series retained their original sponsors in a continuing state of euphoria. Second, she initiated a national script contest for *Dr. Christian* with annual prizes and the purchase of winning stories for the show. Several writers came out of the contests; one was Rod Serling, who created *Twilight Zone*, *Night Gallery*, and many other science-fiction radio and TV stories.

I could finally confide my problems with the Engineer to someone who would listen impartially. She said exactly what I knew to be true, "It is your own doing. You have allowed yourself to be knowingly manipulated. When you really want to be free, you will get free."

The Engineer queered his "in" with Mother about this time with one vulgar gesture.

She belonged to the Santa Monica Swimming Club, a charming old complex down on the ocean next to the Beach Club and Marion Davies' colonial mansion. It was a beloved, unpretentious place with a starry membership roster, including Johnny Weismuller, Dick Powell, Joan Blondell, Allen James, Cary Grant, Billie Dove, the young Hearsts, and many other film personalities, as well as a group of old Los Angeles socialites. The food was excellent and the members were friendly, without being self-conscious about fame, wealth, or even obscurity.

With Rod Serling, winner of the *Dr. Christian* writing contest at a benefit for young writers, c. 1960

The moving to California had not cured the Engineer's wild penchant for mischief. Any formal situation or conventionality brought out the worst in him. The Swim Club's dining room had a hard and fast rule about men wearing shirts to lunch, and no bare feet, a fact of which our friend was well aware.

This particular day I was out on the beach while he and Mother were having brunch. When the waiter asked him politely to put on slippers and a shirt, he went to the locker room. When he returned, according to Mother, he whipped out a jock strap and threw it across the room where it landed in a wealthy old member's soup.

The next thing I knew, we were in Mother's car headed for Beverly Hills without our stunt man. From then on he took to hanging around in the bushes, but never made it inside again. When Mother was through, she was all through.

CHAPTER 15
CHEERS FOR MISS BISHOP

My country and I share a peculiar attitude. We embrace and enshrine our defeats. As a country, we laud Bunker Hill, Gettysburg, Remember the Maine, and The Alamo, and never forget Pearl Harbor! As a person, I can recall my failures with a clarity that brings back the original perspiration and hiccups.

I remember well that my first film test was a surprising defeat. RKO had tested me for the part of Judy Price. Since I had been playing the role of the beloved Dr. Christian's nurse for two years on radio, it never occurred to me that the little scene I had to play with Jean Hersholt was anything but a formality. I was surprised to see another young lady (Dorothy Lovett), dressed in a nurse's uniform, on the set. I introduced myself, hoping she was a REAL nurse, there to bring me around if I fainted.

Not at all. She did the same scene with the good doctor that I had. The studio notified me the next day, in effect, "One potato, two potato—out goes you!" I was hurt and furious, but done's done, and eventually I lucked out in a different direction. The few Dr. Christian films were badly made and no one heard of them after they crawled out of RKO.

Meanwhile I was substituting for Martha Scott in a radio series recorded here while she was preparing for *Cheers for Miss Bishop*. She had made an enormous hit on Broadway in Thornton Wilder's *Our Town*, and was very much in demand. She was the kindest and most generous actress I have ever met and never missed an opportunity to help me, even though she had many personal problems and demands on her time.

One day she called me to say that there was a part for me in her new film. I had a gift for mimicry and had successfully imitated her voice in her series and, of course, had my drawer full of accents, as we all did in radio.

The part was that of a 16-year-old immigrant girl who was accused of cheating in an examination on the Preamble to the Constitution, her defense being total visual recall of whatever she saw in print.

I met Tay Garnett, the director of *Cheers for Miss Bishop,* an Irish pixie who had a fine reputation, and such social charm that he almost concealed his concern about me. He knew I had never been in films and also that I was much older than the girl he was casting. He liked my reading of the part and suggested a screen test. Martha said, "No, Tay, I want her to play the part, but give her a make-up test if you like." After my experience with "screen tests," that was very kind. She knew I needed to feel secure.

Martha fussed over my wardrobe, battled for the salary she thought I should have, even let me use her bungalow for a dressing room. Her thoughtfulness and her example have reminded me to pass on what help I could give to young people, even when it was not comfortable to do so.

The make-up man on *Cheers for Miss Bishop* was Don Cash, one of the most remarkable artists I ever met in Hollywood.

He did years of rehabilitation cosmetics in the Veterans' hospitals for men whose faces had been burned or mangled. This was a complicated procedure involving first, plaster masks, and then from those he would make thin, flesh-like rubber appliances that could hide disfigurement, or even replace missing features. When plastic surgery could go just so far, or when it failed, Don enabled many a wreck to return to society. He worked with children who had birth defects, or bad accidents. He donated his time to the hospitals and gave many an unhappy human being a new outlook, and a new self.

I saw him only a few years ago when he had been doing that kind of work for 30 years. He was an artist in human flesh and commanded a big studio salary at one time. But the hundreds of "alumnae" who can testify to his skill and generosity probably meant more to him than his screen credits.

His job on *Cheers for Miss Bishop* was not simple, as everyone in the film (and it was a big cast) aged 50 years. Each one had to have "death masks" made. That melancholy phrase simply means that you lie quietly, GREASED, while the make-up artist pours plaster over your face with little straws in your nostrils for breathing. It is uncomfortable, because as the plaster hardens, it becomes very warm. But if you can keep from sneezing, and think only calm thoughts, you will have a dandy replica of yourself. Of course, it is not very cheerful because you look sound asleep, or, let's face it, DEAD... hence the name.

For me, Don put little plastic triangles behind my ears to make them stick out. They skinned my hair back in a braid—no make-up—a good gaffer, and lo! I was no longer 31, but a 16-year-old immigrant girl of the 1880s. Then for the reunion banquet at the end, Don made me fancy crepe jowls to go with a gray wig.

The scene went very well. How can you lose, with two minutes of close-up saying, "Ve holt dese troots to be self-evident, dat all men are kvee-ated eekval..." etc.?

For the first time, and perhaps the only time, I heard applause for ME, in the projection room. My trophy case of bronzed Failures now included one modest Success, and a long career in films had begun, thanks to Martha Scott, Don Cash, and Thomas Jefferson (who wrote my lines).

CHAPTER 16
MY HOST

Perhaps for each of us there is one kind of face that is dangerously attractive. The magnetism is so compelling, so irrational that it seems to emanate from some former life some fateful reincarnation... "When you were a king in Babylon, and I your Egyptian slave."

My fateful face is a descendant of some Tartar marauder. He has high cheekbones, wide apart eyes of any color, olive-hued skin, and a curly mouth that is rather cruel. A Yul Brynner kind of face.

Maybe he is every woman's Nemesis, the prototype of the Hunter. I don't know. I never hung around long enough to watch the other girls' symptoms. Knowing instinctively that such a face was Surrender, I had always urged my knees to carry me to the exit before it was too late.

But in 1939 I met the Face—face-to-face—at a rehearsal of the radio show he was producing. I was locked in with a contract. He was very matter-of-fact, crisp, no lingering glances, no favoritism. I thought, "This will wear off. I can handle it. I don't have to watch him, sit beside him, or listen to his voice. I will be busy with what I have to do." This went on for two months. Then one day he looked at me coolly and said, "Stay a few moments. I want to ask you something."

My heart pounded and my hands got wet. The show went off the air. He stayed in the booth. I collected my things and went to the door. He caught up with me and, looking straight ahead said, "What are we going to do about us?"

I needed to lean against a wall, or sit down. I wanted to say something smart, like, "Us who?" But my throat closed and I couldn't answer. I never did answer. Neither of us found any solution. He was married and the Engineer dogged my every move. The only times we could meet were when we walked our dogs in Roxbury Park at dusk. We'd sit in the swings and whisper and sigh; two not-young love-sick children. There was no way out for either of us. I could never live with him after the emotional damage done by the Engineer, and his wife would never give him up.

The Dr. Christian Show moved to New York for two months that summer, marking a recess in this frustrated romance. When I had been there a week, Dorothy McCann took me aside and said, "Rosemary, the man you've been

With Jean Hersholt and John Charles Thomas at 21 in New York

seeing is dangerous for you. He's in New York now and called the office asking for your hotel. Mr. McCann's attorney tells me his wife is preparing an ugly lawsuit. Please think this relationship over carefully."

I was horrified that she knew—that anyone knew. I was angry, too. What was the matter with me? Where had I spent the years when other people were falling in love and getting married? Had I been too compulsive a worker? Rehearse, rehearse and never meet reality? Was I such a Late Bloomer, or a case of Arrested Development that I hadn't found love until all the good ones were taken?

I swallowed my anger, because I knew she cared for me personally, in addition to her radio show and its public image.

The last time I saw the Face was at dinner in an obscure little restaurant on the East Side where most of the furniture was painted on the walls. It was "Good-bye" though he didn't know it then. He made it easier for me by picking his teeth and snarling at the waiter.

The light on those high cheek bones and the delicious curl of his cruel mouth lingered a long time in my memory.

In the house of my life there are private rooms whose doors are seldom open to visitors. But even the most casual guest is entitled to know something of his host.

"My host" has been the other half of me for over 50 years. We are one and two. We are three and four, and sometimes more. We met when we were young, parted, and met again.

We were college seniors; he at Stanford, I at Mills. He was an SAE nicknamed Sad Eyes, always involved in some outrageous scenarioed prank with his "brothers" against other fraternities, or professors. That whole class of '32 was so feckless and unpredictable, it's a marvel they became the solid citizens most of them managed to be. I think John was called Sad Eyes because no matter what mischief or con game was afoot, his big brown eyes remained grave and melancholy.

That gravity is probably responsible for the astonishing "fan mail" he occasionally gets from some of the criminals he has sentenced. They read like this: "Judge, you done right I am going to get parole soon becuz I been good here," or "I remember what you said judge you felt bad you sent me up but I am ok now hope you are the same." It must be that he sentences them so sadly that they feel he is not vengeful, but disappointed.

Back in the spring of 1932 we had had a juvenile romance, spoiled by a quarrel over Wordsworth. I had fallen in love with his "Ode to Intimations of Immortality" and kept chirruping, "Not in complete forgetfulness, Not in utter nakedness, but trailing clouds of glory, we come..." He wearied of this (as who wouldn't) and said, "Wordsworth was a dope who went to a dedication of a railway in England, and then wrote a poem about it 'rolling down the grooves of Time. He was a hack who didn't know a rail from a hole in the ground!"

That concluded what must have been a very frail relationship at best.

Eight years later Mother and I were living in her beautiful old Spanish mansion on North Linden in Beverly Hills. She and Dad had bought it years before and kept it rented. Garbo lived across the street and her friend, Dr. Hauser, leased our house for a while. A nosy neighbor insisted that Greta visited him barefoot, but so what? Why shouldn't a legend walk free?

The house had a lovely entrance over which hung an openwork iron lantern. A little yellow finch (to whom I will always be grateful) built a nest in there and hatched out two fledglings. A newspaper friend did a story, with a picture of me on a ladder with the birds. It was rather "ickey-poo" but pleasant. John saw the picture in the *Los Angeles Times* and came to call. We were married eight months later.

He was an attorney and had just been appointed city judge of Torrance. Since his doctor-father had died, and his brothers married and gone, he lived with his mother in the old family home. His eyes were still sad and his mouth still mischievous, and he was utterly dear and lovable.

John and I on our wedding day (1941). Joan Cannon was the bridesmaid and John's brother Fred was best man.

What fabulous good fortune! I had stumbled through years of wandering, had many shabby encounters, unrewarding hard work and loneliness, to come full circle and find darling Sad Eyes. "My bridges all were crossed... The losing dice were tossed... I found you just in time."

My mother planned a perfect wedding, but I made it a very difficult time for her.

The gown—it was "gown" then, never "wedding dress"—was an obstacle for me. I was 30 years old, 105 pounds, five feet two, and jittery. The white traditional outfits made me look like a Maison Blanc boudoir. Finally, 10 days before the wedding, I told Mother she must make me a soft pink, long dress and jacket. Dear wonderful dame! She did it, hemming 10 yards of rose gauze by hand, plus a waist-length veil for my hat. It was so lovely and original I wore it many times and still have the lace jacket.

I became increasingly nervous and fearful as the date drew near. This was not just another public appearance. No play acting; it was real, and for keeps—forever. John and I had a long session with Reverend Stewart of the Beverly Hills

Community Church, which did nothing to lessen the solemn overtones, and merely made me more timorous.

Three days before the ceremony, I asked Mother to cancel all the wedding invitations and invite the guests solely to the reception at our home. I know she must have asked herself if there was going to be a marriage after all, but she said, "Of course, if that's what you want."

Suddenly it seemed very important that our wedding be private; that just our mothers, a brother apiece, and Joan Cannon, my bridesmaid, and the minister be there for those vows. However, we forgot to notify the church that the attendance would be for seven people instead of 250, so I faced a long candlelit aisle and 'way down by the altar were my mother, John's mother, his brother, the minister, and Sad Eyes himself.

I leaned on Jerry, my brother, trying to match his stride. My bouquet was a huge wired affair that rattled like a bunch of maracas. We marched slowly past all those empty, flower-bedecked pews toward the tiny group at the front of the church. Then there were the classic, murmured words, and it was over. I felt as though my heart would burst with joy and relief. John's coat felt so warm and safe when he put his arms around me. He smelled of soap, and his eyes weren't sad at all.

We heard the reception was quite a bash, with hundreds of people dripping little ice cream brides and grooms on each other. Apparently they danced, and drank, and sang until all hours. We barely said, "Thank you, and good-bye" before creeping down the outside staircase to a hidden car. The night was warm and beautiful as we drove along the coast to the old Del Mar Inn.

Four days was all we had before I was due at the *Jungle Book* location. The war was coming closer, and we both had a lot to learn and re-learn about each other. Fortunately, we were old enough to realize it.

CHAPTER 17
TIGERS IN MY LAP

The filming of Kipling's *Jungle Book* lasted from July to December of '41. For those of us involved, it seemed as long as an elephant's gestation.

This was the project of Alexander Korda, whose imagination and elegant taste had produced some of the cinema's finest classics: *Elephant Boy*, *Henry VIII*, and *Thief of Bagdad* among them.

The preparation of *Jungle Book* took several years for good reasons. The original classic was written by Rudyard Kipling, an Englishman; an American, Lawrence Stallings, wrote the screenplay; the scene was laid in India; the world was well into World War II; and it was produced, directed, and designed by three Hungarians.

Of all these causes for confusion, the latter may have been most valid. There are those who will tell you that one Hungarian is too many.

The Korda brothers were extraordinary people, combining more talents than any family in the world of motion pictures.

Alexander Korda—Sir Alex, as he became—was a brilliant financial manipulator; at least, he seemed able to get huge financial backing with ease. He had matchless taste, but was also a ruthless people-manipulator. It's probable that the film would have been done in England or India except that Sir Alex was rumored to be in debt to a British insurance firm for so many millions that he could not return to England, or the Commonwealth, and still retain any of his assets. Whether the rumor was true or not, *Jungle Book* was filmed in California and was beset with financial problems from the first weeks of shooting.

The extravagant sets, the enormous cast, plus erratic changes in the shooting schedules, were likely causes of the "red ink" as we all realized during those wild, hot months in the summer of '41.

Vincent Korda had a marvelous talent for design. His costumes, palaces, idols, villages, caves, and temples were Angkor Wat, Ali Baba, Scheherazade, and Indian Raj combined and rewoven into his own dreamlike fantasy.

Zoltan Korda was the director. He was a gentle-appearing man with green-opal eyes and a sweet smile, who could NOT be hurried. He also had a remarkably foul vocabulary. Zoltan in crisis, with a bullhorn, could frighten us all. The child extras were told to stuff their fingers in their ears.

I had been in only two pictures before my interview with Zoltan; *Cheers for Miss Bishop*, and *Hold Back the Dawn* where I was a pregnant Austrian woman trying to get over the border to have her baby in the United States. They were

As Mowgli's mother in *Jungle Book* (1942)

"showy" parts and I had received some praise for my work, but why Korda wanted me for Mowgli's mother, I still can't understand. Sabu, with his beautiful East Indian face, was starring as Mowgli (the lost boy raised by the jungle beasts), whereas I had light eyes, freckles, and Western features.

Zoltan Korda looked at me with his absent opal stare. There was a long silence. Then he said, "Ah, yes. She vill be da mudda of Mowali. But da eyebrows is too tin." Another pause, then, "And maybe too tin here." He made a vague circular motion in front of his chest.

There it was! Flat-chested was what he meant! I blushed, more from anger than embarrassment. That surprised him, and perhaps won him, for he stroked

Mowgli (Sabu) drinks from a well in *Jungle Book*.

my shoulder and smiled, "Don't vorry. Ve fix dat. You de mudda. Good-bye. Tank you."

This happened a few days before John and I were married. After a four-day honeymoon, my hair was dyed blue-black, I was fitted with rubber breasts, and I reported to Sherwood Forest up near Calabasas for the first day's filming of *Jungle Book*.

All of this is simply factual. The five months that followed are swirling images and fantasies that overlap reality. The great tiger, the black leopard, thousands of pigeons dyed apricot, turquoise, and rose. Curtains of dust. Odors of incense and excrement. Painted elephants. A huge lagoon threaded with track for the great mechanical snake, Kaa. Trees draped with real orchids, perfumed jasmine, and jungle vines. "My" village of haystack huts... the fire... the running. Running barefoot over buffalo and elephant turds. Night, and the all-over scrub with bar soap and cold water, trying to remove the brown make-up. Eating in tents. Sleeping in tents. Wondering if my new husband missed me—or if he would even know me in my long black hair and eyebrows, no longer "too tin."

Some crazy, implausible realities intrude on those images—comic now but shocking then.

Jungle Book (1942) with Sabu and those two "Tigers in My Lap." This photo is courtesy of Gloria Jean.

That first day of the picture I was dressed in a beautiful gauze sari. It was plum-colored, banded in silver. I had silver earrings and silver ankle bells. My hair was satin smooth. Ann Fielder, my wardrobe lady and friend, brought me to a chair near the camera to show Mr. Korda the costume and get his approval. He was busy so she turned away, and up came Louis, an old Hungarian animal trainer, carrying twin Bengal tiger cubs. They looked like tiny bears, with round ears and pink tongues. So darling. I begged Louis to let me hold them. He looked around nervously, then grinned and put them in my lap. They were warm and playful. I scratched their bellies, they relaxed, and evacuated handsomely. Ann Fielder saw the damage and screamed. Louis grabbed the cubs and danced about yelling, "You so lucky! All our life iss luck when da tiger does it in your LAP! You lucky lady!" He was steadily backing away, fearful that the assistant director would punish him for my ruined wardrobe.

With Sabu and Jerome Cowan before he ran off with the head hairdresser and was fired from *Jungle Book*

Secretly, of course, I cherished the "lucky lady" legend. There may be something to it, for my good fortune is, to me, unparalleled and I don't know anyone else who has had one tiger crap in her lap—let alone twins.

That was the first day.

The heat up there in old Sherwood Forest (so-called because an early version of *Robin Hood* was filmed there) was appalling and certainly abetted our first disaster.

George and Gordon Bau, two talented and inventive make-up men, had evolved a new stain to color all of us the same shade for the erratic and inconsistent Technicolor film of that period.

The big crowd scenes, which were to be filmed first, involved every principal in the story, as well as a lot of extras. Central Casting had sent a hundred or so assorted Hindus, Muslims, Sikhs, Touchables, and Untouchables, with no regard or awareness of their religious differences. These were to surface later into mayhem.

The first four days everyone seemed to get along. They were dressed in unbleached cotton singlets and dhotis (this is a diaper-like drape) for pants. Then everyone was stained with the new make-up, regardless of color, sex, or whatever.

The same scene from *Jungle Book* as I plead for Mowgli's life with John Qualen, Frank Puglia, and Joseph Calleia (who replaced Jerome Cowan)

The margin for error in those early years of color was widened by the inability of the lab to get the "rushes" or "dailies" processed and returned in less than four days.

The assistant director broke the news to the Bau Brothers at 6 a.m. on the fifth day that it all had to be done over because wherever the men had perspired, the make-up had turned their body fluids bright green in Technicolor. To the naked eye the moisture had just appeared as natural sweat.

I wish I could have heard the commotion when those first scenes were run in the projection room. All those "natives" flapping around with green groins and armpits must have been a sensation... especially at, say, $1,000 a foot.

So it was "Change the make-up! Round 'em all up and shoot the four days of crowd scenes again!"

While this was being organized, Zoltan Korda shot some scenes in the lagoon which did not include the dhoti-draped extras. But the switched schedules disturbed the sequence of the scenes and the delay in seeing the daily footage left gaps in what could be used.

Every time we shot in the lagoon, it was $18,000 worth of orchids, and a crew from Hollywood to work all night on "golden time." When the director decided we had finished the lagoon, he would call for the village to be put back in its place. Orchids and water out—straw huts and village back. Then they would discover the lagoon footage was incomplete. So it was, "Take out da willage! Put back da lagoon!" or "Take out da lagoon and put back da willage!"

Just as the first four days were completed for the second time, disaster struck again. The villain, Buldeo, played by a well-known character actor (Jerome Cowan), ran off with the head hairdresser. Buldeo was the one character, besides Sabu (Mowgli), who ran through the entire picture and was vital to the story.

The whole company was brought to a halt. We had all watched this rather boozy romance develop, but had thought it the usual "location syndrome" of lonely, middle-aged people passing the time. Rumors were rife—"They had gone to Mexico," or "They had an auto accident," or even "They've been waylaid."

After three days they returned to face the combined Korda wrath. We never knew what happened but within hours, there was a new Buldeo, the excellent character actor, Joseph Calleia. Once more we had returned to square one. It was, "Shoot the crowd scenes again!"

By now things went quickly enough as everyone knew where to stand, or run, or fight. But some of the village and lagoon scenes had to be partly redone. So, "Take out da willage and put back da lagoon" ate up more thousands of dollars.

Meanwhile the Muslims, Hindus, and Sikhs were chasing each other with knives after dinner. The screams of the aggressors and the wounded became a nightly lullaby. The Kordas went home to sleep, so they did not realize how our little war was heating up, until one wild night a leaping Sikh threw his curved sword at a Hindu. Lives were spared, but the weapon overturned some candles and the big restaurant tent burned to the ground.

The next day, while we worked and ate lunch outdoors, a new tent was brought in and at seven o'clock, 500 people ate dinner inside, as usual. Efficient, but expensive.

The last sequences filmed in Sherwood Forest were bizarre and hilarious.

The scene was, once more, the lagoon. A herd of elephants was to come to its edge and rescue Mowgli from a "great fire in the jungle."

The lagoon was one-half the size of a football field, laced with track for the mechanical serpent. It had a cement bottom and held water to a depth of three feet. The bank around it, on this particular day, accommodated a crowd of people. There were cameramen, crews of greenery men, gaffers, agents, most of the company, a few relatives, and many onlookers. But today a new group had arrived—pacing up and down with ill-concealed anxiety. They were bankers and financiers, broiling in their dark New York suits, brushing dust, wiping perspiration, and swatting at the multi-colored pigeons. Someone said they would probably run off with the cans of film—or hold the Kordas for ransom.

The lagoon itself was serene and beautiful, reflecting the hanging vines, the banks of reflectors, cameras, and platforms for directors and crew.

The herd of elephants was waiting nearby in a grove of oaks. The poor creatures were so warm and dusty, they kept swinging their trunks back and forth in restless misery. Their "mahout" was a wiry little Bengali who had explained to me on one of my idle days the social order of his beasts. "Deez," he pointed with his prodder at five or six of his herd, "Deeze not smart. Deez not from circus. Deez dumb elephants. But dis one," he patted a ragged-eared monster with benign yellow eyes, "Dis is Rosy. She dah leadah. All de elephants do what Rosy say. She veh old, but veh smaht." He let me feed Rosy some grapes and told me to watch out for her feet.

Today she stood in front of the herd waiting for the mahout to prod her into the shot.

I heard the cameraman and director discussing the feasibility of a rehearsal. Zoltan said, "No. Ve shoot it and use vot ve can. Maybe dey vont do it again." Very prophetic.

Everybody geared up for the elephants' entrance to the big pond. The "Speed!" calls came over the bullhorn. The mahout gave Rosy a swat on her rear and she started forward. He ran around prodding the other beasts into line.

Then came utter madness. If only I could have a slow-motion film of the next five minutes.

Rosy ambled over to the edge of the water and kept right on coming. The mahout tried to stop her but she tripped on the underwater track, fell down and rolled over, spewing water from her trunk high in the air.

Then it was "follow-the-leader" for the other six monsters. They all sloshed into the pond, tripped, and rolled over. There's something hysterical about an animal that big, stubbing its toes and falling down. Everyone on the sidelines had started to laugh, but were suddenly doused with waves from the shallow lake now overflowing with thrashing elephants. Cameras, platforms, agents and financiers all went over backward in one wild wave of water and confusion. Those who were still on their feet were bug-eyed with amazement, or doubled up with laughter.

In the lagoon Rosy and her gang were rolling, spraying, and trumpeting with joy—so cool at last. So happy!

In early winter, when we had assumed *Jungle Book* was finished and on its way to the theaters, I got a telegram

Another shot with Sabu from *Jungle Book*

saying, "Are you available to work in water November 21st? (Signed) Korda." That odd language is practical contractualeeze for female performers.

So—to paraphrase a cliché—"Meanwhile back at lagoon..." they were preparing a new sequence for the big fire in the jungle.

This time the lagoon had been rebuilt in a giant tank at General Service Studios in Hollywood. It was smaller and deeper with a little sandy island in the middle. Sir Alex Korda was directing by bullhorn. Zoltan was nowhere in sight. I was made-up, dressed in my old sari, and told to wade in and make for the island. The water was waist-deep and chilly. There were huge fans blowing red powder so that the air looked fiery and the water reflected orange light. The effect was marvelously colorful. The whole sky and forest seemed to be burning up except that the water was getting colder and my teeth chattered.

When I reached the island, the Great Sir Alex "Bullhorn" bellowed directions that could surely be heard at Hollywood and Vine: "Look this way! Look that way! God damnit! Look agonized—you are losing your little boy again!" It was humiliating; everyone in the studio could hear. Meanwhile grips, prop men, and stand-ins were swimming past me with antlers or water buffalo horns tied to their heads. Since this had to be done dozens of times, we had plenty of quips, such as, "I'm glad my old lady can't see me with these here horns," or "Hi, Rosemary, you're lookin' in the pink, kid." The red dust gave everyone a kind of weird, hectic color. I wondered how long we could go on breathing that stuff. Sir Alex was getting crosser and crosser. Louder, too.

It was maddening that I could not talk back to the bullhorn. I had no dialogue and was not wired for sound. A make-up man would occasionally wade out to mop off the red dust. He would tell me any news, and I would say "You tell that Sir Loudmouth to quit yelling and swearing at me, or I'll quit." But I knew he would never deliver the message.

We finally finished. I said "Good-bye" to darling Sabu on the little island, for the film, and for life. He lived only a few more years after *Jungle Book*.

In spite of all the blunders and incongruities of that filming that have disappeared like the waters in the fake lagoon, *Jungle Book* lives on as one of the world's classic films, a gift from the Kordas' genius. The great tiger still stalks the jungle, and the beautiful native boy rides laughing between the water buffalo's horns forever.

CHAPTER 18
LONG MAY IT WAVE

When the Sherwood Forest location ended, I was faced with sudden domesticity.

My mother and dear Mina Shidler, my mother-in-law, whom we called Shy, must have been aware of my inadequacies as a cook and housekeeper. John had always lived in a male-oriented world of father and three brothers, with Mother to care for them all. Fraternity life at Stanford had meant just another well-run house with regular meals and clean bathrooms.

Our most welcome wedding gift had come from Shy, who had returned to nursing at the Good Samaritan Hospital in Los Angeles after giving us her lovely old two-story home in Torrance.

It was suggested we put an ad in the paper for a cook and housekeeper. I had the weekly broadcast and three good pictures about to be released, so we could afford to have done that which I didn't even know HAD to be done.

Our ad was answered by a beautiful, calm black girl named Bee Millet. She and her husband Bill came to live with us to make our home and our lives pleasant.

John was city judge there in Torrance and had a small law office near our home. The friends and neighbors were friendly and generous, although I knew there must have been a lot of gossip and surmise: "The Judge married that actress who had her king-size bed flown up the outside of their house," and "She brought two black people to live with her!" All this was in 1941 in a quiet town of 10,000 people whose mores were rather those of Nebraska than Hollywood.

We settled into a happy period of playing house. John's stories of his court and law problems made "How was your day?" a game of a "Thousand and One Nights" with endless variations.

He was moderately interested in my "Who-did-what-on-the -set-today" gossip. However, I must have realized then, just as I knew 50 years later, that the action in court is real and is played for higher stakes, and is also far less predictable than the action that takes place in front of the camera.

That fall we ate Bee's wonderful dinners and then listened to records in the twilight. Bee would say, "Miz Shidler, I cook all day and then you eat my work in 15 minutes. Seems like you ought to make it last."

I wish we could have made it last.

I wish we could have made that whole lovely interval last for a much longer time, but Warner Bros., and ultimately World War II which was close at hand, eliminated those quiet months forever.

A studio glamour portrait from the 1940s

Do you recall that perennial greeting card with Jimmy Cagney in a soldier suit, Walter Huston as Uncle Sam, Jeanne Cagney and Joan Leslie wearing stars and stripes, and me as the Statue of Liberty in a white muumuu, with lots of flags waving in the wind? That "still" is over 50 years old. Joyful and dynamic, it exudes a dauntless spirit. That was the last day's shooting of the picture *Yankee Doodle Dandy*.

The overused photo on Fourth of July greeting cards—Jeanne Cagney, her brother James Cagney, Joan Leslie, Walter Huston and me, the Statue of Liberty in *Yankee Doodle Dandy* **(1942).**

The first day on that film was a very different matter: a dark set, bare stage with a few work lights. The camera and crew were standing still with grave faces. Jeanne Cagney, Walter Huston, and I, made-up and elaborately costumed, were staring at a little radio emitting the sound of President Roosevelt's voice, along with a lot of static.

Mike Curtiz, the director, and Jimmy Cagney came in through the freight dock and walked across the big soundstage toward us. When they reached the set, Mike started to speak, but Walter held up his hand. The President finished, with the grave news that we were now at war with Japan and Germany. Then the national anthem blared forth. Some of us got to our feet and sang the words hesitantly. At the end Jimmy said, clearing his throat, "I think a prayer goes in here... turn that damn thing off!" Someone did. We stood in silence for a full minute. Jeanne and I dabbed our made-up eyes carefully. Mike bowed and with his inimitable accent, said, "Now, boys and girls, we haff work to do... we haff bad news... but we haff a wonderful story to tell the world. So... let us put away sad things and begin!"

That began the first day of the film *Yankee Doodle Dandy*, the day after Pearl Harbor, December 8, 1941. Throughout that picture all of us worked in a

Yankee Doodle Dandy—Jeanne Cagney, James Cagney, me and Walter Huston

kind of patriotic frenzy, as though we feared we might be sending a last message from a free world because the news was very bad indeed during those months in the winter of '41 and '42.

We had three weeks of dance rehearsals during which Jimmy was a great example for all of us. He came through the main gate every morning at 6:30 in his modest old Ford, wearing a sweat suit, with his lunch in a paper bag. He worked out and danced (creating most of his own choreography) till noon; took a half hour to eat, a half hour to rest, and then danced tirelessly till five.

We all tried to live up to him. For Walter Huston, it was less difficult. He was that graceful combination of Dodsworth, Father Knickerbocker, and Uncle Sam, and he had danced and sung on Broadway for years. Joan Leslie, Cagney's *Yankee Doodle Dandy* sweetheart, and a lovely, gifted, and popular redhead, became a dear friend.

For Jeanne Cagney and me, it was different. She was 18, beautiful, dimpled, and gray-eyed, and could sing and dance adequately. I was 31 and back-of-the-bus all the way.

The weeks of rehearsal helped. Johnny Boyle, assigned to whip us into shape, was patient and determined, having been a "sidekick" of Jimmy's in his New York song-and-dance days. I felt I was the company "klutz," but everyone

Yankee Doodle Dandy—As the Cohan family clowning around, with Jeanne Cagney, James Cagney and Walter Huston

was very dear and generous to me. When we finally filmed the numbers, we were a joyful and well-coordinated team.

In those days, the songs were recorded in a soundproof studio with the entire orchestra, then on camera the actor or actress "lip-synched" the words to match the song coming from a box, somewhere out of sight.

The other three "Cohans" had sung the original song emanating from the box. Since I can hardly sing "Happy Birthday" on key my voice had to be "dubbed" by someone else for most of the numbers. Consequently when it came time to match my lips to the canned music I was in strange territory.

Ray Heindorf, Warner Bros.' Academy Award–winning composer and conductor, said to me several musicals later, "Jeeze, Rosemary, I don't see how you get by. You don't even have a downbeat." I gave him my best innocent stare and said, "What's a downbeat, Ray?" He fell off his stool laughing, "Never mind. You've got luck. You don't need a beat."

The best fun was on the *Yankee Doodle* rehearsal stage when I could sit next to Walter Huston and coax him into reminiscence. He must have been in his late 60s but so attractive—a handsome, lanky Yankee with merry blue eyes and a wry mouth. He recalled his best times as his years in *Dodsworth* and in *Knickerbocker Holiday* where he had sung " September Song." For me however, his performance in *The Devil and Daniel Webster* was one of the greatest I had ever seen.

I asked him about the "close-ups" of that role. His eyes had been electric—hypnotic—though in real life they were a mild blue under heavy brows. How had they lit his eyes to create that lightning–like intensity?

He took exception to my implication that it had been lighting alone. "Rosemary, m'dear, I discovered in the test for that part, a rather remarkable trick. Most actors in front of a three-inch lens will stare, allowing the light to open up their eyes to give a kind of liquid look. That's passive, and in most cases, uninteresting. I realized, that for the Devil, my eyes must be restless... moving, flickering, bright and intense. So I narrowed 'em and never held 'em still. I must say, with a small 'eye light,' the effect was good. And I think it has helped me in other film roles."

It is rare for an actor to divulge such information. I was especially interested because for one thing, I had had very little experience acting for the camera. For another, I'd just had quite a shock when I saw the "rushes" of my first day on the picture.

In the scene, I was lying propped up on pillows (no one in films ever lies flat, have you noticed?). As Mrs. Cohan, I had just given birth to little "George M." Walter Huston, the baby's father, was standing a little behind the bed and to my right. I knew all about "upstaging" and realized I was at a disadvantage when told to look up at him. He was the star. Had I known him better, or been more experienced, I could have avoided the neck-craning. Anyway, on film, I was horrified to see that when looking upward, my eyes appeared to be crossed! No one mentioned it, and there was no possibility of getting a re-take. So I learned that day how NOT to turn my eyes in my head.

Rather wistfully, I mentioned something about that shot to Walter. He looked at me and smiled, "Yes, m'dear.

With Walter Huston as the parents of George M. Cohan in *Yankee Doodle Dandy*

I noticed what was happening, but I thought Mike would cover it in a close-up. He didn't... So, my apologies."

During those weeks he spoke of his delight at the prospect of working with his son, John Huston, and Humphrey Bogart on *The Treasure of the Sierra Madre* in Mexico. We didn't guess then that this film would become an all-time classic—though it could hardly fail, with John Huston directing his father and Bogey.

Those were happy intervals, listening to Walter. I cherish what I learned from him, and whenever I hear "September Song" I can close my eyes and see his face as I hum along with him, "For it's a long, long time from May to December... And the days grow short as you reach September."

Mike Curtiz was a remarkable director and an exhilarating personality. He was very sentimental about Home, Mother, Birth, and sometimes Death. Nevertheless, he was a ruthless authoritarian, with an eagle eye. He could walk on a crowded set with extras, and instantly spot the one with a missing earring, or twisted tights, or runny mascara. If some actor was hurt, he would first call for a replacement, THEN call for First Aid. Production always came first. He must have been a soldier, because his bearing and manners were Austro-Hungarian circa 1912 with lots of heel clicking.

Since Mike was a dramatic and successful figure, he evoked a good deal of gossip. Stories of his sexual prowess were rife, but I never knew anyone who admitted first-hand knowledge. His wife at this time was Frances Marion, a delightful woman and a top scenarist for many years. Jokes about his accent were always good for a laugh. One concerned Mike's phone call to Frances on a night in '39 when Southern California was drowning in a big storm. As director, he had to attend a sneak preview somewhere in the San Fernando Valley, and he called Frances to say that he might be late. Her front lawn was under water, so she said, "Mike, have you got your oars?" to which he replied, "No, no, dollink, no girls!"

He was always on the set before the camera crew and never ate lunch, or so the legend had it. The noon hour for most directors is used up with seeing dailies, film editors, and production problems for the following day, so a conscientious director seldom indulged in the social hour. Mike quit work at six and needed refueling at once. An assistant director told me he had eaten a late dinner at a chicken shack with Mike and had seen him eat all of the chicken and then crunch up and swallow the bones! Probably fiction, but it fit.

His loyalty to the brothers Warner was deep and constant. They had brought him from Europe and he never forgot the debt, which may have been a detriment to his career. In my opinion, they wore him out on many pictures that did not merit his talent.

After months of work on *Yankee Doodle Dandy*, we all assembled for that big finale—the one that appeared on the greeting card.

Jimmy Cagney performed his incomparable "Dandy" number on the apron in front of the camera, while the rest of us marched endlessly on a huge treadmill behind him. There were dozens of flags blown by the giant wind machines. My Liberty Torch was so heavy they had to wire my arm up. I don't know how Walter kept his Uncle Sam hat on his head. Darling Jeanne and Joan sparkled and swung their arms in rhythm.

Yankee Doodle Dandy goes on and on, appearing year after year, every Fourth of July. The film is black and white and is growing gray and grainy, but the theme of Red, White, and Blue goes on thrilling audiences, as we who were fortunate enough to be in it, to go on singing, "the emblem of... the land we LOVE, the home of the Free and the BRAVE."

The scene is so upbeat and affirmative it is hard to realize that as we were filming it the Philippines had fallen, and General MacArthur was escaping Manila in a submarine, leaving his army to begin the cruel chapter of Corregidor. Our forces seemed to have lost the war in the Pacific three months after it had begun.

The original caption for this photo stated: "Helped by makeup magic, Rosemary DeCamp turns from a young woman to an elderly matron in *Yankee Doodle Dandy*."

CHAPTER 19
MEXICO TO CANADA

Unless you were a Nazi, 1942 must have been one of the world's cruelest years to survive. The underlying ugliness was lack of hope—the certainty that everything would get much worse before it would end.

But in February, the war had not yet touched our lives. When I finished in *Yankee Doodle Dandy*, John and I spent a belated two-week honeymoon in Mexico. It was heaven.

I suppose Pearl Harbor had ended most tourism south of the border because wherever we went we were almost alone. With a car and driver, we drove south through Pueblo toward Vera Cruz. We swam undisturbed in the gardenia-strewn pool at Fortin de las Flores, marveled at Orizaba's snowy top in the sunset, drove to Cuernavaca and lunched in sight of Diego Rivera's murals, had cocktails at Madam Berthe's in Taxco. Then we were surprised five miles outside of Acapulco by runners begging us to stay at various hotels.

We were two of perhaps 10 guests at El Mirador. Everywhere we walked or shopped, there were Japanese posters and a few from Germany, exhorting in Spanish to join a triumphant Axis.

On the return trip our car broke down near Taxco. Our little driver, Trinidad, insisted that if he could just get the "skeen of a peeg," he could repair the broken something-or-other. No "peegs" in sight, we were forced to ride into Mexico City, leaving Senor Trinidad to repair his car and get our luggage to us before the next morning's flight to Los Angeles.

This sounds rather naïve now but he was as good as his word and arrived at four in the morning, just before the five o'clock deadline. We were airborne with baggage, plus two sisal hammocks full of primitive masks and tin candlesticks which we learned to deplore during the long re-entry proceedings.

Getting back into the United States was difficult in March 1942. The first surprise was landing in Palm Springs instead of Los Angeles. The second jolt came when we were prevented from going to the bathroom before the three-hour trip in the rain to Van Nuys, where the military had taken over an airport facility for immigration screening. I was understandably short-tempered during the questioning and body search that followed.

We were glad that they were so thorough, remembering the pro-Axis propaganda in Mexico, but John was surprised when he spoke to a young of-

With Edward Arnold in another 1942 film, *Eyes in the Night*

ficer he had known at Stanford, Dusty Allen, and received a fishy-eyed stare. Maybe he thought we were peddlers with our corny sacks of trinkets. We finally passed all the doors with peep holes watching us, got to the lavatory, and met our waiting families.

That day widened my experience a good deal. Now whenever I see films of Ellis Island, I get a shiver of empathy.

The next few months were hectic because I was pregnant. and John had decided to run for the 17th Congressional seat now vacant because of a death in office.

This was not simply a matter of filing to run. We first had to get 15,000 signatures to qualify for the ballot. It was a very large district and there were 12 other candidates canvassing for signatures. Most of them were using professionals to get the registered names, at 25 to 50 cents a head. We couldn't afford that so John walked hundreds of precincts, getting his own signatures. I helped him when I was able, but he did most of Wilmington, San Pedro, and Torrance by himself. That is one way to really learn your district.

We have been in many political campaigns since that one, and smile at some of the armchair activists who talk about their political efforts. Most of them have never walked a single precinct door-to-door, but we learned a lot the hard way, which helped us years later in the Helen Gahagan Douglas and Kennedy campaigns.

John had tried to enlist in the navy before we were married; his eyes were 20-400 and he was rejected. Now, of course, he was in the draft. His Board had promised him they would not take him until after the election. We naïvely took them at their word.

Meanwhile my friend and agent, Harry Tattelman, had arranged an interview with Lester Cowan. He was a remarkable young producer who was about to make a picture with Paul Muni entitled *Commandos Strike at Dawn*. John Farrow was directing. The part I was being considered for was that of a Norwegian woman whose husband is discovered to be a traitor in league with Nazi occupation forces in Norway.

By now I was visibly pregnant, wearing thinly disguising maternity smocks. The interview was very lighthearted. Cowan, being a high roller—a what-the-hell, take-a-chance kind of moviemaker—slapped his thigh and cried, "Great! You look wonderful. You're going to be a Norwegian peasant. Who cares if you're fat?"

This was encouraging, but then he said we were all to go to British Columbia and that the whole picture would be made on location around Victoria. Since the only "location" I had experienced was *Jungle Book* (difficult enough even when I had been thin and tough), I said, "No, thanks" and wished him luck.

But Cowan had an answer for everything. "We'll take your mother along. You'll get double your salary. You'll be living at the Empress Hotel, all expenses paid. John Farrow's wife, Maureen O'Sullivan, is going and she's pregnant, too. It will be like a holiday."

Obviously he knew nothing about pregnancy—the war apparently presented no obstacle—and he was a gambler who loved risks. Besides, we needed the money for the campaign; so, with apologies to our unborn child, I tentatively accepted.

That evening at a family dinner I waited till dessert to mention the interview with Cowan. When John saw my mother's face light up at the prospect of going to Canada, he concealed any reservations he may have had and said, "I think you should go. It will be easier than staying here and campaigning."

In bed that night when he said, "I'll miss you," I cried knowing it wasn't wise to go, but the decision had been made. The machinery was in motion.

Two weeks later I said good-bye to John, and with my mother left on a crowded train for Canada—in war time six months pregnant. Victoria, British Columbia, was shining in the sun when my mother and I got off the ferry from Seattle. Flowers were everywhere, in window boxes, around lamp posts and lining the walkway to the old Empress Hotel, so close to the dock, towering up like a medieval castle. Each turret was flying a banner or international flag. It was hard to realize that this was a part of the British Commonwealth, engaged in a war that had been going on since 1939 which would destroy thousands of its best and brightest. The assistant director met us in the lobby, which was sort of a combination of Grand Central Station and the Victoria and Albert Memorial. He said the hotel and the whole city were excited about the movie company in residence—that my rooms were on the 10th floor—that I must rest and meet Mr. Farrow and Mr. Muni the following day. This was welcome news because the three-day trip had been exhausting. Also, I was depressed to find no mail at the desk, the clerk explaining that censorship delayed all letters.

When we entered the baroque elevator, we were assaulted by a knee-buckling wave of perfume. Since there was no visible source, I growled, "What is that?" The operator laughed, "Ain't 'at somethin. 'At's Miss Lillian Gish, as was just 'ere, Ma'am. I'm used to it meself... but at first, it's a bit 'eavy."

Whatever it was, it was with us for six weeks. I admire Miss Gish, her charm and talent, but the scent WAS 'eavy. It was a great ad though. We always knew where she was.

The next few days were lively and pleasant. I met John Farrow and his lovely wife, who was pregnant with Mia Farrow's older brother. Paul Muni seemed grave, but had a surprising boyish quality when he smiled. His wife was very reserved, and reputed to be a formidable negotiator in her husband's behalf.

The first day's filming was on a remote part of the island in a beautiful wooded section on a bay. The exterior of a small Norwegian village had been skillfully tucked in among the trees. Actors in Nazi uniforms patrolled its paths. The extras were all recruited from Vancouver or Victoria's society—thrilled to be a part of the story.

The first scene we filmed was a grim execution involving all of the cast and villagers. My "husband," Louis Jean Heydt, and I watched the Nazis hang a man in the village square. In the story he had been our close friend. Later, Louis Jean is discovered to be the traitor who'd reported him for helping the British.

Most of *Commandos* was filmed outdoors so there were many locations in the beautiful forests on Vancouver Island. One day we had box lunches in the woods with the spectacular Black Watch Highlanders, loaned by England for the picture. They were to see grim duty later in New Guinea and the Lowlands, but that day they were blithe and bonny. I marveled at the skillful way they could sit on the ground, balance a lunch, and maneuver their kilts in total modesty. We watched closely, and never "caught them out" as the Canadians say.

With Paul Muni in a scene from *The Commandos Strike at Dawn* **(1942)**

Whenever someone mentions The Black Watch, I see them marching with their bagpipes on the deck of the battleship *Prince David*, their kilts "awaggin'" in the wind, and their music tearing every eye. The film seems to miss the impact and the beauty of that day—the snowy mountains ringing Princess Pat Bay—the gaunt sailors and crew—the solemn actors—and the Highlanders, so handsome, blowing on their pipes.

The location was beginning to take its toll on me. Though I was physically healthy, I couldn't sleep at night. The mail came rarely and was heavily censored. Then one evening John phoned, saying he had been taken in the draft to Fort MacArthur, six weeks before the election. He tried to be humorous about it, saying he had been transported in a bus along with some of the men he'd previously sentenced. He must have been the only judge drafted in the company of his unsuccessful litigants. For me, it was not comic. I knew he would not be detained long at MacArthur and that our location would last another four weeks.

Why had I come? Now the money for the picture seemed a poor excuse—payment for election expenses we might never incur. John would be off to war. I was alone, with my child to be born into a world I could not map or envision. The news from Africa and the Pacific grew worse daily.

Every other night John would attempt the long-distance call to the Empress Hotel at a set hour. He could get through only part of the time. When we talked, everything we said was recorded. If I mentioned the weather, even obliquely, such as, "The part in my hair is sunburned, it was so hot today," we were immediately cut off and a strange voice would say, "Start again, please." It is very hard to talk to someone you love under those conditions. I would leave the phone thwarted and disconsolate.

The daily problems of filming seemed to grow tougher. Along with many others, I had to climb up and down the landing nets on the sides of ships—run through forests—be ready, made-up, and costumed by seven o'clock every morning. The clothes were growing tighter and I was growing larger, sleeping less and less. Every night I would try to wait until my mother was asleep before I began my chronic weeping.

Despair is the ultimate selfish sin. All of us experience it at some time. Some of us give in and let it flatten us, sit on our chests, eat into our minds. It stifles laughter and kindness; rots love. It is a rejection of all the beauty in the world; a negation of life.

My despair during this period was a demon existing only in my own mind, and had no real basis. I was well cared for, gainfully employed, doing very pleasant work with congenial, creative people. The Empress Hotel was the lap of luxury; its food was famous, and its gardens were prolific with extravagant displays of flowers. The weather was sunny and the scenery magnificent.

In retrospect, I can only guess that my gloom was organic. I was 32 years old and about to have my first child. Maybe my hormones had ganged up on me. It's easy to rationalize now, but the blues had me by the throat.

I survived the melancholia for several reasons: my Mother was kind and protective; the Ernie Westmores were full of fun and practical jokes; Mr. Muni was thoughtful. Later he wrote a dear letter to Margaret when she was born, telling her of his affection for me and that he had "worked with" her before she was born. All of this helped, but I got one shock that forced me to forget my own misery and self-pity.

It was the Dieppe raid and its effect on Victoria. This was an attempted commando raid of British and Canadian forces on the French seaport of Dieppe. The news accounts led us to believe the Germans were forewarned and were waiting for the commandos.

For weeks after that raid there was a black wreath on almost every other door in the city. It was then that I stopped weeping for myself and managed to pity people outside my personal world.

The last few days of shooting went more quickly, but there was one big scene which turned into a real stomach growler. Louis Jean Heydt and I were proprietors of a hotel. This was a dolly shot of a long smorgasbord table loaded with food, and the cast lined up helping themselves to the various dishes. It was a sort of Last Supper tableau, with Heydt, the traitor, as a Judas. Every head turned toward him as they finished speaking, and then he had the final speech. The shot ran eight minutes, which was long for those days. A dozen times we completed that scene right up to Heydt, and then he would blow his lines. There was a lot of pressure on him, as he was end man, and we were all sympathetic; that is a situation that makes actors, cameramen, crew, and especially the director, very twitchy. My little baby was objecting, too. We finally got the scene, but we all were older.

The acceleration of the last week had a happier glow. John phoned that he would be held in California for basic training. The Westmores and cast gave me a beautiful baby shower of elegant hand-embroidered English woolens and linen. The picture was reported to be good. My clouds had lifted. It was time to leave our make-believe Norway and catch the ferry for Seattle.

The last hurdles were the Seattle blackout, the fog, and the customs. Mother finally threw a hundred dollar bill to the quarrelsome inspector for the imported baby clothes, and we found a cab which would crawl through the darkness to the train station with minutes to spare.

Train travel in 1942 consisted of soldiers sleeping standing up, and long lines of people waiting for food that ran out. I was fortunate in having a lower berth, but Mother had to climb her little ladder at night, and then hang upside down to see if I was still breathing.

Never mind the discomfort! At last we were California-bound for JOHN, and HOME, and BIRTH.

CHAPTER 20
"A PEARL IS A PALACE BUILT TO PAIN"—KAHLIL GIBRAN

We live a thousand lives within, our exteriors experience only a few—backward and forward in time, in touch, in sight, in full or wasting flesh.

We rush about, playing dolls, assuming roles, devising dramas, in a frenetic preoccupation with our outsides meeting other outsides.

The real confrontations are taking place inside our bodies; the "Star Wars" of diseased cells fighting healthy cells, blood shooting the rapids near the heart, the contraction of the duodenum doused with alcohol, the lightning explosion of nerves exposed to fear, or flame, or ice. All those battles are ignored for make-believe games far from the killing ground.

In pregnancy and birth I discovered the sobering truth of where the action is.

The luminous look of a pregnant woman is so evident, so remarkable. It must be that she is listening to the inner conflict. She has a divided attention between other human beings and the busy life within.

My first labor began about 37 hours before birth. I gradually realized that pain can be so complete, so all-encompassing, that it verges on euphoria. You can float on it. It is actually levitating. In the latter stages you can reach a disengagement that puts you on the ceiling, pitying yourself below.

I had to walk endlessly for two days and a night. This sounds worse than it was. Actually the trudging was lightened by the rhythm of the pain which elevated me from point to point—table to chair—to bed—to patio—up the hall—back to room—back outside.

The walking was external. The great force was inside—a large child fighting its way down a narrow tunnel to life and breath.

The last four hours were eased by cones of anesthetic which were placed over my face a few seconds at a time. The delivery room was beside a patio with a door open to sun and flowers. Goldie, my nurse, was beside me. My mother-in-law came to measure my feet for slippers she was crocheting. The doctor was in and out. It was a cheerful, matter-of-fact scene that helped me to believe the pain must be normal—that I would not die under the ether cone—that the compulsive spasms would cease—and that I could eventually reach a longed-for unconsciousness.

Of course, after birth the memory of the pain is wiped out more quickly than a film cutter's splice. Otherwise no woman would ever conceive again and the race would end.

What's more, when the warm little traveler from inner space lies on your breast, there is no inkling of blame, no connection between the agony and its cause. You are both exhausted survivors of a terrible battle; a team resting a little while for the longer life struggle ahead.

That night about 2 a.m. my husband slipped into the chair by my bed, wearing a crumpled rain-soaked uniform. My brother had picked him up in the rain outside of Camp Roberts and driven him 200 miles to Torrance.

With Nana (Margaret), our first daughter, on her first birthday in 1943

We whispered and laughed for hours.

"Have you seen what I... er... we have produced?"

"Yeah. The night nurse showed me a funny little beat-up doll. She looks like one of those toys they make out of dried apples."

"Oh, really? Everyone says she's the image of you."

"No, I think there must be some mistake. Ours was probably out for a snack and they just keep this one around for visitors."

"Well, we can't take it back. She's no-deposit-no-return. Though come to think of it, there was quite a large deposit."

"Cheer up. They'll bring you the real one in the morning. This one looked like a dealer's model with a lot of miles on her."

It was so fine to see him, though he looked thin and smelled very wet. He slipped a silver infantry ring over my wedding band, kissed me and said he had to go. I think he was AWOL, but we didn't talk about that, or "shipping out," or when we'd meet again. He left just as it was getting light.

When my mother came in about eight o'clock, I said, "John was here last night."

A family portrait with our second daughter, Martha, and Margaret in 1947

She touched my forehead and murmured, "There, there. Of course he was with you in spirit, all the time." Then she trotted off to get the nurse.

When I kept insisting, the nurse put a thermometer in my mouth and began writing on the bed chart.

I waved my new ring at them. But even then they were dubious—doubting a stranger could breach their sacred halls so easily. Three years later, after the wars on both sides of the world had ended, Martha, our second daughter, started down the birth canal during a movie, 10 miles from the hospital. Remembering the last interminable labor I decided to stay for the end of the picture. We arrived at the hospital with a very small margin to spare. It was all so easy and so different from the first child—and the third. And the fourth.

Fourteen months later I spent the longest night in the hospital I hope I shall ever have to endure. Dr. Beeman, our same, one and only doctor, was not happy about this pregnancy. I felt fine, but he kept taking X-ray pictures and listening to my heart. He measured and probed until I grew angry and sent him, as well as my nurse, Goldie, to bed. Climbing on and off examination tables, with my bulk, was wearisome and awkward. I assured them that I was in great condition. "Go get some sleep. I certainly intend to. Let me be!"

Our three daughters, Margaret, Martha, and Valerie in 1950

They left me in bed, in the same room I had had during the two previous births. After a while, I got up to go the eight or 10 steps to the bathroom. Suddenly I heard my blood pounding rhythmically "thrum-thrum" on the tile floor. My mind was slow to grasp what was happening. I moved to the head of the bed to pull the emergency light and leaned there—waiting. But no one came. I looked at the floor, marveling that I could contain so much bright fluid. Then there was nothing. I just faded out in shock.

When I came to, numb and flat, there were a lot of faces around the bed. During that painless coma, I had had a "Cesarean" and a perfect third daughter. For me, it had been almost cinematic—dissolve from bloodbath to surgery—out to recovery.

A nurse I had known years before had entered the hospital that night to begin her 11 o'clock shift. She saw my name on the register and came down to visit. What she found apparently produced a flurry of doctors, nurses, and surgery. They proudly announced it had taken only an hour. An hour? What's time in a coma?

The emergency light in my room was shorted out and had not registered on the main board. So I really owed my life to a chance visitor. Oh, lovely circumstance—to save two lives—a subsequent baby, and at least 30 more years of this dear world! Thank you always, Helen Nelson. You came from the outside and saved the inside.

The fourth birth was really rather jolly, relatively speaking. Which may prove one can become accustomed to almost anything.

If you have had one Cesarean, the medical profession refuses any normal births thereafter. I suppose they fear the abdomen and uterus walls might tear, though they are very vague and just say things like, "It will be much safer and simpler, etc." Certainly Cesareans are easier for the doctor to control. They can schedule a 7:30 a.m. operating room birth and skip any 3 a.m. emergency calls. Also, playing God, with a set time for birth, ensures a free weekend. I'm not too cynical. The practice has solid precedent. But skepticism sets in when the little baby appears not quite "done"—eyes slightly fetal—body too small for the size of the head.

Walking on the backyard croquet field in 1953 with Valerie, Nita, Martha, and Margaret

However, Nita Louise, our fourth daughter, arrived prearranged in a happy and successful morning surgery.

I was given a spinal anesthetic and listened, bemused, to the operating room bustle. Those medical shows that portray a solemn hush are way off the mark. It is more like *M*A*S*H*. There is a God-awful lot of noise in the O.R. Banging metal—swearing doctors—jokes—greetings—cheerful comments on the cutting process. I could see, in an overhead reflector, most of the procedure. The sound of the little vacuum cleaner used to suck up extra blood was a noisy buzz. One doctor, Cliff Easely, failed to show up and was cursed out calmly and steadily by Dr. Beeman. My husband's brother, Jim, was serving as a medic on the vacuum cleaner. The reflector grew dim from the steam of activity beneath it. My calm was that of a spectator with just a mild interest in the outcome. I felt only a few solid shoves as the baby was removed and I was sewn up.

No one had told me a Cesarean baby has no color. So when Goldie held the little body up for me to see, I was shocked and saddened at the clay colored face—eyes closed and a single drop of blood on its forehead.

Christmas 1954 with my four beautiful pearls

I thought, "Oh, she's dead. How sad, and she's so beautiful."

But she was perfectly all right and had that strange color because of missing the normal birth struggle, which reddens the face and body.

Now she is grown and as lovely a person as the other three—two normal and two Cesarean. I've often wondered what personality differences would become apparent from not having experienced the fight to be born. So far no generalities seem valid.

There are many "old wives" beliefs—regarding Cesarean sections and the humans who arrive sans a struggle. These people are said to be divine optimists, courageous, and unaware of opposition. This fits Caesar all right, who seemed blind to Brutus' widespread conspiracy. However, as to my daughters, I see no apparent differences in attitudes or strength of character—optimism or pessimism. Each of the four is different; strong and humorous, with a fine mind and a charming personality. The manner of arrival probably has little effect on the predestined soul of the newborn except in the minds of astrologers and spiritualists.

My daily *laudate deums* include profound gratitude for the four beautiful pearls from inside this oyster.

CHAPTER 21
UNIVERSAL BEFORE
THE BLACK TOWER

My husband was at Camp Stoneman on the verge of being shipped out to the Pacific. The baby and I lived with Mother in the big house in Beverly Hills. The war seemed endless and we had no income, so I went back to work.

In the 1940s Universal was like a happy little village. No—make that a sanitarium. It had cottages and awnings, and cozy, shabby little offices for make-up, hair, and costumes. You knew everyone's first name, at least.

"Good morning, Joe." "Norm, has the coffee gone through yet?" "Hey, Don! I saw your dailies. Just great!" "Betty, I'm late but I need a shampoo." "Didja hear? They're trying to get us a five-day week! Imagine having Saturday off!"

"Listen, they'll work ya till dawn so you'll have to sleep all day to catch up."

"Yeah, Norm said last week they left for location at five with a 'having-had' call.

"You never had a having-had call? Well, luv, that means you leave at dawn having-had breakfast, so they don't have to feed you."

Those Universal days were fun, filled with a kind of familial warmth. Most of the actors were contract players, or else the casting director liked us and kept calling us back because the film directors were used to us and knew what we could do.

It was a snug little nest for errant and gifted children. The stars and crew had time to play practical jokes on each other. The hours were very long, and most of us seldom saw our real families—so we adopted make-believe relatives.

By 1944 every studio in Hollywood was attempting to ride on the coattails of the successful *Yankee Doodle Dandy* and its story of a poor but talented vaudeville family that worked its way to fame through innumerable production numbers. Universal Studios joined the trend by producing *The Merry Monahans*. The cast included the beautiful child-singer, Ann Blyth, plus Peggy Ryan and Donald O'Connor, along with Jack Oakie and me.

Donald O'Connor is one of the most skillful dancers who ever came down the runway, and 50 years later Old Featherfoot is still hanging in there with wit and grace. It's that heel and toe that makes him go, I guess.

The Merry Monahans **(1944) — driving in a "merry Oldsmobile" with Jack Oakie, Ann Blyth, Donald O'Connor and Peggy Ryan.**

Ann Blyth had a fabulous operatic-trained voice at 14, and Peggy Ryan was a skinny little twinkle-toes who could match, if not surpass, O'Connor.

Jack Oakie was the big star to sell the picture. He and I were the father and mother of Peggy, Donald, or Ann; my recollection is a little hazy about which one, as this particular plot tends to blur through repetition. In time-proven fashion our vaudeville act inevitably wound up wildly successful on stage in a finale of Tapping Toes, Trilling Notes, Top Hats and Tails, but only after many Trials and Tribulations.

Why I was in the cast with such great singing and dancing talent was moot. Apparently Universal bought the Yankee Doodle illusion that I could sing and dance.

Louis DaPron was Donald O'Connor's choreographer and coach. He was young, imaginative, and a fine dancer. He was also endowed with such patience and courtesy that he did not show his horror when he discovered I could not even do a time step without counting out loud.

Jack Oakie and I were to do an old-fashioned music hall number early in the picture just to establish that we were show biz folks. Louis rehearsed with me endlessly. I had an hour with Jack the day before the shooting.

With Jack Oakie at the dressing-room door in *The Merry Monahans*

Now, Oakie was so much fun that he was a little dangerous. With him you got to laughing, applauding, trading jokes, and showing off so happily, you weren't aware those twinkling little eyes in that jolly round face had you wrapped, ticketed, and ready for delivery. Jack was a born con-artist and probably was saved from a life of crime because of his talents, which were enormous, as well as by his wise wife, Victoria Horne.

We rehearsed the dance and in between laughs, I remember his saying something about how "we had better spread out a little." I thought, "Why not? I can count 'one-two-three' over here just as well." Then I'd forget and move closer on the turns. He smiled and said, "Honey, I'm going to be wearing some clown shoes and you may need a little more room."

A little more room! Holy Cow! You should have seen him when he came out of his dressing room. He was wearing a kind of hobo-leprechaun outfit with tight pants dwindling down into the most incredible flappy red shoes I had ever seen.

Remember Pinocchio, whose nose grew longer every time he told a lie? Oakie's red shoes were like that. They literally ran along the ground for a yard beyond his toes. They looked medieval, as though they came from the Comedia dell'Arte, or some ancient engraving by Hieronymous Bosch. In the circus they would have been just old clown shoes; to me they were an impossible hurdle I would have to jump.

It must have been difficult for Jack to dance in those appendages, but he did everything with such skill and style it looked easy.

For me it was like dancing and skipping rope at the same time. On each turn I was jumping to miss those long red worms. To hell with "one-two-three"—just don't trip on the rotating flappers. Every time I turned toward Oakie, he would up-end one shoe like a ski, look at me in the eye and laugh. He was fun and I finally got the hang of it—jump rope plus time step. We stumbled through to a finish in four or five sweaty takes.

It was a lot of work for little gain as the camera was way back in a music hall set crowded with extras who thought we were wonderful. But the story had to move on to Ann Blyth and Donald O'Connor and our ultimate success as a family act. Several years later I met a man who had seen *The Merry Monahans* 14 consecutive times and was understandably tired of it. It was a windy night in New York, and Edie Phillips and I were searching for a cab near Sixth Avenue and 58th when a fierce gust blew something in my eye. Edie, a young Paramount lawyer at that time, was a born and bred New Yorker who could solve any emergency. She herded me into the Barbizon Pharmacy to get drops, advice—whatever. When we reached the prescription counter, a neat young man in his white jacket looked at me and said, "Oh no! Not you again!"

I said I thought that rude, and please do something for my eye, mopping the tears.

He removed a gnat and gave me some drops, while explaining he had just returned from some lonely base in the Pacific where *The Merry Monahans* was their only movie. He had seen it every night for two weeks, even offering to do some of the numbers to prove it. Edie and I thanked him and declined, leaving him to his night shift prescriptions and memories.

Unlike the returned GI, I never saw the picture even once (until recently) for some reason or other and I always wondered how Jack and I and the red shoes looked in the weird little dance. A few months after *The Merry Monahans*, Universal decided to do the same story again. Like the old school yell, "Hit 'em again—Harder!"

This time the cast included Turhan Bey, Maria Montez, Susanna Foster, Donald Cook, Frank McHugh, and Jack Oakie. Its title, *Bowery to Broadway,* tells you all. My memories of that one are fragmented; dark and light, happy and sad, and perhaps some are just malicious.

Turhan Bey, an exotic Oriental-cum-Turkish leading man, had a crew cut that had to be blacked on top before every shot because he was getting bald. If he perspired, the black ran down his neck.

Turhan Bey, Susanna Foster, Frank McHugh, me, and several players in a scene from *Bowery to Broadway* (1944).

Susanna Foster, a beautiful young singer, was late every morning. Her car was bashed and damaged in some new way each day. At the end of the picture, one of her headlights was hanging by a thread and her right front door was missing. We often speculated as to what she did nights. The guesses ran from drag racing to a parking-lot-attendant lover. The wonder was that while the car looked worse and worse, she survived the accidents, could still sing, looked great, and could cuss out the help like a mule skinner.

Maria Montez, a lovely Tintoretto Madonna, spoke very little English and had a low boiling point. She was always fighting with the front office, the assistants, or the wardrobe people. The poor girl seldom won any of her battles. The studio had her on a long-term minimal wage contract that was virtually slavery, occasionally farming her out at a big salary which they collected. The grapevine had it that her revenge was to crap in the wastebaskets of her dressing rooms. This rumor may have been false, but possibly it was true, because she was a "primitive." Those of us who did not have to do janitorial work applauded.

Many of the *Bowery to Broadway* scenes were shot in the old Opera House on the Universal lot where Lon Chaney had starred in *The Phantom of the Opera*. It was a musty, romantic abandoned stage. There were tiers of red velvet boxes, magnificent chandeliers, gilded rococo panels, pervaded by a musky

Having lunch on the set of *Bowery to Broadway* before running off to do *Dr. Christian*. Jack Oakie looks on.

odor of perfume and decay. When you stepped inside, out of the sunlight, you knew you were in 19th century Paris. The wings behind the dusty curtains were haunted by evil villains and tragic lovers. You could almost hear the rustle of the Phantom's cape high in the catwalks. The whole place had an air of Dumas gloom and DeMaupassant romance.

It had rats, also, and it was unwise to leave your doughnut or sandwich unattended.

One of the worst days I can remember came toward the end of *Bowery to Broadway*. It was June 6, 1944.

I was in my dressing room near the opera stage with a radio monotonously repeating news of the Allied landings in Normandy. Everyone was grave and quiet, gathered around their sets. My wardrobe lady had gotten me into a beautiful Can-Can costume with long silk tights and a heart-shaped bodice.

I learned of my father's death while wearing this costume during *Bowery to Broadway.*

Just as she fastened the velvet hat with ostrich plumes in my hair, a messenger knocked on the door with a telegram from Spring Byington, Dad's lady love. "Your father died early this morning. I was with him till the end. Will call you tonight. Love Spring."

Half my life was over with his death. My childhood had been sitting on his shoulders, riding in front of him on his horse, driving in a car while he showed me how to steer. He taught me to dance—first putting my feet on top of his when I was little. He'd hold my arms and do all kinds of dips and whirls; later we would tango and waltz. He had been so handsome and generous—loving and cherishing me until I was grown.

I remembered his taking me to Honolulu when I graduated from high school, even though he was ill then with TB and the silicosis that finally ate away most of his lungs. Best of all was the memory of his laughter. He told wonderful stories and laughed a lot in the telling, showing his strong white teeth and wiping tears of joy from his big hazel eyes that were just like mine.

My father had been ill for years but never admitted it or gave in to fatigue or his chronic cough. He lived at 12,000 feet in Bolivia and managed mines that were even higher in the Andes. His heart had enlarged by a third when he finally returned to the States. After his death the doctors showed me x-rays of his lungs that revealed almost no healthy tissue free from scars. But his will was so much stronger than his body that he was determined to come back to see his granddaughter and me, and to spend his last days with Spring.

I thought of what he must have been like as a little boy working in the mines when he was only 10 years old. I thought of how he looked when he had come out to the house in Beverly Hills a few months before his death. He took pictures of my daughter in her playpen. Standing a careful six feet away, he said, "I'm not going to risk giving her what I've got, but I want some pictures of her as she is now."

He and my mother had communicated entirely through lawyers for the past five years, so it was a comfort to know that Spring had been with him those last days. She had been his childhood sweetheart and I suppose they never stopped loving—at least the memory of—each other. I know my mother's bitter comments indicated that he and Spring had corresponded for 40 years.

That June 6th was a bad day for all the world. The radio was telling the news now about how many men had been lost in the D-Day landings, but I was far back in the past, and none of the present seemed real; not the slaughter on Omaha Beach, not even the news of my father's death. I wouldn't really realize he was dead for days. I was encased in a costume, in a dressing room, in a situation with a built-in momentum of its own.

The director, Charles Lamont, came to see me and was kind and sympathetic. He offered to let me go home if I wished, but I knew there would be household details and phone calls, and my mother's closed face. There really wasn't anywhere to go, but to work.

The make-up man repaired my eyes, I pulled up my tights, and we finished the day's shooting, which included a Can-Can dance with darling Frank McHugh and a lot of lighthearted dialogue.

I had always assumed "The Show Must Go On!" was a crude Shubert policy to save money. But grief deserves undivided attention, so finishing some necessary task may be the only way to enshrine or handle sorrow with fitting concentration.

The last feature I did at Universal before TV and *The Black Tower* was called *The Treasure of Lost Canyon* starring William Powell.

Aside from its star, the most interesting quality of the film was the original script adapted from a Robert Louis Stevenson story. In "The Treasure

The Treasure of Lost Canyon **(1951) with Tommy Ivo and William Powell**

of Franchard," a gambler and a dance hall girl have grown old and left the Barbery Coast to retire in the mountains. They adopt an orphan (Tommy Ivo, a very talented child star) who discovers a buried treasure which complicates everyone's lives. The script is rich in '49er memories, visually beautiful, and has a moral. I remember a scene in which Bill Powell plays a piano for me to dance. A candle is overturned, the house catches fire, and we dash about trying to save our old antiques—running through smoke and flames with clocks, mirrors, and bird cages.

The dance scene was staged with charm and gaiety by the director Ted Tetzlaff, an ex-cameraman who had a genuine love of the pictorial. To him dialogue was like sub-titles—O. K. if you need it but not really vital. He wanted me to dance around the piano and finish by leaping into Powell's lap as he sat on one of those little whirl-around stools. I knew that Bill had had a colostomy operation and worried about how to land on him without harm. After a few cautious rehearsals, he gave me a penetrating look and said, "Rosemary, stop being careful!"

Dear man. He knew and let me know that he knew. After that it was High Ho! and Adagio.

The exteriors were shot where the Universal Hotel is now. At that time in 1951, it was rolling green hills and valleys. An ancient fire brigade with horses

The Treasure of Lost Canyon **would be William Powell's last starring role. In this scene our house is ablaze.**

and dozens of leather buckets tried to put out the blaze but our little cottage burned to the ground. (Of course, with hand-passed leather buckets!)

The sad part of this film was that it was William Powell's final picture of his contract with Universal, so they let it creep out under the studio door, giving it minute publicity, budget, and less mention.

But I often think of our little make-believe cottage in those green hills, where there was a running stream, a vegetable garden, and where I was a retired dance hall "girl" who cooked, and washed, and danced for one of the brightest and biggest stars that ever shone over Hollywood.

CHAPTER 22
THE WALDORF AT MGM

Most of 1944 had gone and it was December. The Allied world was fighting for victory, with a heartbreaking lack of success at Bastogne. My brother was somewhere in the Bulge getting his feet frostbitten. My husband was in an army air base mopping up after P38 tragedies. My little daughter and I were still living with Mother in Beverly Hills, and like everyone else we were caught up in the war and were buying war bonds, observing rationing and shortages, and queuing up for meat and coffee and gas coupons. But during my working hours at MGM, I was living in luxury.

The war-weary public was eager for escapist movies, and MGM was doing a modern version of *Grand Hotel*, their big hit of 1932. The cast was filled with stars: Ginger Rogers, Lana Turner, Walter Pidgeon, Van Johnson, Edward Arnold, Phyllis Thaxter, Keenan Wynn, Robert Benchley, Xavier Cugat, and numerous others. It was titled *Weekend at the Waldorf*, and the New York Waldorf Hotel had sent experts to make sure it was accurate. There were floor plans, swatches of fabrics, even menus, under an agreement with the studio that everything, except the occupants of the rooms, would be exact replicas of the original.

I found out how grand this production was the first day of shooting when I asked the first assistant director if I might leave the set to go to wardrobe. He looked like Walter Pidgeon, Saville Row tailoring, with a touch of black sapphire here and there. He smiled frostily, looked at his watch, and said that the limousine was coming now and he would take me. I murmured something about not troubling him, and he replied, "It's no bother. The limo picks me up at 9:05 every morning to go to the lavatory."

Wow! And he was just the assistant director! I was really impressed.

The set designer must have been Louis B. Mayer's cousin, because the mirrored room we were working in was next to impossible to photograph. There were mirrors, mirrors, mirrors, everywhere. The cameraman swore softly to his crew; his lights and camera showed in every set-up because of the angle of the mirrored walls.

I stood viewing myself in three mirrors, and saw three views of a little brunette endomorph, wearing a maid's black uniform trimmed with white ruffles.

As Ginger Rogers' French maid in *Weekend at the Waldorf*.

There were three views of Ginger Rogers in molten gold and satin, sleek and beautiful, draped on a chaise lounge holding a hand mirror.

Big Bob Leonard, the director, marched up and down, chewing on a cigar.

Ginger drawled, "My hair is really lovely, Bob. I'd rather not change it. Besides, it's all lacquered."

Bob grunted. "Hell, honey, I can't see your beautiful blue peepers with all that gilt pastry hanging over them. Get Sidney down here. We've got time. It's gonna take weeks to shoot anything in this damn fun house!"

He was right. The struggle with the mirrors would take days.

Sidney Guillaroff was Ginger's hairdresser. He was a daring and original genius and he must have been something of a hypnotist, too, because most of the big stars demanded him and then sat still for some incredibly exotic creations. The problem was that Sidney had to keep topping himself; each hair design had to be more fantastic than the last. When Bob Leonard called it "gilt pastry" he was not exaggerating; he could also have added golden doughnuts, satiny croissants, gilt noodles, and bangs to the nostrils.

Undoing one of his masterpieces presented a problem in time. The demolition alone meant shampoo, plus conditioning, then drying, then on to curling irons, back combing and three coats of lacquer. Something not to be attempted in a hurry. No wonder Ginger protested.

My part as Ginger's French maid was not too demanding, although I had to spend a lot of time on the set. Concurrently, I had a long-term contract with the *Dr. Christian* radio show, every Wednesday afternoon. CBS was a good half-hour away by car from Culver City, so I had to leave MGM by three o'clock to make the first broadcast for the east coast.

My part as a maid was not too demanding, but it was fun working on *Weekend at the Waldorf*.

One day my car developed a cough and I left it at a garage outside the gates, where they swore they would call for me before three, without fail. They were late. I stood outside between the two big soundstages, getting so nervous I could feel the vibrations of my heart in my feet.

Just at that moment I had one of the nicest surprises I have ever had. Around the corner came a big black convertible with red leather seats, and out jumped Katharine Hepburn. She strode toward the soundstage door, then stopped and looked at me. "S'matter, Kid?" I told her I was late for a broadcast and waiting for my car. She lit up with that wonderful grin, turned and threw her car keys onto her front seat and said, "Here, take mine!" Then she went through the door and was out of sight.

My car came finally and I made the show on time without testing my Hepburn luck. Mentally I say, "Thank you, you dear generous human being" every time I see her on film or the stage.

Weekend at the Waldorf ground expensively on, but it was fun. Ginger was agreeable. So was Van Johnson, who played backgammon continuously with the Waldorf Hotel supervisor. Lots of stars come on the set to swap stories with Bob Leonard. The *finis*, or "wrap" for the cast was celebrated with a glorious

A 1940s studio portrait

party on the Waldorf set for all the stars in the picture as well as most of MGM's roster of contract celebrities.

Everyone was elegantly dressed, or made up to look smashing for the newsmen, out in force with their cameras. The great mock-up lobby glittered with stars, who moved among the marble pillars. I remember Ava Gardner, and beautiful Lana Turner, warm and gracious, then untouched by time and tragedy.

The crowd was so fascinating I became the total Observer, no longer a part of the cast.

I think character actors are usually Watchers. Stars are Self-Builders and each function or process is equally vital to the creation of a good film.

The Watcher notices, files for copy—poses, mannerisms, little facial shadows of fear and jealousy, tricks of speech, and physical attitudes.

The Self-Builder works on his image—tests his volume, remembers his best mirrored smiles and expressions. He keeps careful track of which press, producers, directors, stylists, and cameramen can aid him in making that image bigger, and more hypnotic.

Being a Watcher made my conceit no less than that of Ginger Rogers or Keenan Wynn. It was simply that I had a built-in superiority of awareness as well as social and family security. I had lived among Hollywood personalities for many years—had watched them come and go—rise—flame out—and disappear. I still love their flamboyance, courage, and humor. It is an affection that is sharpened and saddened by the certainty they can't stay center stage for long. Whereas, we Watchers hang around until carried off on stretchers.

That phony "reception" in December 1944 was a fabulous party—perfumes, luxurious food and drink and music—never to be duplicated. When I enter the Waldorf Hotel lobby now it certainly doesn't measure up to the MGM fantasy. But then of course the guest list is cheaper.

My career gained a boost that month with a call to go to Warner Bros. for a part in *Pride of the Marines*, with John Garfield and Eleanor Parker. The catch was that the part was so good Warner's conditions included a seven-year contract, a miserly salary, and hidden clauses that allowed them to use me in as many pictures at a time as they chose. Also, like all long-term agreements of that time, the studio had the option to cancel, but the performer did not.

What I did not know did not hurt. I was thrilled to be on my way as a top featured player.

CHAPTER 23
THE PROJECTIONIST'S MONTAGE

Everyone probably runs his own movie theater on closed eyelids. But it must be less confusing to show straight memories and not have the program mixed up with filmed features.

My Projectionist, like any subconscious, is seldom obedient. He is a NAG and keeps reminding me of stuff he hasn't shown yet.

I try to ignore him because every time he's given his head we spend hours wallowing in old films that have worn out their re-run welcome.

He's whispering now, "Don't you want to see yourself stumbling over the border, pregnant, when in real life you're not even married?"

"Don't be coy. You mean *Hold Back the Dawn* in 1941. Yes, I see that parade in Tijuana with a Mexican band playing 'The Marseillaise' and Victor Francen carrying the tri-color with real tears rolling down his cheeks. It was May 1941 and all of France had fallen to Hitler."

Upstairs in a cheap hotel Paulette Goddard looks out the window at Charles Boyer below in the street. But he is watching Olivia De Havilland standing by her station wagon. Walter Abel, an immigration official, is watching me moving slowly toward the customs office, very pregnant, on my way to give my child birth on US soil.

My mother had given me a cotton bag she prepared full of BB shot to tie around my skinny front. It was heavy, realistic, and made me look nine months pregnant-plus.

Hold Back the Dawn was one of Arthur Hornblow's finest films. It won eight Academy Award nominations and several Oscars. Whenever I hear the theme song, "Marie Elena," I see that parade on the lot at Paramount, filmed in the beginning of WW II, and I see the faces of those marvelous actors.

Mitch Leisen, the director, told me I was his "good luck," but I suspected it was a ploy he had often used to get actors to do his bidding. It certainly worked with me. A few months later he cast me in a comedy with Fred MacMurray and Claudette Colbert, called *Practically Yours*. It was a tragic little part in a very funny film.

With Claudette Colbert in *Practically Yours* (1944)

Mitch was a charismatic stranger; a hyperthyroid mystic who was an interior decorator, and also a formidable authoritarian on the Paramount lot. I saw him a few months before he died at the Motion Picture Home. They ran *Hold Back the Dawn* for him, and he asked me to come. It was a poignant experience.

The scenario of that film was the actual love story of Ketti Frings and her husband Kurt, taken from her novel by the same name. It is one of the Projectionist's favorite re-runs, but by now the writer and the cast have gone their separate ways: Boyer, De Havilland, Goddard, Mitch Leisen—all of us.

The Projectionist wheezes, "What about Elizabeth Taylor? Don't you want to run *The Big Hangover* again?"

No, I don't. Though Elizabeth the legend is worth a hundred re-runs, in memory, every time I see Dear Violet Eyes I get a whiff of Grand Marnier and crêpe suzettes. During *The Big Hangover* we sat around a dinner table for an entire week drinking brandy and eating crêpe suzettes. The crepes were prepared with elegance and style every morning, but they had to last all day, and Leon Ames, Van Johnson, Elizabeth Taylor, Fay Holden, Gene Lockhart and I became mighty tired of them before the week was up. The writer, director, and producer, was Norman Krasna, and this was his first directorial assignment, hence the week of crepes, brandy, and burnt sugar.

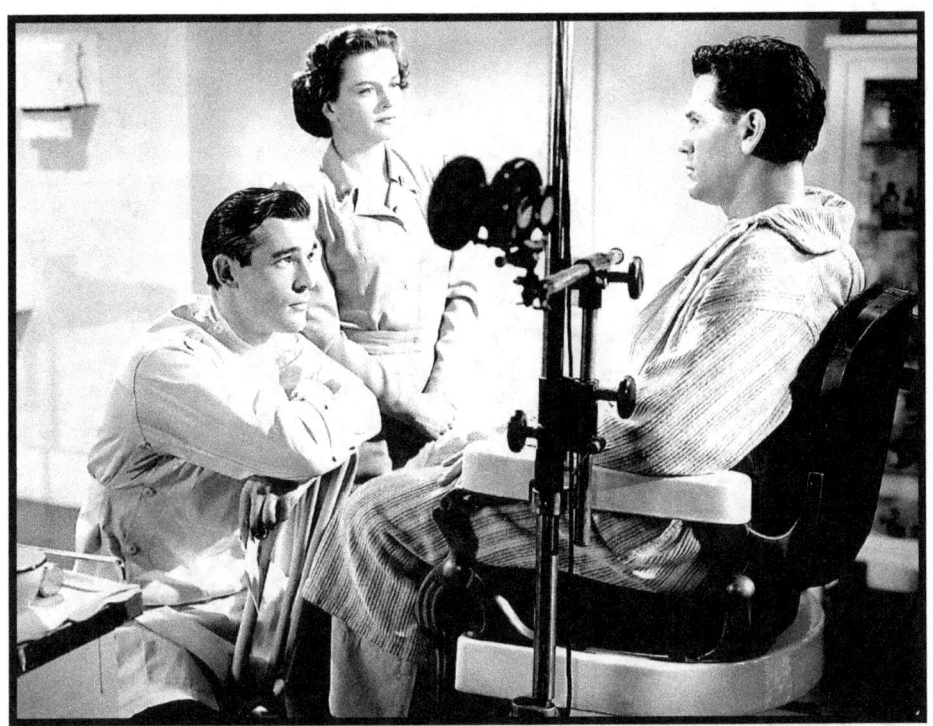

Pride of the Marines (1945) with Rory Mallinson and John Garfield

Dear friendly Van Johnson! He was the only star I can remember at MGM who stayed late to do off-camera lines for lesser actors.

As for Violet Eyes, it was enough just to have her there, she was so lovely. In *Cat on a Hot Tin Roof*, her performance was so utterly smashing, I found it disconcerting. I would rather just have her be there, over the crêpe suzettes, not doing anything but being beautiful.

Now the Projectionist is running scraps of film that don't match. I yell at him on the talk-back, "What's the matter with you? Why all the bits and pieces? You been playing in the cutter's wastebasket?"

The black and white film rolls on: part of *The Postman Always Rings Twice*, *Four Daughters*, a scene from *Golden Boy*, then *Body and Soul*. Now a news still of Lucille Ball with a group of reporters. Finally there is Lillian Hellman at a podium receiving an ovation.

My memory screen goes to black and there is a big close-up of John Garfield. I'm impatient. "Fine, fine! But get to the point, or is there any connection?"

Ah, now I see. John Garfield, or Julie Garfinkle as his friends knew him, is the one who binds the scenes together.

The whole montage is a set of folding mirrors. Just touch them and they reverse on people, scenes, headlines, black books, red books, vicious faces,

With Moroni Olsen, Dane Clark, and John Garfield in *Pride of the Marines*

weepers, and then the tight, strong face of Garfield. The bandages around his eyes are unwinding—there are his eyes now—open, bitter, and blind.

In 1944 when I first met Garfield his personality was strong enough to withstand all the roles, the adulation, and the success. When he walked on the set in *Pride of the Marines*, his compact square body, his rare, sweet smile and laser glance brought everything to a halt. The script girl would drop her book, the cameraman smile. The grips would stop moving lamps or eating. or whatever they were doing. Actors moved closer. He would say something trite like, "What's going on here?"—as if he weren't the star, fully aware of his part and his relationship to everyone else.

He was so real I was terrified to sound a false note. As his nurse in the story, I had to guide him around, write letters for him to his girl, encourage him, discuss the doctor's plans and prognosis. I also had to dissemble a cheerfulness that I did not feel about his blindness. So it had to be a false optimism that sounded honest to him, which was tough for me to do with the eye of the camera and the ears of Garfield demanding the truth.

Delmer Daves was directing, and this made *Pride of the Marines* a memorable experience for everyone. I had never before met such an affirmative di-

As John Garfield's nurse in *Pride of the Marine* I wrote letters to his girl.

rector—with eyes full of light—he was a warm, cheerful, cinnamon bear of a man. During an emotional scene, he would sit under the camera with a box of Kleenex, prepared to weep; and weep he did, take after take. It was encouraging to know you were going to move him that much. When he whispered, "Action," my throat would swell and the words would come out right—the sound disguised, trying to comfort the blind soldier. When Garfield spoke, it was tense; seeking hope, demanding the news, good or bad. His darn husky voice carried us all, and forced us to give him what he needed.

That picture proved to be a traumatic experience for Johnny. Warners was said to have canceled his enlistment, and the army brass to have informed him he was more valuable to the war effort in films. Whatever truth there was in the rumor, Johnny minded playing a part in uniform when he was not a soldier; he minded a lot.

The day we spent shooting at the San Diego Naval Hospital tore him up. Some of the shots were done in the courtyard where the wounded lay on cots in the sunshine. His head was bandaged and I had to guide him through lines of paraplegics, burn victims, and dozens who slept, or called out to him. He would whisper, "Jesus Christ! Look at that guy! What am I doing here?" or

"Here comes the make-up man with the phony sweat, right in front of a guy with no legs! I don't belong here."

We finally got through the day, and eventually the picture. It was fine and honest and won several Academy nominations. Eleanor Parker was beautiful and moving as the blind Marine's sweetheart. In the next year or two Garfield starred in *Body and Soul*, and *Humoresque*. Both became classics, adding to his remarkable record.

In the late '40s his daughter died suddenly of some undiagnosed illness. A close friend told me that Johnny went crazy; wouldn't see anyone or talk for days. Then one night he took all her toys, clothes, and pictures out in the backyard and burned them.

About that time Senator Joseph McCarthy and the House Un-American Activities Committee began their insinuations. Most of us couldn't understand what they were looking for. Spies? What was there to spy on? Communists? The Communist Party was legal in those years. The only valid complaint that HUAC and the FBI had was pitifully weak. They claimed that certain Hollywood writers portrayed wealthy people and big corporations as greedy and corrupt, and conversely, the poor were shown to be hard working, honest, and oppressed by the powerful. Since this plot was as old as the fables of Aesop, it was extraordinary the havoc that the investigations caused.

Garfield had started his acting career with the Group Theater in New York, and was still close to the old friends he had made there. When the Great Red Herring Spy Hunt began, the character assassins leaned on Johnny to tell of meetings, to name names, and discuss ideologies. He laughed at them and gave them nothing. The studio (Warners) suspended him, which at that time meant "Out!"

He died of a heart attack in the early 1950s. The square little kid from the streets of New York died lonely, ill, and unemployed, because he had ignored the opportunity to betray his friends. His work will live for a long time.

What about Lucille Ball and the reporters? How did that picture get in the montage the Projectionist was showing me?

Oh, I remember. It was also during the witch hunt. Now that was a very remarkable episode.

Stars were being expelled from the Hollywood heavens. Reputations were blackened, or reddened, with no basis in fact, merely with a grimace or a lifted eyebrow. Writers had their work and FUTURE royalties confiscated. Fear was rampant. Congress seemed to have forgotten the Bill of Rights and civil liberty.

However, Lucille Ball, who had a popular television show with her husband, Desi Arnaz, was a match for the whole pack of hounds.

Someone noticed that our Lucy was listed as a State Committeewoman for the (then legal) Communist Party. Well, whadda ya know! Our Lucy? None other.

She and Phillip Morris, her sponsor, called a press conference, during which she gave, as always, a great performance. She was witty, charming, and cool. Her grandfather, she said, was a registered Communist in California, and had put her name on the ballot without her knowledge or consent. She was not, nor had ever been, a Communist. So put that in your pipe and smoke it, Phillip Morris and Senator McCarthy!

She won. Phillip Morris wanted her, because the public wanted her, and to hell with red smears! She named no names; said she had attended no meetings and please, let's get on with the show.

The case of Lillian Hellman showed a different facet of political involvement. Miss Hellman was no Communist. In fact, she had a deep distrust of their methods, their recruitment, and the whole machinery of the US Communists. But she was a true liberal with an incisive mind that saw through political lies and the machinations of the Pentagon and the arms merchants. Her books and plays gored them. The McCarthyites hated her honesty, and convinced themselves that she was against them—ergo—she was "red." Her protests simply tightened the chains around her and her friends.

It is possible that in cases similar to Lillian Hellman's, martyrdom was welcomed. Many of the Unfriendly 10 or 12, or 12 Dozen, reached for the crown of thorns after finding no recourse in denial. The drama of the pillory must have appealed to some, but I don't think any of us realized how long it would be before they were let out of the stocks. Most of us had hopes that our Constitution would pull up its socks and defend us. We were sure that "guilt by association" was a temporary nightmare. Surely Civil Liberty was still alive in the United States!

But the House Un-American Activities Committee continued to fly around like a Halloween monster, destroying everyone it called on. Big, bad HUAC. The only one of its members who marched to the top wearing the Pumpkinhead was Nixon. One member of the Committee was jailed after being caught with his hand in the till. McCarthy and the rest were exposed, or faded from sight after Judge Welch pounded home the truth in the Senate Censure hearings.

Now the Halloween costume hangs in the American attic, hopefully forgotten. But it's there, on a nail, waiting for the next demagogue.

CHAPTER 24
JOHNNY COMES HOME

The afternoon of the atomic bomb, August 6, 1945, began quietly enough in our living room at 805 North Linden Drive in Beverly Hills.

Four of us were living there then. Maurine, Mother's beloved black housekeeper, was listening to the radio in the kitchen. She had worked occasionally for Nelson Eddy, Ronald Colman, and Bugsy Siegal up the street. But after Bugsy was machine-gunned through his living room window, Maurine swore the neighborhood was ruined and moved in with us full time.

Mother sat near the window mending a black-out curtain. She was a full-fledged Air Raid Warden now, with badge, arm bands, helmet, sand buckets, and flashlights at the ready. Every night she spent hours berating neighbors for light chinks. In her 60s she had found a vigorous vocation and relinquished popularity for clout.

Our daughter, Nana, two and a half, was trying to stuff the cocker spaniel into one of her baby sweaters.

I was reading a script with only half a mind, wondering when John would get leave from his Grizzly Peak look-out station—wondering if my brother Jerry was safe in Germany—wondering too about John's three brothers in and around Okinawa.

Suddenly there was a yell from the kitchen. Maurine came running down the hall shouting, "Miz DeCamp! We dropped a big bomb! We wiped 'em out!"

Mother dropped her sewing, "What bomb? Where'd you get this?" She moved toward our radio. Maurine was clapping her hands and laughing, "Those yellow rascals gonna quit now! We've won the war!"

The news announcer's excitement matched Maurine's, but he became decently grave with the possible casualties, and even graver about the mushroom cloud and radiation.

We were stunned—guilty, too, for the immediate joy that the long years of war might be over. What was an atomic bomb? How had such a secret been kept? How many dead?

The radio voices kept saying "...estimated to have saved a million of our soldiers' lives..." in between reports of bomb tonnage and civilian casualties. There were statements by Air Force generals revealing nothing but a desire to share in the glorious destruction.

No one said very much the rest of the day. Maurine sang "The Battle Hymn of the Republic" untroubled by our silence. Nana went on teasing the dog into her cast-off clothing. Mother was quiet. Once she said, "I wonder if Jerry knows in Germany?"

"I think the whole world knows, Mom."

She was thoughtful. "Yes, we've been heroes—a lot of sacrifice. I wonder if we'll be heroes now?"

The crazy quilt of John's army life and our three years of now-and-then marriage rolled like film across my memory to my first visit with him at Camp Roberts, an infantry training base, when I was

My husband John Shidler in 1942

eight months pregnant. His feet were blistered and bloody, but his enthusiasm for bayonet practice was startling. He trudged me off to the obstacle course and said, "Watch this!" Holding his bayonet he galloped over a wooden barrier, a big dirt mound, and harpooned a swinging sawdust dummy. Then he ran back panting, "It's important y'see, to stab 'em right in the middle." He glanced at my bulk and grinned, "Sorry, nothing personal y'understand."

Aside from wringing out his bloody socks at night, he really enjoyed the combat training—the barricades, the rifle practice. It was so aggressive—exhaustive and stimulating for a chair-bound attorney. I felt out of it—a big cow looking over the fence at the action.

He said, "Y'know, a funny thing happened. I sentenced a guy in Torrance for stealing mercury out of oil rigs. The only eyewitness was a Japanese truck gardener. I gave the accused six months in the county jail a week before Pearl Harbor. Then after I'm up here at Roberts for a while, my buddy on the rifle range says, "You sent me to jail on the word of a Jap! Judge, I coulda killed you for that—but you never recognized me. Now I guess we both hate the Japs, right?"

When John saw my face he laughed, "Oh, hell, darling, it didn't matter. At this camp we don't even have live ammunition for our wooden rifles."

Then I remembered the day in February of '43 when he called me from Camp Stoneman saying he had orders to ship out to the South Pacific with a combat outfit.

I screamed, "Don't those idiots know about your eyes!?" His vision was 20-400 and he had failed to get into any of the services before being drafted. "No, they're getting to the bottom of the barrel and need everybody who made it through basic training. I have two days leave. Can you come right away?"

Mother said she'd care for the baby if I would dress up in my best, and for heaven's sake stop crying. Somehow she got me to Union Station for the long train ride up the San Joaquin Valley. Then there on the Pittsburg platform was Johnny, thin, brown, and smiling.

"I've got reservations at the only good hotel. It's great you're here. We'll have 20 hours."

But when we reached the hotel desk an army corporal sneered, "PRIVATE Shidler? This hotel is for officers only. No enlisted men allowed."

I could have sprung for the clerk's throat but John led me away muttering that he should have known. In the army they even had separate toilets for non-coms and officers. It took all afternoon and most of our cash to find a cab and a hotel with a vacant room. It turned out to be a kind of a crib, with canvas walls, near a pier in Port Chicago.

Ah, but we had a happy loving time that night with a lot of added entertainment. Our canvas wall was also the wall of a huge sailors' lavatory on the other side. The acoustics were amazing.

The next day was Sunday—inch-thick flapjacks at a greasy cafe, and an hour to find a cab and get to the depot. On the station platform we were jostled by hundreds of hurrying soldiers and kept staring at each other, wondering if it was for the last time. I was afraid to ask when he would ship out. Then he kissed me again for the baby and I climbed into the moving train. He was still standing on the platform looking for me, but the windows were too dirty to see in.

I must have prayed all the way to Los Angeles, knowing there were millions of women all over the world praying for their men. I wondered how many circuits were open—and what had we done to deserve special favor?

Two days later he phoned. I could hardly recognize his voice. It was exuberant. "Guess what! I was sitting on my duffle bag at the dock when a messenger comes tearing up on a bicycle with orders from HQ for me to report to the legal office for work on a court martial!—Are you there? Can you hear me?"

Then I remembered him going off to Officers Training at San Antonio, Texas, the same week I reported to Warners for *Pride of the Marines*. He had created a useful income tax manual for all GI tax problems. It became standard for the entire 9th Service Command. His grateful colonel, George Ginsberg, helped him transfer from the Infantry to the Army Air Corps.

Weeks went by with no letters or calls, then finally I got a telegram, "I'm going to graduate on the 15th. Can you come?" Warners wouldn't release me for the date of the ceremony but I could have three days right away. I got a train ticket for one day and two nights to old San Antone to have four hours

Watering the garden at our new house in the mid-1940s

with a paper cut-out of a husband—dear and thin and nervous. He showed me all the drills, sang all the songs, and kept backing up to the wall to see if his spine was straight.

So it was Kiss-me Kate-I'm-Late, and he was off to camp for bed check or whatever. I caught the milk train back to L.A. and the brothers Warner—but it was better than nothing.

Now, a year and a half later he was an officer in charge of look-out stations in northern California. I wondered if he was listening to the radio.

The Afternoon of the Bomb was over. Shadows were turning blue green in the patio. Nana stood close to me and whispered, "Why are you crying, Mom?"

"I'm crying because I ought to be happy—because Daddy is coming home. Because maybe we will have peace."

She didn't understand at all. When Johnny came home from the separation center in Sacramento it was a disruption of her whole life. He and I spent every free hour together. She was lonely. She had been a princess in a palace surrounded only by women who adored her. Now there was a male, firmly giving orders. The OCS voice was very compelling.

She ran to her grandmother one day and deliberately said within his hearing, "That man spanked me!" Mother lined up with Nana. I was on John's side. Then we realized we had to move out of the palace and turn the princess back into an ordinary child.

The day we bought The House was sunny and warm. On the Palos Verdes Peninsula orchid geraniums climbed tree trunks and spilled out at the top. There were masses of pink, yellow, and cerise ice plants over miles of empty hills.

With Nana (Margaret) in 1943

We drove into an area called Hollywood Riviera—an almost-deserted real estate development from the 1920s. It had a mile of beach on the great Santa Monica Bay and formed the south end of Torrance, where John was once again a practicing attorney and the city judge. On Camino de las Colinas (street of the little hills) there were only three widely separated houses. One had a FOR SALE sign on it. We went in and looked it over but there were too many small rooms with dark wood beams. It didn't seem to be a part of the sunny world outside. We drove to the third house. It was white and beautiful—set down from the street and surrounded by big black pine trees and flowering succulents. We were surprised to see a discreet FOR SALE sign on the iron gate.

The front door was wide and paneled with a bright brass bell and knob. It opened and a handsome white-haired woman said, "Yes? Well, hello! John Shidler, come in!" She had been a friend of John's mother and was about to retire to Pasadena. Our meeting was pure coincidence.

The house was remarkable. It had two-foot-thick walls, big windows with views of the sea and the pines, several fireplaces and nothing between it and the beach but salt bush and sand. We gave the five bedrooms and baths a quick glance and bought it in 15 minutes for $22,500 and have lived there ever since—making it larger—filling it with children, friends, and relatives—planting its yards with flowers and trees.

It is the only real home I've ever had. Its basement and attic closets are packed with 35 years of costumes, books, trunks, pictures, and children's toys. That 15-minute purchase in 1945 was our Great Bargain.

Though now I was pregnant again and faced a 60-mile round trip to Warner Bros. in the Valley, when there were, as yet, no freeways.

CHAPTER 25
MOMMY TO MANY

Publicity is often gross and self-inflating, but it has long been considered a personal necessity for actors. Even the IRS agrees it is a deductible expense.

I have had several "public relations" men who did good work for me at a high price in dollars, embarrassment, and time. Time was the biggest extravagance, because, for instance, fashion sittings at photographers took days of fittings, and sittings, and make-up. Then showing up at "openings," awards, or charity events, Boy Scouts, Girl Scouts, Y.W., Y.M., or Y Not, all took hours of driving, dressing, phoning, and smiling, when I was tired and longed to be home.

Some of it was fun, because I love the men and women of the press. Almost every interviewer in 30 years was a person I would have enjoyed knowing better; most of them were witty, cynical, and honest.

However, without exception, they would eventually ask me one of two questions, and sometimes both would come up in an interview.

"Why do you think you did not become a big star?" was the first one, which was phrased in various ways.

I became adept at handing out several different superficial answers: "I opted for character parts even when I was young." "They are richer and more interesting." "The 'leading lady' roles in plays I rehearsed at school, or in little theaters, were literally straight!" "Love interest allowed few variations and no humor. Now 'leads' are far better written and have more than two dimensions." Another factual answer was: "The beautiful, predictable ingenue was already too young for me by the time I had graduated, taught in college, and struggled through the Depression toward employment."

But the real reason is buried deeper and is even more prohibitive. I am shy. Shy about sex, or making love in front of a camera, or an audience. That must sound like a terrible admission, in this day, but it is the truth.

In 1945 during my Warner's contract Steve Trilling called me into his office and gave me a sudden insight into my own character, though I was married and had a three-year-old child. "Rosemary," he said, "I think you are a very sexy dame. Now we have a part for you that, I think, will open up your career. I want to talk to you about it."

I was horrified. I could barely mumble, "Uh... thank you, Mr. Trilling. I don't think that's my-uh..."

A *Dr. Christian* radio rehearsal with Neil Reagan (Ronnie's brother)

He said, "Why not? This is a good part. It's honest. There's a very hot love scene between you and..."

I nearly choked, but I got it out. "No! No! Don't tell me. I don't want to regret it. I just couldn't... in front of a lot of people. Please..."

He laughed, got up and put his arm around me. "OK, but I think you're wasted always playing 'Mom.'"

I was nervous about his arm. What was he doing? Testing? The interview ended pleasantly, but a month later Warner's dropped my option. They often re-hired me after that for character parts, usually someone's mother, so I think the decision I made that day defined the rest of my career.

Questioning my feelings didn't occur to me. I already knew that "making love" before a camera and crew would be impossible for me. "Why" was too deep to go. To me, physical love, sex, between a man and a woman is a very private thing. I was simply not enough of a dissembler, or unself-conscious enough, to consider it.

The other question involved the Mamma-to-Many theme. "Now let's see," they would say as though they had just discovered an original idea. "Let's do a

As Ann Blyth's mother in *The Merry Monahans*

story on how many famous children you have mothered. There's Jimmy Cagney, Sabu, Ann Blyth, Bob Hutton, Dwayne Hickman, June Haver, Ronald Reagan, Doris Day, Shirley Jones, Marlo Thomas..." Here I would interject. "How about an article entitled "Princess Many Faces? Lookey, all the different faces I've worn. Lookey," I was tempted to say, "all these faces I can make if you don't stop all this Mommy slop!"

But they paid me no mind. I have files of articles and clippings about Mommy-to-Many, and only one tattered rotogravure spread extolling my Many Faces. I suppose they tagged me correctly as to what would be printed, but I am wistful about having played some Non-Mommies that were pretty good, and receiving no kudos for them.

A family Christmas portrait from 1960

Consequently, to all interviewers I can say I honestly chose to be just a character actress who often got star billing, in a career which spanned time and various media: radio, vaudeville, Broadway, films, and television. The unusual features of my life and work, besides the variety, are that I have had a private life, a 50-year marriage, and four daughters concurrent with my work. This has all been grist for the publicity mill.

There is a supportive group of people in the filmmaking industry who work long hours, wear make-up and costumes, and are essential even though they are not publicized. They get minimal pay, no billing and are often treated as if they were furniture, or non-persons. These are the stand-ins.

All stars have them, as do the featured players. They are matched for height, general build, hair, and complexion, so that the long periods of lighting can be done as accurately as possible without the actual actor getting messed and sweaty.

Ideally the star and his associates are busy rehearsing their dialogue, although, unfortunately, this is not always the case.

Once, a long time ago, some nervous second assistant director called the actors into their scene, when the lighting and stand-ins were through, like this: "OK! Will the real people take places, please!" There was a stunned silence, then laughter, after which the assistant was drummed out of the regiment. From that day on the terms have been, "First and Second Teams."

I have had several stand-ins who have been affectionate, generous, and willing, and have become my friends. One in particular, Eleanor Urcan, was with me for years. She made my working days much easier, often bringing my lunch to my dressing room so I could rest at noon, as well as call sheets for the next day's shooting. She would arrange my chair as though it were my office, bringing me bulletins and gossip, take phone messages, and, in short, be a wall of comfort and protection. For at least 15 years she clipped every mention of my name in "the trades" and magazines, so she was virtually a public relations bureau, as well as a dear companion in films and television.

Certainly she was a REAL person!

Valuable as publicity can be, sometimes it goes off in odd directions. Like a faulty firecracker, surprises sometimes evolve from an innocent story.

One day in 1953, the publicity man hired by the *Dr. Christian* radio show begged me for "An item—anything!" Poor fellow, no wonder he looked tired and badgered. The show had been on the air for 16 years, and Jean Hersholt and I were so square, we seldom did anything startling in our private lives. Besides, the PR man was not supposed to plug any films or television that we were doing.

"Oh, I cannot think of anything," I said, "the only news at our house this week was that Nita Lou (18 months) ate some of our butterfly collection."

He looked shocked, but happy. "Good God! Dead?"

"Nita Lou? No, she's fine. She took the wings out and nibbled a few."

"I meant the butterflies, of course. Well, thanks, I'll head it 'Rosemary's baby has butterflies in her stomach!' Yeah, I can use it. I'm that hard up." And he was off.

A month later John and I were in San Francisco and heard on a news broadcast. "The infant daughter of Judge John Shidler in Los Angeles has eaten his butterfly collection." No mention of *Dr. Christian*, and no mention of me. Just a straight UP bulletin. Then we began to get clippings from friends all over the country, even one from *Stars and Stripes* in Germany, telling about this poor judge whose child ate his priceless collection. Then came a lovely mahogany box from Java containing two exquisite blue velvet moths, with a note of condolence, on the Judge's loss. There were no inquiries as to the child's health.

So you can see "public relations" is like the old game of gossip. By the time the story makes a complete circle, it is barely recognizable.

CHAPTER 26
LOTSA LIVES

In my basement there's a big box containing several hundred movie stills. I am told they are worth quite a lot of money. Why? Is it just one of those vagaries of fads in nostalgia which seem to recur in cycles, like the length of women's skirts?

The market price of an old black and white still today runs from $2.50 to $6.00. The garish, colored lobby posters can bring $150 or more. The other day I saw a woman put down $45 on "layaway" for an obscure Judy Garland poster which even those of us who adored Garland wouldn't have around.

Mike Fitzgerald, a knowledgeable young man, has produced an elegant tome, *Universal Pictures*, which is the only definitive work on that fertile studio's history. One day he spent digging around in my basement, and came staggering up the cellar stairs carrying two cartons of stills and grousing, "Why did you give all those years of stills to the University of Wyoming?"

"Because they asked for them, son. And I was flattered that they wanted me in there with Will and Ariel Durant, Dean Martin, and all those other biggies."

"Yeah? Well, they'll just bury them in a vault and that's the end of it. I need that material for my new book on *Films of the Forties*. I need all your Warner Bros. stuff. How long were you there, anyway?"

How long? It must have been several lifetimes, off and on. Other people's lives that I was playing, or living, vicariously.

Mike and I looked over the boxes he was carrying, and he left me with the collection after I promised to grab them first in case of fire or earthquake.

The contents of the boxes are interesting to me for several reasons: (a) vanity, as I am in all of them, and (b) they are reminders of films I have forgotten, and (c) they induce a warm affection for times and faces that are gone.

Two of the stills are priceless to me. One is of Paul Muni and me, conspirators in *Commandos Strike at Dawn*. He looks so young and vulnerable. Another favorite is of four people: Mark Stevens, Henry Morgan (aka Harry Morgan of *M*A*S*H*), Joan Fontaine, and me. The lighting is skillful and captures the poverty and anxiety of the original story by Clifford Odetts, which was called "All Brides Are Beautiful." How that picture became RKO's *From This Day Forward*, a film that was merely a series of beautiful close-ups and two-shots of the stars, is another Hollywood might-have-been story.

From This Day Forward (1946) with Joan Fontaine and Mark Stevens

Our director was one of the best I have ever encountered. The name he used was John Berry. He was a fellow traveler, or a genuine Communist, or possibly he was just close to those who were. Early in the McCarthy era he pulled up stakes and went to Paris where he worked in film for years. Simone Signoret merely mentions him in her book; I wonder if she knew how good he was.

We rehearsed two weeks before we filmed, which was unprecedented in 1946. He was a "method" director in that he made us dig deep into who we were, our pasts, our relationships, our poverties and riches of spirit and possessions. The result of his work and ours was fine—honest and moving. But what he accomplished on the set was wiped out in the projection room where Joan Fontaine and William Dozier (head of RKO and soon to be husband of Miss F.) spent an hour a day viewing and editing the dailies. Miss Fontaine's perfect features and young Stevens' photogenic profile became reels of classic heads and luminous eyes gazing longingly at each other.

Perhaps Dozier and Fontaine were right. Maybe the public in those years wanted to forget the pain, the wrecked careers, and even the absurd humor of that era, and preferred to watch pretty human beings glow in soft light wrapped

With Warren Ashe in *Smith of Minnesota* (1942)

in music. But Berry became grimmer and gloomier as we neared the end of shooting. Possibly it was the final cut of the film that drove him out of the country, and not his politics.

Clifford Odetts, having sold the script, no longer had any connection with it. He was busy with Luise Rainer and eventually testified against some of his colleagues in the HUAC hearings.

There are five stills from a film called *Smith of Minnesota*, whose importance I failed to grasp when I was in it, and even now have to have it explained to me. Apparently it was the first honest portrayal of a famous athlete. Bruce Smith, a remarkably handsome All-American halfback, played himself. Columbia did the story of his fame and family with disarming honesty. The reviews were more than generous and claimed it to be "cliché-free."

Three pictures from a Warner film entitled *Too Young to Know*, starring Bob Hutton and Joan Leslie, show me to be the nice dowdy lady with glasses, silver temples, and rather plump. Why not? I am pregnant, 34, and am playing the mother of 24-year old Hutton. That anxious expression I wear is because I am due over on Stage 8, where I have to switch make-up, cinch my corset, and play the neglected wife in *Nora Prentiss.*

Ah, here are some funny ones from *Look for the Silver Lining,* starring June Haver and Gordon MacRae, with Ray Bolger, Charlie Ruggles, the Wilde Twins— Lee and Lyn, and me. It must have been another version of the *Bowery to Broadway* plot based on the life of Marilyn Miller, though, of course, minus her alcoholism, because no one seems to have a care in the world. We are all prancing around in knee britches, hoops, white wigs, and toothy smiles.

Too Young to Know **(1945) with Robert Hutton, Joan Leslie, and Arthur Shields**

Look for the Silver Lining **(1949) with Lee Wilde, Lyn Wilde, Charlie Ruggles, and June Haver**

***Night Unto Night* (1949) with Ronald Reagan, Broderick Crawford, and Viveca Lindfors**

There is only one still from that endless film, *Night Unto Night*. It shows Ronald Reagan, young, brown, and handsome, with Broderick Crawford, huge and benign, watching Viveca Lindfors and me. A happy moment.

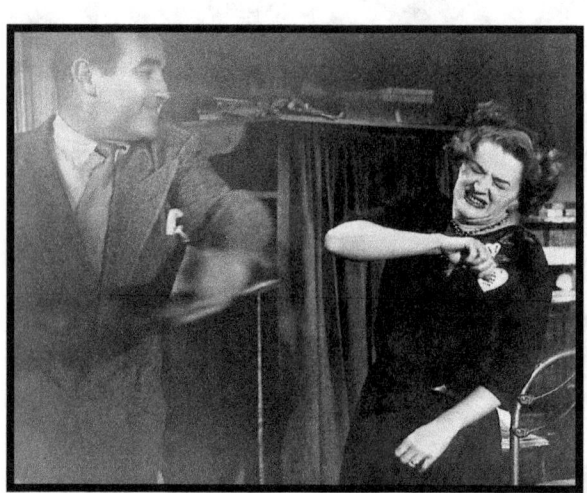

Broderick Crawford knocks me across the room in *Scandal Sheet* (1952).

The picture of Jimmy Cagney and me looks crisp and new, the corner unmussed, so it is surprising to see the inscription on the back, "1945 *Blood on the Sun*." I was flattered that Jimmy wanted me in his own production, but I regretted I had to be killed early in the film and stuffed in a trunk. Oh, well... Hi ho!

Speaking of an early demise, here are some shots of *Scandal Sheet*. I was a rotten, blackmailing bitch

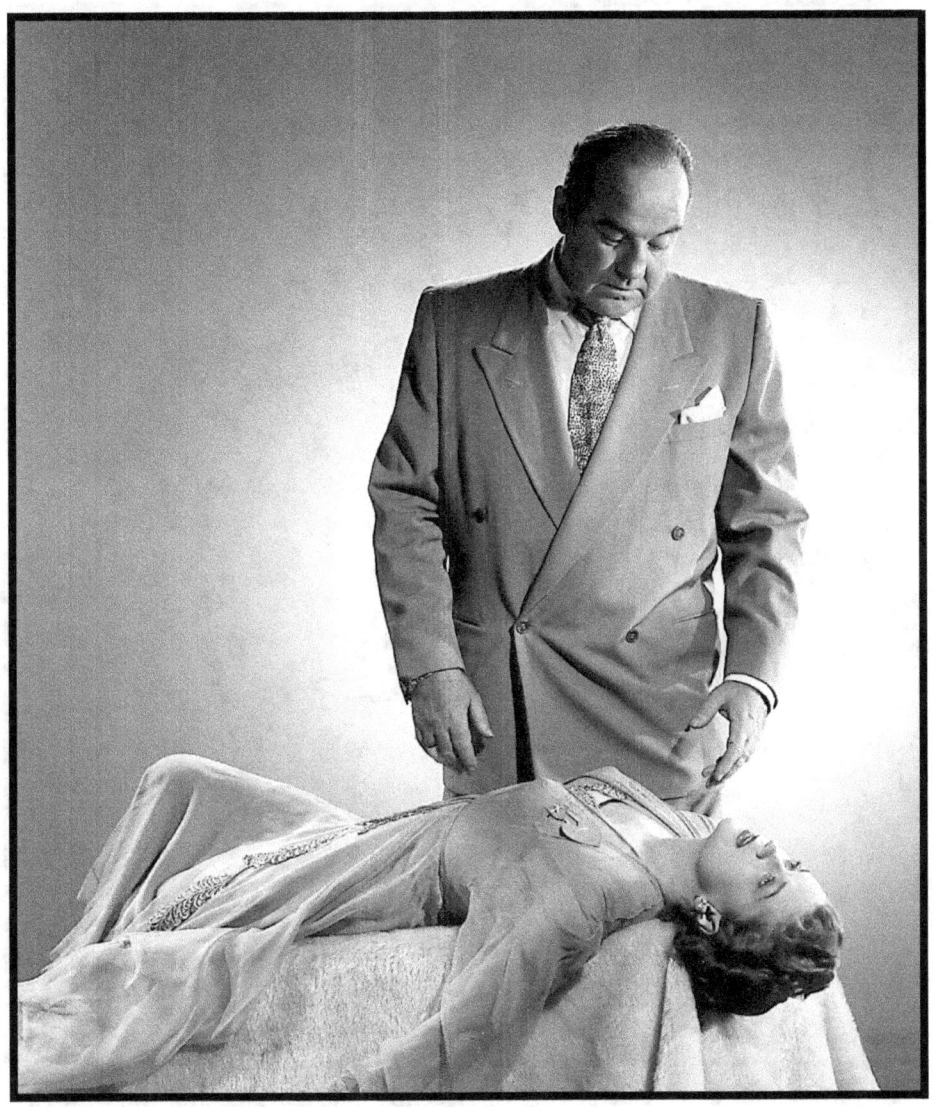

A posed publicity portrait for *Scandal Sheet*. Unfortunately, it didn't lead to more slutty parts.

in that one—and very proud of this departure from all my icky-sweet Momma roles. Broderick Crawford left me to drown in a bathtub after an eye-gouging, knee-in-the-groin fight, which he finished off by knocking me clear across the set. I thought the results were splendid, and hoped for a whole new career of tacky whore parts, but I never got another. I remember having a black eye for Mother's Day after the beating scene. It was my own fault for begging Brod to "really hit me," After a few halfhearted swats, he decked me with a hand the size of a bowling ball.

Ray Milland kisses me before my early demise in *Night Into Morning* (1951).

There was another early demise in a film with Ray Milland called *Night Into Morning*. I kissed Ray one morning a few minutes into the story and went back into our house, which then blew up from a faulty gas main, or some such prosaic but final device. The two things I recall are that Nancy Davis (later First Lady Nancy Reagan) was in it, and that Ray Milland said to me with charming curiosity, "I know you came from Jerome, Arizona. How does anyone get out of such a place and arrive here at MGM?" Wasn't he fortunate I didn't answer?

Along with almost everyone in Hollywood at that time, I was in a William Castle horror film. Bill never skimped on publicity, so I have almost too many stills from that one. It was called *The 13 Ghosts*, and starred Donald Woods

William Castle's *13 Ghosts* with Jo Morrow, Donald Woods, Martin Milner, and Charles Herbert

and me with Margaret Hamilton, Marty Milner, and Jo Morrow. Our acting consisted of playing Ouija board tricks, screaming, hiding, and yelling "Boo!" All of this while waiting for the big horror finale where the ghosts were supposed to emerge in a kind of double exposure overlay.

Maybe it was like Peter Pan: You have to believe, or you can't see the fairies. At this preview, I couldn't see the ghosts at all. The Emperor had no clothes on for me, but our children all swore they saw them clearly.

Here's a still I had forgotten. There is a brunette midget (me) standing between a giant and a dark-haired man in buckskin. Oh, now I see the giant is Jim Arness, thin and young, and like seven feet tall—before *Gunsmoke*. The other fellow is Robert Taylor, who must have been the kindest and least troublesome star on the MGM roster. A publicity man at Metro told me that when Taylor was young, he was so beautiful that of all the glamour girls, Garbo was the only one unafraid to share a two-shot with him. Taylor's wife, lovely Ursula Theiss, bore him a son, Terry, and a daughter, Tessie, who inherit a great set of physical beauty genes, but also warm memories of a dear and gentle man.

Eyes in the Night was an original detective story called "The Odor of Violets." This film was Fred Zinneman's first assignment at MGM. Edward Arnold played the hero, a blind detective. I was a hysterical maid. The cast was

***The Big Hangover* (1950) with Elizabeth Taylor, Leon Ames, and Van Johnson**

memorable: Ann Harding, Donna Reed, Allen Jenkins, Reginald Denny, Barry Nelson, John Emery, and Peter Lorre. That last name is not listed in the cast, but I remember him being all over the set, mischievous as the devil himself. The last name is "Himself" played by "Friday"... so perhaps it was Peter. Or maybe Peter just came to visit us so often he seemed to be one of us. I had only seen him in *M* at the time (1942), so my laughter at his pranks was wary.

I am sorry the still I have is just of Eddie Arnold and me. It would be wonderful to have a picture of that precious Zinneman when he was young. And, of course, a shot of Peter Lorre looking tricky over his great love—beer.

Here is a beautiful still of Elizabeth Taylor looking lovingly at Van Johnson. Leon Ames and I are upstaging them across a small table, not the vast banquet board on which we ate crêpe suzettes for a week while making *The Big Hangover*.

I see several stills from *Rhapsody in Blue*, with Morris Carnovsky, Robert Alda, and Herbert Rudley. I am there, but I don't belong. I was not right for Momma Gershwin physically, but I could have been. Warners had a horror of portraying anything as Jewish—any lilt of speech or mannerism. It was the pathological anti-Semitism of the Semites. Why couldn't they have said on film, "How wonderful is this Jewish family!" But they chickened out. I was

Rhapsody in Blue (1945) with sons George (Robert Alda) and Ira (Herbert Rudley) Gershwin

not allowed to shrug. I couldn't say "So..." before any statement. I couldn't lift my hands or use any inflection to make Momma Gershwin a believable Jewish woman. The orders came through the director, Irving Rapper, but they originated at the top. Oh, well—the music was great.

It all came back to me when I looked at the face of Morris Carnovsky, the darling. I'm sitting beside him with gray hair. We are listening to "Rhapsody in Blue," endlessly. Oscar Levant is pretending to be George Gershwin on the soundtrack. Bob Alda is pretending to be George Gershwin on camera. Now there is a scene with Oscar Levant pretending to be Oscar Levant, friend of George Alda Gershwin, while the soul of the real Gershwin pours out of the speakers in rolling, minor chords that build and build until the music reaches a wrenching climax.

Next is a flare of color... a red curtain... a bugler... "I gotta get up. I gotta get up..." It's Irving Berlin and "This is the Army, Mr. Jones. No private rooms or telephones!" Oh, what a show! Every member of the cast a big name in show business. There's George Murphy in a WW I uniform. I'm kissing him good-bye. Me, a Democrat, kissing George Murphy! There's Mike Curtiz straightening a show girl's tights, and I can imagine him saying, "Aright, sveethearts, ve haff a great show." And it was. A great variety show with little pockets of plot here

This is the Army **(1943) — a little cheesecake for the boys overseas**

and there. I was Ronald Reagan's mother for a few minutes. (No doubt the direct result of kissing George Murphy in WW I.) There was a swirl of color, beautiful girls, and music that was wow!

Then there is Kent Smith's face, scarred and made over. I am on the witness stand looking a little pale and tight-lipped. (Good reason, I am pregnant and Warner's has me corseted tightly and is also working me in three pictures at once.) Ann Sheridan's warmhearted beauty made her the pinup queen of GIs around the world when she made *Nora Prentiss*.

Those contract days at Warners were difficult for me. The weekly stipend was better than modest, but I hadn't realized they could work me in more than one picture at a time. My agent had secured the Wednesday afternoon release so I could do the *Dr. Christian Radio Show*, but every

With George Murphy in *This is the Army*

With Wanda Hendrix in *Nora Prentiss* (1947)

week the studio screamed as though they had never heard of it before. Being pregnant with our second daughter was certainly not in the fine print, so every Wednesday I would get that old heartburn trying to get free in time to make the broadcast 10 miles over the hill at CBS. I also had to pray that the make-up I had on would not be incongruous for the *Dr. Christian* audience. The old lady face I wore in Bob Hutton's *Too Young to Know* did not fit the young nurse, Judy Price.

The third picture I was making at this time was... must have been *Danger Signal*. Now there was a basket of squirrels! Bad luck dogged it from the start. Ann Blyth, playing the ingenue, had a toboggan accident. She was replaced by Mona Freeman, and two weeks had to be re-shot.

It was the story of two sisters who fell in love with the same man, but he loves neither. Faye Emerson was starred along with Zachary Scott, Bruce Bennett, and me. Faye had undergone an amazing metamorphosis from a gray little contract wren, who did tests with all comers, to a silvery blonde siren with sultry lips, sexy eyes, and sinuous movements (try that on your lisp). This all happened in one year. It may have been Warners' ploy, but the change was so complete I had a feeling that the real siren had been hiding in Faye all the time.

The plot blurs in my memory. Robert Florey directed. I was a psychiatrist, and I think Zachary killed someone. Bruce and I discussed clues. Jimmy Wong

Danger Signal (1945) with Bruce Bennett

Howe was the cameraman, and a real star. By that time he had collected five Academy nominations for excellence, and felt a little above the *Danger Signal* shenanigans.

After we had been re-shooting a week, Faye Emerson flew off to the Grand Canyon and married Elliot Roosevelt, the President's son. This took several days and everyone came back hung over. Then Jimmy Wong Howe had a tantrum because Florey was critical of Faye's close-ups. Apparently the great cameraman was unable to disguise the effects of the honeymoon, so he walked off the set for three days.

Soon after Jimmy was coaxed back to work, Colonel Roosevelt notified Faye he would fly over his bride's soundstage before noon. Half the cast and crew climbed the fire escape to the roof to wave at Elliot. Three hours of that

Strategic Air Command with **June Allyson, James Bell, and Jimmy Stewart**

and we fell five hours behind. Two days later President Roosevelt died at Warm Springs and the Colonel wired Faye to come to Washington. And so it went.

There is a colored still of June Allyson, Jimmy Stewart, James Bell, and me dining out somewhere in *Strategic Air Command*. Jimmy looks so dear and young playing the life of Ted Williams.

The still of Kathryn Grayson and me from *So This is Love*, is odd. The film was supposed to be the life of the opera star Grace Moore. But what is Kathryn, or Grace, doing in bed? I was her aunt in the story. In real life I had a fat guarantee and a two-week minimum. The film was budgeted by Warner's at five million. In 1953 that was not shabby, even for a big musical. However, halfway through the first week someone in the front office discovered some figures on how many Americans were staying home watching television. Well! You never saw such a change in tempo. It was as though Jack Warner pressed a button to undercrank the camera. Everyone began running instead of walking. Even when you sat still, you had to do it quickly. The budget had slipped to three million; consequently, we were all urged to do our scenes rapidly and get off the payroll. Grace—or Kathryn—had to get out of bed and get the lead out.

Now I am at the bottom of the box and looking at a sad dame standing between Linda Darnell and wonderful old Sara Allgood. This still is from *City Without Men*, a story about a rooming house near a prison full of women wait-

City Without Men **(1943) with Linda Darnell and Sara Allgood**

ing for their husbands, or boyfriends, or sons. I am there to wait for my son's body as he is about to be electrocuted. Remember when they used to do that? I don't mean in a Frankenstein film, I mean in the "big house."

I hoped no one would notice when I did that one, and I doubt anyone did. I needed the money. Mother and I had just returned from *Commandos* location in Canada. I was eight months pregnant, and my husband was about to be shipped out of Camp Roberts in an infantry company scheduled for the South Pacific. We had saved my salary from *Commandos*, we were living in Beverly Hills, but no one knew how long the war would go on. I could net almost a thousand dollars from this job and could pay off John's congressional campaign debts with enough left for the hospital. So I did it. And it was not all that hard, though I was afraid the implausibility of a 32-year-old pregnant woman playing a 60-year-old mother of a condemned criminal would show. I don't think it did. It just seemed like a melancholy charwoman with a slight pot. If I had known the still would be around 35 years later, I might have taken more pains and at least combed my hair. I was trotting around the Warner's lot, changing wardrobe and make-up every few hours, wondering if our baby would be born before *Danger Signal* ever got in the can, but loving every minute of it.

Somewhere in 1947, Warner's dropped my option, which was a relief to John and gave me a little more time to spend with our children. Also, a few months later they began hiring me back for more money and only one picture at a time.

Night Unto Night with Ronald Reagan and Viveca Lindfors took so long to finish that a friend of mine said, "I notice that the styles changed during that picture." I hooted with laughter but he gravely insisted, "Oh, yes—the hems dropped six inches."

There were a lot of reasons for this—not the hems but the endless weeks of production. The film technicians' strike was blamed primarily, because Reagan as president of the Screen Actors Guild was negotiating at night with the Brown-Bioff insurgents, the I.A.T.S.E., and other factions, to bring some kind of peace to the industry. Then Ronnie, with very little sleep, would have to get up at dawn and be taken through the picket lines, as we all were, in armored cars.

The Warner Bros. entrance was guarded by riflemen standing nervously "at the ready," wondering what or whom they were supposed to shoot.

But there were internal reasons for the delays. The producer (Owen Crump) was a reasonable intellectual who lacked the necessary steel to shove production ahead. Don Siegel, the director, was an assistant on his first assignment as director. He fell in love with Viveca during those endless months and eventually married her.

Viveca Lindfors was a thrilling actress, but a tiger lady with a firm jawline. Don would look into those limpid sea-green orbs and move the camera wherever she wished. He and Owen Crump also would move the dialogue around for her—ostensibly because she was learning English.

Even the basic plot was changed, erased, substituted, sifted, simplified, then obfuscated beyond belief, for an entirely different reason.

Phillip Wylie's original novel, *Night Unto Night* was the moving story of a man who discovers he has epilepsy. In 1948 you hardly said that word aloud, let alone on film. One day after we had been in production a month or so, someone in the Warner front office realized what this picture was about.

Suddenly the atmosphere changed. Lots of men in dark suits invaded the set wearing tight little frowns. They behaved as though we all had epilepsy and it was contagious.

When you do a picture about a man who has a catastrophic and progressive disease and then decide midway not to identify it, the behavior of the principals becomes very foggy and bewildering.

The penultimate cut of the film shows Ronald Reagan, a handsome, healthy-looking male given to fainting fits. He seems to have some of the symptoms of pregnancy, or a light touch of rabies. You keep wondering why

Night Unto Night **with Broderick Crawford and Ann Burr**

Viveca is so sympathetic—why doesn't she just pull up stakes, or take him to a good vet.

Anyway, summer drifted into fall. The strike was settled, but the script problems were not. Around Christmas we had a lottery on the set. There was rumored to be a grand prize. For the first time in my life I held a winning ticket. My slip read "19." I yelled, "Here!"

A large aggressive character woman pushed forward and said, "I have 19." Then she leaned on my shoulder and pointed to a ticket and growled, "Yours is 61."

There was one of those inquiring silences while a stand-in handed me a huge bundle of white crochet, covered with lumpy roses. So this was the prize!

Reagan and Siegel looked nervously at me. I looked nervously at "Big 19," and managed to be a rapid loser, expressing appropriate regret as I surrendered the load of needlework.

It turned out the whole 10-foot tablecloth had been made during the filming of *Night Unto Night*, lumpy roses and all.

Whether the picture was ever shown on TV I can't say. It had a splendid preview, but the reviews were confused. Like the song says, "Oh, dear, what

The Story of Seabiscuit **(1949) with Shirley Temple, Barry Fitzgerald, Lon McCallister (on the left), Donald McBride and William Forrest under the horse statue, me, and Pierre Watkin**

can the matter be?" Ronnie wasn't too long at the fair, he was just ailing with no diagnosis. It could all have been summed up as a load of crochet.

When David Butler directed work became fun. He was the dearest and most understanding of all Warners filmmakers. He was mad about horses and determined to do the story of Seabiscuit. He owned a lot of stock footage in color of many of that brave little horse's victories. This was 1948 and almost all of the news film was still in black and white. Consequently, Dave had to adapt the story to match the film he owned as well as to shoot new angles which would blend with the old "coming down the stretch" reels.

Butler named the picture quite simply *The Story of Seabiscuit*. We learn that an expert trainer took charge of an unpromising colt and led him to many unprecedented victories. Shirley Temple, Barry Fitzgerald, and Lon McCallister played sweetheart, trainer, and jockey, in whatever order you like. I was the owner, Mrs. Howard.

We settled in at the Santa Anita racetrack, sharing stalls and eating outdoors with a lot of fine horseflesh, accompanied, of course, by horse manure and horse flies. Dave Butler was so in love with the Seabiscuit story that he didn't notice these minor distractions, and made the location a happy four-footed picnic.

By the Light of the Silvery Moon (1953) with Leon Ames and Doris Day

The best fun I had during the Warner years was playing in the two Doris Day musicals *By the Light of the Silvery Moon*, and *On Moonlight Bay*, both based on Booth Tarkington's "Penrod" stories.

Again the director was Dave Butler. He had been a romantic star in silent pictures and then went on to have a long and successful career as a director in sound, specializing in comedies and musicals. He lacked the inherent conceit of many male stars, and yet knew actors' problems from the other side of the camera. A big man with a Francis X. Bushman kind of head and x-ray eyes, he had a rat-a-tat tempo when he was in the cage with the big cats. And we had some big cats on those pictures, at least we thought of ourselves that way. There was Gordon MacRae with his warm golden voice, and Leon Ames, who was a skillful veteran, plus Doris Day. Even smaller parts were played by fine talents with well-known names: Mary Wickes, Russell Arms (on loan from his "Your Hit Parade" video duties), Maria Palmer, and Merv Griffin, who had too little to do. Both the casts were full of favorites.

Dave could handle us all, even getting along with Marty Melcher, Doris' producer-manager husband. When we had too many games and tricks going, he would swell up and play the martinet over delays and too many takes, but even when he screamed and swore, we knew he was one of us, an actor before he

On Moonlight Bay **(1951) with Billy Gray, Mary Wickes, and Doris Day**

became a boss. He was a dear, funny man, and one of the greatest storytellers in Hollywood, both on film and in conversation.

One long scene, with Leon Ames in bed and the rest of us twittering around him, took forever. The set was hard to light, and there were camera delays as well as equipment failures. When we finally neared the end of a good take, Leon was sound asleep and missed his line. On the next take we tied a thread to his big toe and yanked it on his cue. He let out a howl, Dave yelled, the cameraman went to the toilet, and the front office phoned down a curse.

I always wondered how the news got around that studio so fast. It was as if Jack Warner had a console of peepholes to spy on every stage. He knew instantly if an actor blew his lines, or held up production. More than likely he had his own little CIA network of assistants with walkie-talkies.

Knowing Doris Day during those years was a door to light and fun. She is not only amazingly talented, but honest and invigorating. Her dancing, and that vibrant voice, made everyone around her alive. Her religious faith inspired and awed us.

Toward the end of one of the "Moons"—Harvest, Silvery, or whatever—a whole soundstage was converted into a woodland snow scene with trees and ice

By the Light of the Silvery Moon with Doris Day, Gordon MacRae, Billy Gray, Leon Ames, Mary Wickes, Howard Wendell, Walter Flannery, and Geraldine Wall

and skaters. Doris, Leon, and I (her parents) had to come circling into a long boom shot in an old-fashioned sleigh. The top of the boom was 'way up in the catwalks to catch the hundreds of extras, who were costumed for the year 1913 in furs, boots, and woolens—all very expensive. The long shot opened wide, and then zoomed in on us, for a close three-shot.

This was during the first Adlai Stevenson campaign for the Presidency. I think Doris and I were the only Democrats in Burbank. We had some big colored Stevenson buttons which we kept hidden. As soon as Dave yelled "Cut! Print!" and climbed off the boom, we pinned our buttons conspicuously on our chests and waited for him to come up to the sleigh. His eyes, which missed nothing, saw the buttons immediately. Doris assumed an innocent look, and I kept my face blank. Dave began to rant and rave about the "cost of the shot," and "idiot actresses," and went on to what he thought of "God damned politicians," until his face became a dangerous purple. Then we told him his shot was OK. I don't think he believed us until he checked the dailies.

When I see these two pictures on television, I realize it is the only period in my long career that I would like to live over again. We were all a part of a lovely reproduction of an age of innocence in our country that may never really have existed, except for us, at Warner's in 1953.

CHAPTER 27
LIVING THE LIFE OF RILEY

One day in the fall of 1948, Irving Brecher asked me to play Peg Riley in a feature film he was making at Universal of *The Life of Riley*. Brecher is a very funny and complicated man, who had created this perennial favorite years ago. If I could have foreseen all the difficulties and opportunities "Peg" would open—and shut—for me, well, I would probably have gone ahead anyway. Intermingled with the pain there were a lot of laughs.

I responded with, "What's the matter with Paula Winslow? She has been playing that part on your radio show for seven years."

Perhaps my motives were not altogether altruistic, but the memory of having been cut out of the *Dr. Christian* pictures still rankled, and, besides, I honestly admired Paula, who was a fine comedienne.

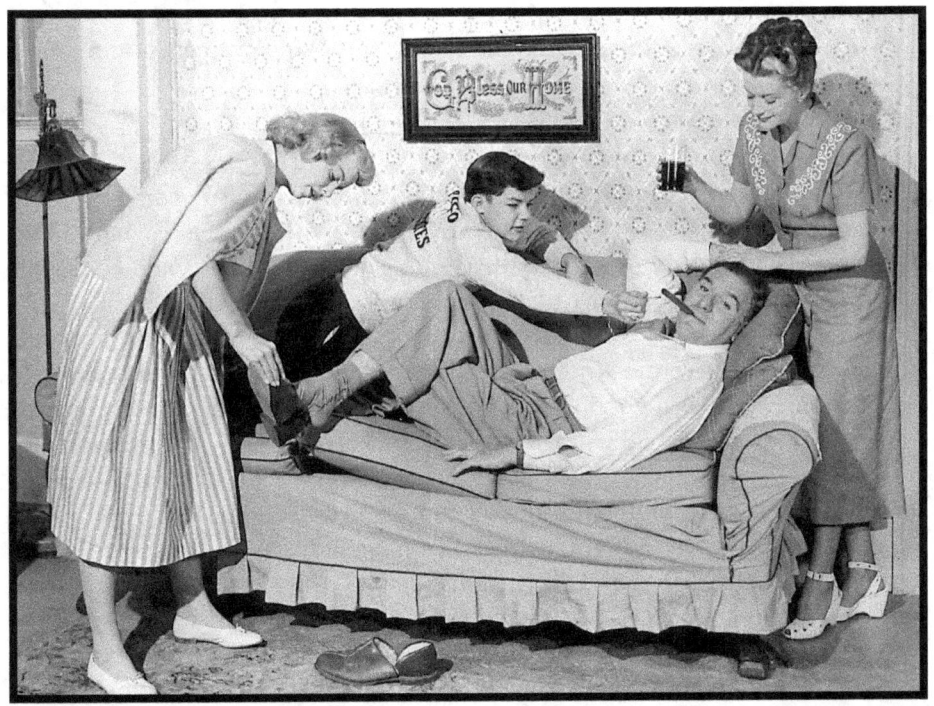

Living the *Life of Riley* (1949) with Meg Randall, Lanny Rees, William Bendix, and me.

Life of Riley **with Meg Randall, Richard Long, me, William Bendix, and Lanny Rees**

Brecher said that she'd had no film experience and did not want to do the role, so that is how I came to play "Peg" to William Bendix's "Riley."

Three people emerge clearly from that picture: Irving Brecher, a tall, thin, myopic blond with the sweetest smile I ever saw; William Bendix, built like a hyper-pituitary angel with a barely discernible sense of humor; and Harry, the prop man, who was a grouchy realist slaving in Fantasy Land.

Life of Riley was a distillation of some of the radio scripts Brecher had written. Now, to have the writer also be the director was hell for us actors. In the first place, if he is a good writer, it is safe to assume that film is not his first tongue, but something he learned later. In the second place, a writer-director knows every word of your lines better than you do, because he has squeezed them out one by one, and loves them better than Home and Mother.

Brecher, being very bright, learned fast in an industry that has a high price tag for every foot of film and each minute's delay. Directing *Life of Riley* was his first solo flight. (Make that first time in a link trainer.) He was loyal to radio actors because he had worked with so many of us for years, but it never occurred to him that a radio actor can become a crumpled wreck when metamorphosed into visual action in front of the Big Eye.

Life of Riley with William Bendix, me, Bill Goodwin, and Victoria Horne—Bill couldn't say "flame."

The radio-actor-turned-movie-actor has to learn to stop on a taped mark without looking at it. He has to memorize lines which he formerly read with ease; learn to use props; discover how small to play a close-up; how big to play a long shot; and so on, ad infinitum.

One scene in that picture I shall never forget. Neither will Harry, who was head prop man. "Head" may be a euphemism for "the" as this was a low-budget, black and white film, and Universal was notoriously cost-conscious.

A prop man, as you may know, is the person who handles and provides the physical things that are used on stage or in a film. He does not have jurisdiction regarding set decoration or special effects. Sometimes this becomes a fine line of distinction. If an art director wants a certain kind of fireplace, the prop man is responsible for the fire that burns therein, but if the fire is to smoke, or explode, or do something unusual, the special effects department is involved. The prop man also takes care of the daily needs of the director and stars, such as water, aspirin, pop, cigarettes, and so forth. It is the overlapping of gray areas that is confusing. For instance, one frosty morning during Christmas week I was in a frontier story out at Columbia Ranch. A stagecoach had to thunder past on a village street. Something was wrong with the camera, so the director called for another take. The coach and horses were brought back for a new start. Inevitably they had left manure in the road. The assistant yelled, "Hey! Props! Clean up the horse apples!" The prop man strolled over to the smoking pile and said, "Nope. If it's steaming, it's special effects!" The sound man fell off his boom, laughing.

A scene in Riley's living room involved Bill Goodwin, a well-known radio announcer, recruited by Brecher to play the part of Riley's old friend who had been invited to dinner. Bill was supposed to be a well-to-do heel who brags of his success, and climaxes with a dig about having been Peg Riley's former sweetheart.

Goodwin was tailored to his dewlaps and smoking a big cigar. The scene was a long one and, unfortunately, Brecher wasn't experienced enough to gloss over the cigar at the start. No. He established it in a big tight two-shot with Bendix. About three pages of script later, Bill Goodwin was still waving the cigar and talking a mile a minute. The ash was getting longer and longer. The camera moved in for the joke. Bendix was following the ash with a tray to catch it before it fell on the rug. The tag was to be that at a certain line the guest would flip the ash and miss the tray.

But all the while Bill was acting, Brecher was stopping him and correcting his dialogue. This made Bill so nervous he was sweating like a wrestler. The

***Life of Riley* with Meg Randall**

Riley (Bendix) tells Junior (Rees) to hit him on the head so he can collect insurance—Peg (me) reminds him his policy lapsed!

payoff line was, "Yeah, didn't you know, old boy, your wife used to be an old flame of mine?"

There we stalled again and again because Bill had some kind of mental block and he could not say "flame." Maybe his mother had beat him for playing with matches. He'd get to "fl…" and stop cold.

I have never seen an actor blow so steadily at the same place. We did take after take, up to this point where the ash was an inch and a half long, Bendix chasing with the dish, and Bill getting more and more nervous.

For every take, Harry, the prop man, had to run in with a new stogie to match the ash. I didn't pay too much attention to him until about take nine, when I noticed he was wobbling as he walked.

He was working off a mantel near the camera with a test tube rack, like those used in a chemistry lab, with a cigar in every hole. He'd go quickly up and down the line puffing on each one to keep the ash forming. He was like a man playing some kind of a weird xylophone. He'd puff, and put it back; puff, and put it back. Then they would yell for him and he would run into the scene with a cigar the right length. But poor tired Bill would get to "fl…," quit, and Harry would lunge back to his rack and start puffing again.

Sometimes when they were ready for another take, Goodwin would beg for a throat lozenge or a drink of water. This also being Harry's department, he would sneer, put the cigar in the rack and run for the pill or the water, then hurry back to puffing so his cigars wouldn't go out.

When the assistant would yell "Quiet!" Harry would trot back into the scene with a new cigar.

It required 19 takes before Goodwin got out the word "flame" and dropped the ash on the rug at the right place.

After that they wrapped up and moved to another set. I looked over at Harry. He was swaying like a palm tree, only he was greener.

"That was rough, Harry. How do you feel?"

He swallowed and said, "I'm sicker 'n when my appendix bust. And y'know the lousy part of this whole operation?"

I said, "No," expecting him to blast actors as he usually did.

"Well," he gulped, "what makes me really mad is I invented a machine that smoked six cigars at once! And you know what happened? Somebody stole it!"

I was tempted to suggest to Harry that he look in some other prop man's locker. A six-cigar-smoking-machine is not an item that would have many takers.

William Bendix, who was "Riley" for so many years, was an enigma. Like many famous comedians, he was rather gloomy. He worked hard and said very little. His craggy features always reminded me of the statues on Easter Island, but he was pleasant to work with because he seldom argued or made any demands. That was unusual in a star.

He and I co-starred in an early TV show, a Ford Theater "Segment," about a psychopath who held a piece of broken mirror to his wife's throat for two days until the police broke in and ended it. I was grateful for his placid nature, because the glass was sharp and we were confined in a small area for a week. Joanne Woodward was our daughter in that play. I remember her as being elegant and impressive, just as she is today.

The Life of Riley feature film made money and enabled Irving Brecher to begin a long and successful career in television. His next venture was the very remarkable *Life of Riley* with Jackie Gleason, which won the first Emmy for film TV. At this point 26 episodes of that series are locked in the NBC vaults because of litigation over re-run payments. Just as in many cases, the death of the principals will eventually solve the legal problem at bargain rates for the owners, or their heirs.

That is a story that may never be fully told, but we can try...

CHAPTER 28
EMMY... WHAT A BEAUTIFUL SMILE!

Making *The Life of Riley* into its first television series proved to be quite a trick. Irving Brecher had five years of radio scripts and a successful feature picture of the same name under his belt. William Bendix, the erstwhile Riley, refused to play, saying that television was "nickelodeon" and wouldn't last. Translated that meant "Not enough money."

Brecher hired one well-known name, who looked the part of Riley, but during the test scene he perspired so much that everything got slippery, including me, his darling "Peg." I whispered to Brecher, who was not only the author but producer, director, and script girl, "I can't work without an umbrella. What's the matter? It jumps out at me!" Without looking up he answered in a loud voice, "It's trying to get back in the bottle."

That did it. The take was so bad they didn't even save it for a blooper gallery. A week later Brecher called me and said, "It's ON! We're gonna go. I got this guy out from New York. He's an unknown night club comic, and he'll be great!"

It was Jackie Gleason. You won't recognize him from this description: slender, black curly hair, beautiful big green eyes, quiet, polite, and a listener!

He didn't know much about film, or he might have taken the next bus back to New York. Brecher used the radio scripts. No re-write. That may not scare you, but it scared me. In radio nobody quit talking to permit a brief silence; the sponsor's one taboo was A Pause. So these scripts went a fast 50 pages with Riley speaking every other line, plus an occasional monologue. And the lines and situations were very funny. They still are—lying in some film vault, as Gleason sued to keep them locked up.

Brecher rented a studio catty-corner from the cemetery at Santa Monica Boulevard and Gower Street in Hollywood. It must have been one of the first soundstages ever built. No. Make that just plain "stage," because someone had belatedly attempted to soundproof it with chunks of felt, mattresses, and old rags glued and stapled to the walls. A lot of this padding was hanging down in tatters. The whole dark barn smelled of old grease and sweat.

We were about to add 26 weeks of new grease and a lot more sweat.

My 39th birthday celebrated on the television set of *Life of Riley* with Gloria Winters and Jackie Gleason.

The shooting schedule became so tight I thought we would have to set up pup tents in the cemetery. We would rehearse four days and shoot on the fifth. Well, you may say, that isn't too bad. No, except that it was continuous. Union rules still did not apply to television crews, so we went right straight through, Sundays included. I had to be off on Wednesday afternoons for *Dr. Christian*, an occasional stint at Warners, and then tack on 30 miles to and from the home John and I had bought near the ocean in Redondo Beach. I had to learn my lines at the red lights.

If I felt my schedule was heavy, Jackie Gleason's burden was intolerable, and I don't see how he did it. He was dieting, on the wagon, and was learning 50 pages every five days. He never seemed to lose his temper, always knew his lines, and was hilarious as Riley. His pals, Sid Tomack and John Brown, were fine comics, but it was Jackie who made the series popular, riding, of course, on the well-known character and Brecher's incomparable dialogue. Our children, Babs and Junior, were played by two talented young actors, Gloria Winters and Lanny Rees. Gloria, still a doll— vivacious and pretty—calls or writes every so often. Not so long ago, a young man came up to me on a Borax promotional tour—and turned out to be Lanny, now living in the northwest.

We made 26 shows, and then one night in 1950 Irving Brecher had the ultimate honor of collecting the first Emmy for Film TV, beating out the Lone Ranger and Silver by a nose.

This event was followed by two surprising developments. First, the sponsor—a beer that shall remain nameless, canceled the show.

Someone reported to us he heard the brewer growling, "Hell, I don't want Art. I just want something for the boys to watch at '21.'"

Then a big flap erupted over "who paid for Jackie Gleason's teeth?"

There were several versions, one of which went like this:

A dentist and Irving Brecher met on a Palm Springs golf course. After a few holes, the dentist confided wistfully that he loved TV and felt he was a part of it. "Oh, yeah?" said Brecher, "How's that?" The dentist explained shyly that he had done "caps" for a star, and although he hadn't been paid, he felt that it was his smile gleaming there on the tube.

Naturally, Brecher asked, "What star? And why not paid?" The dentist admitted it was "Riley," and Brecher cried, "You got paid! I sent him a check for his teeth!"

Then they went round and round. They closed in on Bullets Durgom, Jackie's agent, who had too many places to put the money from the Tooth Fairy.

The punch line of this tale is Brecher yelling at Jackie Gleason, "OK, but when you smile, remember you're smiling with MY teeth!"

Soon after, Gleason returned to New York with a free smile and a suitcase full of scripts which he turned into a brilliant and beloved television show. *The Honeymooners* sketches were close to *Riley*. I know because I had learned some of the lines once, but Audrey Meadows, Art Carney, and Jackie were so wonderful—what did it matter? If Irving Brecher was too busy with *Mayor of the Town* to protest, the rest of us can only applaud Gleason's talent, while at the same time we regret his treatment of the man who gave him a start.

CHAPTER 29
BOB CUMMINGS—HIMSELF

I had only a short rest after *By the Light of the Silvery Moon* when I got a call from Paul Henning to come in for an interview. That was a lucky day for me because it opened up a whole new world of comedy.

The Bob Cummings Show began in 1954 and lasted over five years; years which were loaded with laughter and success. We worked at General Service Studios on Las Palmas near Santa Monica Boulevard in Hollywood. That place was old in 1940 when we had made *Cheers for Miss Bishop* and was even shabbier when we had done the fire in the lagoon for *Jungle Book*.

Now, in 1954, the whole lot was jumping. Every soundstage was busy. I remember *Burns and Allen*, *Private Secretary*, and *Ozzie and Harriet*.

In the Henning-Cummings outfit we all worked to capacity. It was a wholly integrated effort. Each person was sure he was indispensable, and although no one is, that is the perfect myth to produce maximum results.

I still meet strangers in many parts of this country, people of differing ages who will recognize me and clutch my sleeve, while they tell me the plot of one of those shows they loved. I can't remember, but they do. They'll always ask about "Schultzy" (Ann B. Davis), and Dwayne Hickman, and, of course, Bob Cummings.

The first day our cast was all together in one room was electric. We looked at each other and in every eye was a gleam that meant "anything can happen, and it will be fun!"

Paul Henning, genius and child of a man, created and wrote the show, with George Burns as backer and advisor. Ann B. Davis, Dwayne Hickman, Bob Cummings, and I shuffled the scripts and listened to Paul.

The next five-and-a-half years went by like a fast montage, and yet I don't think any of us had ever worked harder before, or with such delight.

Paul wrote 50 pages every week and sometimes twice that. In other words, we did a half-hour a week and occasionally a "back to back" double. That meant a two-part comedy with the same cast and sets.

The planning was brilliant—almost as fine as the scripts. There were many capable people evolving the pattern of rehearsal and production. Joe DePew, a former Our Gang star, was assistant producer. He had the imagination and humor

With Bob Cummings on *The Bob Cummings Show*

to ride herd on those of us who were compulsive mischief makers. After wearing out several very good directors, it got down to Bob Cummings himself.

Now, "Himself" was the star, part owner, and spoke almost every other line in some very rapid comedy. "Himself," in spite of great talent and energy, had never previously persuaded anyone to go more than a few weeks with him.

Bob Cummings, a Gemini, was like many of those charmers, and a very complicated man. In the five years of that show we learned how to recognize and cope with his various personalities.

The kindest was Bob The Father—loving, thoughtful, and proud of his children. He spent a lot of his free time teaching them swimming, driving, or flying. He introduced them socially so gracefully they had a perfect example of good manners.

Bob The Husband was only a rumor. Mary Cummings, the wife at that time (in the 1940s, she was an MGM starlet named Mary Elliott), was busy with their five children and Bob's finances. She rarely came on the set and bothered no one, except Barry the prop man.

Bob, The Guru and Health Nut, was a dazzling pharmacopoeia of kelp, vitamins, curd, placenta injections, exercises, massage, and chiropractics. He persuaded all of us to buy and use many of his hints, but he changed brands and theories so often we eventually became too confused to subscribe.

Bob, The Director, was amazing. He knew exactly what he wanted and could show us how to do it. It may not have been what we wanted, but he was the sole arbiter on the set—by reason of his investment, his leading role, and finally by becoming the only director who could successfully direct himself 26 consecutive weeks a year.

Bob, The Actor, was handsome and skillful; often innovative, sometimes mannered and predictable. He had style and tempo and a great sense of comedy, and he was always completely in control.

Bob, The Star, was the one to beware of. This one was vain, selfish, inquisitive, temperamental, and had a neurotic horror of growing old.

It was imperative to evaluate, daily, which one we were facing and how to survive. Fortunately, we admired and respected most of the "Bobs." He taught us timing, and takes, and movement, and so much about comedy. He also taught us how to get along with a multiple personality.

"Bob Ages Margaret" episode of the show

The pattern of our shooting schedule was unusual and very fast. We would rehearse one-and-one-half days and then film the show in one day. Am I getting through to you? Do you realize what that means?

Every Monday noon we sat down around a table on the set with our script books closed. All lines in the head. This was because "himself" would not wear glasses. Bob had a devoted friend, Eddy Rubin, to pound the lines into his head over the weekend. The rest of us could grab anyone handy, our husband, wife, or the Avon lady, to cue us.

During the first reading, we usually devoted 15 minutes to whatever new vitamins Bob was promoting that week. Then we would zap through the lines, stunning the visiting bit players, who would have just received their scripts.

After that, it was upsy-daisy, on your feet everybody! Scene 1—The Studio—The Kitchen—The Living Room—or whatever.

For those who came late, or were born late, let me outline The About:

This show was about a handsome commercial photographer (you've guessed) Bob Cummings, who was a swinging bachelor. His secretary was called Shultzy—

Margaret (me) tries to keep Bob's mind on business rather than on the model (Leigh Snowden).

funny and bright, played by Ann B. Davis. Bob lived with his widowed sister, Margaret (me) and her son, Chuck, who was Dwayne Hickman. Bob was always photographing beautiful, sexy models, or trying to find a husband for me, or trying to get out of some sneaky trap he had set for himself. I was usually just Reality up against my son's whims and the mad socializing of brother Bob.

It was a beautifully designed framework to attract all ages. The models were a mouth-watering parade of Hollywood's prettiest. Housewives identified with me in my struggle with two male egos. Secretaries and all working women adored Shultzy, who tried to maintain order where there could be none.

Paul Henning wrote a fine line of comedy, where Bob remained funny and still romantic. He never quite got the girl, but outwitted himself somehow, and missed. I don't think Bob understood that distinction, because he was always bucking for more love scenes, yet wouldn't sacrifice the laughs.

If you get the girl, how is that funny? Don't answer, or Women's Lib will getcha.

So much for The About. The scripts were gems of humor and created some wonderful characters, among whom were The Bird Watcher, played by one of my favorite comediennes, Nancy Kulp; and Grandpa "doubled" by Bob.

I got the worst of this slapstick scene with Bob!

It was black and white film time. We used two cameras and two crews. The last three years we had Harry Wilde, a well-named old rascal, who whirled those cameras around like a couple of bullwhips, and rarely lost a face on the edge of a five-shot, or caught a hanging mike. And we went fast!

Monday afternoon till 6 p.m. All day Tuesday till 4 p.m. Then we did it straight through as written, for George Burns, who often brought Jack Benny or some other crony to watch. They were a great stimulus for us. We would go all out to make them laugh. George was stingy with his laughs. He was always figuring out some new twist for a scene, and laughed out loud not more than twice a year. But Jack Benny was marvelous. There was the darling Appreciator of the World.

After they left the stage, and us, with changes to learn, we went through the whole script as it would be filmed. Everything in the Studio—Everything in the Kitchen—Everything in each set. This was for "Wild Harry," the cameraman, who had to know where each one of the set-ups started, and the shooting order. About six or seven o'clock we would go home.

Back at 6 a.m. for make-up—at least Bob and I came early, then Dwayne and Ann. The make-up hour was the fun time—it meant steaming coffee, jokes, gossip, and the lie-back chair with Gene Romer to soothe and smooth talk us as he made us beautiful.

Then it was wardrobe time, and on the set, ready for eight o'clock shooting.

Bob worked out a system that should have been invented years before. There has always been a dead time for actors after the first rehearsal on the set, because then the cameramen have to light the set and the stand-ins. Actors, being like children, go to sleep, muss their clothes, call friends, visit other stages, go out for food, bite their nails, lose confidence, or forget their lines.

Bob, the drill master, eliminated all that by working us endlessly between scenes. He would rehearse us off camera until no one missed a line or a look; then into the lights for a "white rehearsal" (with light for camera); then back out to more rehearsal in the corner; then back for a "pink rehearsal" (just a little blood). Then, while all camera problems were supposedly solved, we repaired make-up, pulled up our tights and went into a "red rehearsal" (more blood), the last go round before film. It was exhausting, but very little time or film was wasted, and we were able to knock off five and 10 minute scenes in one or two "takes."

This procedure went on all day and we would finish the whole show around six or seven o'clock. Such a schedule was very good for one show a week, because you went home Wednesday night, slept Thursday, and got the new script on Friday in time, to learn it for Monday noon.

The rough weeks were the double headers. It was twice as much to learn—twice as many hours—and very hard on the camera crews, who were rolling like tanks—in and out close-up—two shot—doe-si-doe and don't brush fender.

Harry Wilde would get so mad about five p.m. he would turn purple, with language to match. Nevertheless, we loved and respected him, and his skill.

Exam time for all of us was the bi-monthly preview. We would go to a small exhibitor's theater and sit—with an audience—be introduced, and then watch what we had done a week or two before.

It is always traumatic to see and hear yourself on film or tape. Aside from being ego-busting, there is a kind of atavistic horror at seeing yourself separated from yourself. Many primitive peoples, as well as some central European peasants, believe that a representation—a photo or picture of a person—robs that person of part of his soul, or self. And, in a mystical way, they are right. There is a diminution of the id, to be Jungian about it.

However, for practical purposes, the preview, the dailies and the monitor are a great aid in the elimination of bad habits in moving, or speaking bad lighting, unbecoming clothing, or backgrounds. You die a little, but you learn. So the previews were rough, but they were fun, too. There were extravagant, flattering introductions by Bob, questions from the audience, and—most important of all—The Honest Laugh Track.

I don't know how far back in time canned laughter began, but it became an insidious disease that is still of epidemic proportions. The present taped-audience-show has eliminated a lot of falsity, but few producers are above "cranking the gain" on laughs to make a comedy sound funnier than it is. The theory, I suppose, is that if you hear a lot of people laughing at something you thought worth only a smile, you would decide the audience must be smarter than you are, therefore, what you heard is not merely a smile, but a "yuk."

Paul Henning did not believe in cheating on the laughter; hence, the elaborate preview and the honest recording of audience response. He surely was right. The canned, and often unrelated laugh track, is insulting, and creates a backlash against comedy. Who wants to have it decided for him when something is funny?

I am trying to remember a comedy half-hour without a laugh track, and so far have not succeeded. The great feature comedies which were seen in theaters with perhaps 1,500 other people evoked laughter presumed to be contagious.

Probably when television began, its makers said, "There's that poor little fellow and his wife all alone in their living room. They'll be afraid to laugh out loud, so we'll give them company." *Voila*, maniacal laughter from a sound track bought by the foot.

During a successful filmed series, personal problems and entanglements proliferate. Dwayne and Ann and I remained good friends, close enough to know, or sense, each other's anxieties without getting emotional. Without raking any ashes, incidents keep cropping up in my memory.

The writing was the most important factor in the great success of the show. We could hardly wait to read the next script. While Paul Henning rarely came on the set, he knew all about each of us, and tailored the stories to fit what we did best.

One day he gave me a surprise, saying he had acquired the rights to Elvis Presley's soon-to-be-released song, "I'm All Shook Up," and I was to sing it! I moaned and groaned and said if it had to be, I would pay for the dubbing. But he just laughed and said it was not really a song at all. I countered with, "I'm not really a singer at all." In spite of my protests, it turned out fairly well, although I noticed he didn't try that again.

We had a great list of guests; stars, and newcomers who became stars. Angie Dickinson and Connie Stevens, both so young and lovable, carrying their wardrobes in on hangers, and very patient during Bob's intensive workouts. He would put them through grueling hours on a single piece of business. I always marveled that they could play a love scene with him after the stormy sessions

Christmas publicity shot with Dwayne Hickman, Bob, me, and Ann B. Davis

preceding the filming. One sleepy, voluptuous blonde let him have it with some choice gutter expletives. He waited until she was through, then said "There! That's just the energy I want from you. Take it from the top." He was cruel, but knowledgeable, and very thorough. Olive Sturgess, a good actress, played Dwayne's girlfriend—she never seemed to incur the wrath of Himself!!

His character of Grandpa was the most memorable acting in the series. His make-up took three hours, and when he came on the set he was another person. The voice, the walk, the mannerisms were so far from Cummings, we almost found ourselves complaining to him about working conditions and hours.

Over the five-and-a-half years that Paul Henning punched out the show on his typewriter, a word at a time, he had some fine comedy writers with him who went on to do other shows: Bill Manhoff, Dick Wesson, and Shirley Gordon, among others. Dick also was a great comic actor and played the Sailor in the Cummings show—a crude and lecherous, lovable "gob." Both Dick and Shirley have said that Paul wanted them there and paid them well as "sounding boards." He would bounce ideas off their minds, listen to their stories and ideas, and then write his own version all by himself.

The whole concept of collaboration is beyond me. How two people can share the writing of a single piece of work must take closer rapport than that of petals with flowers or leaves with trees. Paul was using three or four writers in his tiny office on each script, and naturally there was a lot of turnover. Writers get restless, but I don't think any of them left in anger; only frustration. They knew Paul was the master craftsman.

There are odd moments, little splashes of light, during those years which have lingered in my mind.

"Harry" the prop man, was a delight. I remember how angry he would get when Mary Cummings, Bob's wife at the time, would show up on the set to check on any props she might need for her household use. One year there was a big flap over a turkey.

The one to be used on the show was baked and beautiful on a platter. But, as is customary, Harry had an identical back-up bird, in case of accidents. The real turkey was dismembered in the scene. However, something, or somebody, got to the back-up bird. It had teeth marks in it, but had to be sent along to the Cummings dinner party. I caught Harry trying to do a little invisible mending on the scars. He was sour, as usual, "Damn! I don't know why the Iron Butterfly wants this thing for her dinner. I told her it was sprayed with Flit, but she just said, 'Never mind.' She must think I got personal plans for this old carcass. We oughta get papier mache birds anyway. You actors are always sneaking a nibble." That was Harry. He and Mrs. Cummings had a cool feud going. Once she told him to order two tank vacuums from a firm that offered one for advertising. Lots of companies did this as a courtesy. But two? Harry said, "What the hell! Now I gotta send both of 'em to her house. Whatta they need two for? His and Hers? Just tell Paul not to write in any more vacuum cleaners. "

One night I came back to the stage around eight o'clock to pick up a script I had forgotten. Harry had the rear end of a horse on a platform, dousing it with some evil-smelling stuff, and growling to himself.

I said, "Hiya, Harry. You gotta little horse laundry here?"

He snorted, "I need a stunt check for this one. Bob says our guest George Montgomery's cowboy outfit is too dark for our old brown horse—so I gotta bleach this sweetheart."

I was impressed, "Gosh, Harry, that's a big job... bleaching a horse! Where's the front half?"

He jerked his head toward the corner. Sure enough, the head and front legs were there, looking like a Minsky stripper, but wet and spotty.

I longed to say, "Oh, Appaloosa, hmmm?" but it was late and he was cranky, so I settled for, "Good night," and resolved to get him a plaque that would read, "EQUINE BEAUTY SALON Tints and set." or "IS YOUR MARE GETTING DARK AT THE ROOTS?"

One show, in the first year, gave me quite a scare. The plot involved a small chimp to be photographed in Bob's studio. The Chimp and I were to be discovered waiting on the bench in his office. I was all gussied up in hat, veil, gloves, etc. The Chimp was dressed in T-shirt, diapers, socks, and Keds.

The "Keds" were the problem. (They were lace-up tennis shoes worn by youngsters at that time.) The Chimp was tired and cross; he'd been in those tight shoes for hours.

Now, I love animals and get along with almost anything that walks, creeps, or flies, but this monkey rolled his eyes and clicked his teeth at me in a very sinister way. The rehearsal went OK. Chimp came through the door to the bench and sat down by me.

But when he heard "Action," that Chimp came through that door in one bound, landed in my lap, and went right for my jugular with those big ivories. Fortunately he was young and not really carnivorous, so they pulled him off in time to stanch the blood, and—more important—save the wardrobe. I've forgotten how the scene finished. Probably they just took the tight shoes off his poor little feet.

The five-and-a-half years finally ended. We were all growing tired—tired of each other, and tired of the work pattern. But the show went on and on into different phases of re-runs. It was known as *Love That Bob* for years. We took our cash residual payments and scattered.

Paul Henning began *Petticoat Junction* and the very successful *Beverly Hillbillies*, taking Nancy Kulp with him. Ann Davis did night clubs, repertory—and *The Brady Bunch*. Dwayne Hickman went on to do *Dobie Gillis* and several great feature comedies. Joe DePew did *The Truman Tapes*, and then returned to supervise *Beverly Hillbillies*.

Bob was later in and out of the news with vitamin sales and problems with the phone company. He continued to play in several TV dramas, but his great skill as a character actor was wasted. His portrayal of his own grandfather in *The Bob Cummings Show* proved him the ultimate artist in "othering" himself. I think if he had been willing to sacrifice the image of his own graceful youth, he could have been a Rod Steiger, a Will Geer, a Ustinov, or even an Olivier. But Bob chose youth, which in Nature's inexorable equation, becomes yesterday.

Whenever any of us see each other now, there are many happy inside jokes, and memories of laughter. It was a lovely time, full of charming, talented people, when television film was young.

CHAPTER 30
HARRY'S MASQUERADE

The feud between Harry, the prop man on *The Bob Cummings Show*, and Lionel Gagswell, the actor, was so comic we couldn't see it was headed for potential tragedy.

Now, to me, Harry is the world's greatest prop man. He's a grouch, but full of gags—grim gags. For example, when we meet, instead of "Hi," he will say, "Print ONE, hold THIRTYNINE!" We've both been there and we know 39 "takes" can age anyone fast in pictures.

Harry might not exactly like me, but he puts up with me because I love his wonderful world of "props."

He has lockers full of everything imaginable: marked cards, gorilla masks, two halves of a horse, brass knuckles, glasses that won't empty, glasses that look full but hold only a swallow, handcuffs and breakaway derbies.

He can get you anything from a bob-eared elephant to Napoleon's Dresden chamber pot. If it's on this earth, he can order it for you; if it's not, he'll have it made. If you need another head, he'll design one for you, at a price, that will look better than your own.

He's also a skillful cook. Once, on *Yankee Doodle Dandy*, I saw him serve eight actors a meal, piping hot, of goulash and noodles. He got that food on the table, looking like a Good Housekeeping ad, for nine takes—and then matched the steam for the close-ups.

He's moody, temperamental, and consistent in only one thing, his deep, dry contempt for actors. He thinks we are all hungry, forgetful, and conceited.

"Actors!" he would growl. "AAAhh! They shadow props, pick 'em up wrong so you can't see 'em. They never stop eating. And worst of all, they forget, forget, forget. Ya gotta do a scene 20 times 'cause some baby star can't remember how to pick up a male puppy, or throw a pie, so it will smack out nice."

No one could remember how the feud began, but if Lionel Gagswell and Harry were on the same set, there were sure to be fireworks.

Of course, I think actors are the dearest people on earth—next to children—and there is not a lot of difference. Most actors are generous, kind hearted, and charming.

But once in a while, in every good group, will come along a stinker. That was Lionel! I say "was" because he has not been around since all this occurred.

I suppose Lionel was not always mean. He must have had moments of charm and kindliness as a child, but those tendencies were no longer evident.

He played "heavies" almost exclusively, and there are some who will swear that this casting "rubs off." Also, he had begun to drink a lot. No one saw him unsteady or anything, but he was getting those little red and purple designs on his nose. He was a good actor, in a florid way, or nobody would have put up with his malice and snobbery.

One day on *The Bob Cummings Show*, he had to go through a swinging door from a kitchen to a living room. He would invariably start talking too soon, while the door was still going "whap, whap."

The sound man said, several times, he could not hear the first line, because of the door noise.

It is part of the duties of the prop department to catch noisy doors by hand. In this particular case, the camera was lined up on the door so that Harry had to lie flat on his stomach in the kitchen so he would not be seen as Lionel marched through.

Actually, it was up to Lionel not to push the door so hard, and not to start talking at once, when he arrived in the living room. Lionel knew it, too. But he was mad at Harry because after he had missed three takes, Harry had said, in a highly audible voice, "You'd think this bird'd know how to handle a swingin' door, now wouldn't 'e?"

Everybody heard it and there were a few snickers. The next time around, Lionel was so mad that he stepped on Harry in the kitchen. Harry held back his scream of pain until Lionel arrived in the living room, whereupon he belted out a great "Yeeowwww!" that bent the sound man's needle.

They finally got the scene, but the gauntlet had been thrown. It was war from then on. Harry had won that skirmish, but he was digging himself a pit, one that almost became his grave.

The next time I saw the two of them was at General Service Studios where another company was getting set for a historical Western with two days scheduled for location.

I walked on the soundstage early that first morning. It was empty except for Lionel Gagswell sitting at a rehearsal table reading his "trades." He looked as hung over as a tenement clothesline.

I sat across from him with no greeting and took out my copy of *Variety*. All was silence. Suddenly over the top of my magazine I saw something crawling across the living room set, behind Lionel.

I blinked my eyes, held on tight to my chair, and checked again. Yes, it was an alligator. For a moment I was stunned.

Then the creature raised up and put a front foot to lips in a shushing motion. I almost laughed out loud—because then I knew it was Harry. That alligator suit had been in his cupboard for years, left over from a Tarzan picture. It was made of rubber and was very realistic.

Closer and closer he crawled to Gagswell's chair. I watched, motionless, as he cuddled up to that chair, the way a cat scratches its chin, rubbing and nuzzling his jaw and sticking his toothy snout around the corner at Lionel.

At first, Lionel just growled, "G'morning, how are you?" and went on reading, but when the snout got between him and his paper, he took one good look at the monster, fell over backward, scrambled to his feet and ran out of the soundstage.

I howled and applauded and beat on the table, until I realized Harry was trying to get my attention. He was standing on his rear legs, making odd sounds, and pointing his paws at the zipper that ran down his tummy.

I said, "What's the matter, Harry. Can't you get out of that thing?"

Just then Gagswell came back on the stage. He walked like Lear in Act II, but when he arrived at the table, I could see he was an off-orchid color and shaking with fury.

Harry was making a lot of "wah-wah" noises, so I unzipped him. It wasn't easy, as the suit was old and the zipper was big and rusty.

When I got him out of the suit, he said, "Boy, it's stuffy in there! I couldn't unzip it with these fat claws."

Harry couldn't resist crowding his gag. He smirked at the actor and said, "Scare ya a little, Mr. Gagswell? Think ya had the DTs."

Lionel looked at the prop man as disdainfully as if he were a barrel of trash. "Funny! Very funny, 'Props.'" It sounded like he meant it was anything but funny.

Harry rolled up the big rubber costume and said, "Mr. Gagswell, I thought as long as you're going to wear this suit, you might as well get acquainted with it before you go out on location together—you and 'Gate here."

Lionel was astonished. "My God! You mean I've got to wear that suit tomorrow."

Harry smiled. "Yes, sir. That's what the assistant told me. They need a talented actor-alligator to chase the horses across that artificial lake. We got some cheap alligators, but you are going to be a super-stunt type to snap at the horses' legs."

Gagswell could hardly speak. His voice broke. "Oh, no, I don't! The assistant said I'd get a stunt check just for wearing a crazy suit and sitting on a rock!"

Harry chuckled happily. "That's right. I don't know about the rocks, but this sure is a crazy suit! Cheer up! The lake's only two feet deep and you'll make a couple of hundred in 20 minutes, while the rest of us sweat for two days."

Lionel was quiet. He watched Harry going toward the prop cabinet, and then with a foxy smile he said, "Say, Harry, you going to be out at the lake tomorrow?"

Harry 'llowed as how they couldn't shoot without him. And apparently that ended it. We went to work and they both behaved for the rest of the day.

The following morning most of the company left on a bus at six a.m. I wasn't in any of the action on location, so I had to piece together the rest of the story from what the wardrobe man and Harry told me.

When the company was ready for the shot of the horses crossing the lake, the wardrobe man, a feeble old sweetheart named Pomeroy, brought the alligator suit to Gagswell's tent dressing room.

Pomeroy told me later that Gagswell fussed around with the rubber monster for a while, and then said, "Pomeroy, go get Harry, the prop man. You're not strong enough to squeeze me into this obscene garment!"

Pomeroy loathed Gagswell, so he willingly trotted off to the prop truck.

Harry was sour, being bothered to do a wardrobe job. However, he was proud of that suit and he didn't want anything to happen to it.

He said that after he got in the dressing room, Gagswell complained of a headache and begged Pomeroy to go find him an aspirin and a glass of water, which he did, leaving the two enemies together.

When Harry tells the rest of the story, he grows almost incoherent. Apparently Lionel told him he didn't see how he was going to get his feet into the leggings, especially as he was a little larger than the prop man.

> Well, I tried, but he seemed awful awkward. I said, "Look, Lionel, like this. It's easy! See?"
>
> What a fool! I put both feet in to show him. Then he said to me, sad-like, "Harry, I'm scared. I can't breathe in there!"
>
> So I say, "Aaah, crumb! There's nothin' to it. Look! Just put your arms in first. Then you reach up and pull the headpiece over your head!"
>
> "Show me, Harry," he says, kind of sweet and nice. I felt sorry for him, so, like a damn dope, I put my hands in the sleeves and hauled the big 'gator head over my own.
>
> Then quick as a flash, you know what he done?

I knew, but I said, "No, Harry, what?"

> That mean ol' cuss zipped me up so fast I never knew how it happened! Then he must a' grabbed some kind a' pin or hook, 'cause I was trapped in there tight. I tried to grab the

zipper tag, but couldn't. My hands was like they had boxing gloves on 'em.

I was yelling all the time, but it was muffled in that big snout.

Pretty soon I could see Pomeroy through the eyeholes. He was just coming back in the tent. But there was no sign of Gagswell. I kept turning around and around looking for him.

Then Pomeroy grabbed me by the right front leg and started leading me outdoors and over to the camera.

I hollered like crazy and danced all over, but I could hear the crew laughing and all the extras calling me "Lionel!" They were gagging it up about my new Brooks Brothers' and how slender I looked in a rubber girdle.

I could hear all right, but the eyeholes and noseholes were my only chance to see. It was confusing having four eyes and none of them. any good.

The director yelled, "OK! Put him in the water. Then show him where the horses are going to cross!"

They threw me in—or I staggered into the water. It was hard to tell. Nobody liked Lionel much, so I guess they shoved me. Anyway, right off I get the news—the water is deeper than two feet. It's more like four 'cause I went down, glug, glug!

The suit was waterproof, except around the zipper and the nose and eyeholes. I figured if I could just keep my snout up, everything would be OK. But the water was rising in the leggings.

Right then I thought of the "other" alligators. It made me awful sore to think I'd hired 'em myself. I'd hand-picked those creatures to give old Gagswell trouble.

Now I might have to fight 'em in this crazy, leaky suit. Talk about the early Christians—Jeez! They fought on dry land.

I figured my only chance was getting up on the bank. Three times I almost made it, but some smart aleck assistant would always catch me and throw me back.

Every time that happened, I shipped another gallon of water. I could hardly stand up, let alone walk around.

Then two lady alligators moved in. The guy I'd bought them from said they were little and harmless. I'd gotten one big male to scare that ham actor, and the owner said all he ever did was sleep and yawn. Anyway, those little females were sure lively. They snuggled and cuddled, and followed me all over the lake. Every time they'd squeeze me up against a rock, I'd put up my snout and bellow. I thought sure the crew would hear me and catch on to who I was.

Not a chance! The director and the assistants were so busy wrangling the horses and cowboys they paid me no mind.

The crisis came when the big bull alligator came after me. I made a date right then to punch that guy in the nose that rented him to me. He may have slept and yawned around home, but he wasn't sleeping around those two females. I caught a glimpse of him through my nose holes, just after I had flipped one of my "lady friends" over my shoulder.

He was coming in about "seven o'clock low" like they say in those war pictures. If I hadn't seen him, I'd a been a gonner sure. He had a set of ivories that looked like two Wurlitzers opening and shutting. Crunch!

I moved as fast as I could, but it was like slow motion. He missed me on the first pass, but I knew I'd need a red cape and a sword to win the next one.

I looked around for a rock and found a medium-sized boulder. It was rough work getting it loose, but I got it between my front paws. Then the trick was to keep wiggling my snout back and forth, like radar, so I could see where he was through them tiny little holes.

He had turned around and was coming in from the back. I waited till he got the old Wurlitzer open wide. Then I heaved the boulder for a strike. It stuck—"Whock!"

Boy! What a relief! This bought me about two minutes of peace.

Just as I was gonna try for that bank again, I heard the director yell, "Hey, Gagswell! Over here now! Over here by the horses!"

I crawled over to where he was standing on a rock and wrapped my front claws around his feet. Any more time in there would be the death of me. I had to get out.

But the rat had a cane, and he started beating my arms and hands and saying, "Get on over there by the horses, Gagswell! What the hell's the matter with you...?"

I was about at the end of my strength. The water inside my suit was up to my stomach now. Like the old joke, I was up to my... uh... hips in alligators.

So, anyway, I give up and wallowed through the water toward where I can hear a lot of splashing and yelling and horses whinnyin'. I held my snout up and saw two lead horses standing behind a big bearded guy on a pinto.

Just then I felt a terrible slap on my tail that nearly knocked me flat. I didn't need to look. Old Buster was back—and without his boulder.

I lurched and crawled as fast as I could toward the horses. It was just a matter of time till Toothy would regroup and make another pass. Far away I heard somebody yell, "Action!"

I caught the second horse by a rope, stumbled over a big rock, clambered up on it and fell over the horse's back. She was so swayback, though, I felt like my legs was gonna be nipped off by that 'gator any minute. Finally I got one leg over and sat up. We were moving through the water at a pretty good clip by this time.

I never thought about how it was gonna look kinda weird from shore, for an alligator to climb up on a horse and ride off. They say they got the film on that, and they are saving it for a studio party.

Harry looked off happily into the future.
I hated to interrupt, but I knew it wasn't the end.
"What happened, Harry? How come you almost drowned?"
"Well," he said gravely:

That big 'gator made a pass at the horse I was on. She reared, and that's all I remember.

When I came to they was squeezin' water out a' me over a barrel. Everybody was standin' around looking real solemn.

The director said, ''Harry, we didn't know it was you. What happened?"

There wasn't enough steam in me to begin to tell 'em the whole mess—till I looked up and caught sight of old Lionel standing behind a bush about a hundred feet past the camera.

I stumbled to my feet and took off after him as fast as I could wobble.

I lost him right away—and nobody's seen him since. The wardrobe woman says she heard he's got a pop stand up near Palmdale.

I still got the alligator suit, but it's got a big bite out a' the tail. You want to wear it some time, you can. Maybe to a masquerade?

I said, "No, thanks, Harry." But I made a mental note to be on hand when they screen Harry's Last Ride—as an alligator, that is.

CHAPTER 31
GOTTA BE LIVE!

"Live" television, as it was practiced in the 1950s, could be classified as cruel and unusual punishment. It was practiced and practiced, but never enough. It was as if a network would say, "Let's get a bunch of monkeys, see? And train 'em for days to do everything we tell 'em. Dress 'em up fancy, then we'll bring in the cameramen and grips and they'll figure out how to follow the monkeys around and take pictures of 'em. And we'll have a great, exciting show, because the monkeys will be scared! Everything will be a surprise. That will give our show real immediacy!"

That was the big word then, "immediacy." Translated, it meant TERROR and BEDLAM.

Of course, we actors were the monkeys.

Most of the frightful fun was the over-rehearsed monkeys and the under-rehearsed crew.

It would always start in some bare hall with a few folding chairs, a director, thick scripts, and the lucky monkeys, chosen from hundreds of eager contenders. The make-believe rooms, streets, or forests were chalked on the floor. Then all of us sat around the table and read the script out loud—till we were told to get up and play in the chalk marks.

While this was happening, a lady would come in with different colored pages. If your pages were white, you might get new blue ones during the first few hours. Then after you had replaced some of your white pages with blue, other colors would come thick and fast. Sometimes two colors in a single hour, so that all those rainbow colors were finally assembled in each monkey's script just in time for the broadcast. It was merely for a souvenir, because if you didn't know all your lines without the papers, they would already have fired you and gotten another monkey.

After several days of running through the chalk marks and saying the words on the colored papers six to eight hours a day, even the dumbest monkey would be letter perfect.

Then came the time to match up monkeys and camera. The cameraman and gaffer could watch the rehearsal, maybe a whole half day. The director always explained the whole thing to the cameraman. Never mind the script. The network cameraman knew that the words meant nothing. Only the picture counted. So they never fuzzed up their minds with what the author wrote.

Our daughters helping John run for Justice of the Peace in 1956

The big mean hour was the dress rehearsal. Sometimes it lasted all day, and the monkeys would lose track of when it was rehearsal and when it was air time.

When the red light went on in the camera, that meant, "This is IT, Monkeys! Millions are watching (we hope)! Do it right!"

Now the really frightening fun began. You moved through a real room, but you could not see your "marks" because a man would be holding a bright light in your eyes and walking backwards alongside you. Another man was on the floor sliding out the track the camera was riding on as it moved with you. You, the monkey, say your words and make lovely faces for the camera, hoping to God you won't trip or step on the track man.

The moves to a new scene were done in utter blackout. So we poor monkeys would stumble around with hands outstretched and sometimes blunder into the wrong set, only to be discovered by the camera's eye cowering in a blaze of lights.

There was a classic case when Tris Coffin, a handsome leading man and fine actor, "died" skillfully in a live TV scene. He was mourned, prayed over, covered with a sheet. Tris waited a decent interval, then got up and tiptoed

Our family blessing their meager meal in 1956

out of the set. However, the camera failed to leave, and dwelt lovingly on his resurrection.

Those were very rough days for us monkeys, because no matter what happened we were blamed for all errors. We were so identifiable. If a grip failed to get his light on a lady monkey and she appeared to have a spotty complexion, he didn't suffer, but she was said to be on her last legs. Just as in Tris' case, when he was blamed for what was a camera error.

All this talk about monkeys and immediacy is me, the actress, saying live television was brutal and unnecessary. It produced very little fine theater. What it did do was create some interesting camera movement: simpler ways of making films; better editing; and some creative mistakes that taught cinematographers fluid techniques for photographing scenery, sets, and human beings.

The attraction those early live shows had for audiences was, I suspect, the same ghoulish orgasm they experience waiting for a racing car to crash or a suicide to jump from a building.

My personal high hour of horror in live TV came in the late 1950s, when I was old enough to know better.

All actors are victims of vanity. That is how producers and directors manipulate actors, by appealing to that built-in vanity. That is why actors have agents who have no vanity and think in numbers instead of words.

Albert MacCleery, producer and director of *Cameo Theater*, sweet-talked me into doing the life of Marion McDowell, a 94-year-old lady who had founded and supported a colony for writers, artists, and composers at Peterborough, New Hampshire.

This experience taught me another truth. Don't do the "life" of someone when you have to explain who she is.

This lady's husband had been Edward McDowell. I was bored at 12 while learning to play "To a Wild Rose," so why did I get trapped by the composer's widow 35 years later?

Albert was very persuasive. Mrs. McDowell especially wanted me to portray her life; she would appear on the program with me; etc., etc.

I must have been completely anesthetized when I signed the contract, because when I read that 10-pound script in which Mrs. McDowell never quit talking, I phoned Mr. MacCleery to scream, "Never!" He had wisely left for Palm Springs.

My husband, my legal advisor, said the contract was binding. So what was there to do but stifle the screams, learn the lines, do the show.

Becoming Mrs. McDowell was rather pleasant. I began to feel dangerously confident. At least, during the five days of rehearsal in a bare hall with chalk marks, metal chairs, and imagination.

My subconscious was wiser, though. There were 27 costume changes in the hour program. My sleep was haunted by the dressing and undressing of Mrs. McDowell. The nightmares increased when I was told I wouldn't see my wardrobe until the night before dress rehearsal.

Then I asked about make-up. After all, I couldn't go from 19 to 94 with the same face, hmmm? The answer to that was also "You'll see the make-up man the night before dress rehearsal."

Oh, but that was scary! I remembered the careful film tests of make-up in feature pictures, the marvelous aging techniques used by Bill Phillips and Perc Westmore at Warners. And by Don Cash and by MGM's Bill Tuttle.

Then we were told the grim news. "Dress rehearsal all day Sunday. Air time 4 p.m." Wow! Now that meant a Saturday night run-through until late. Then home 50 miles and back 50 miles for 8 a.m. make-up and "ready for nine." Then on your feet until "off the air" at 5 p.m.

"Oh, well," I told myself. "I am as strong as a horse, know all those lines and moves. Just a few little wardrobe and make-up details to work out."

MacCleery and his assistant director kept saying, "Now don't worry about a thing. There will be this marvelous NBC floor man in a red vest who will be right beside you, guiding you through every move. Don't forget the red vest. He'll be right with you."

The Saturday night run-through calmed none of my anxieties. The wardrobe lady fitted me with my 27 changes which, it turned out, were mostly to be put on at the beginning and then we would peel... adding a sweater or shawl or whatever in the later years.

Now I am no slender willow to start with. To look 19 at the beginning, I ought to have a waistline, right? I mean I should curve in a little, especially as the period was 1885. It's tough to look young and slim with parts of 27 wardrobe changes attached to your person. I looked like a Goodwill rack with the dimensions of a Russian shot putter.

I kept whimpering that I ought to be able to move fast when young, then slow down and grow heavy for the aged scenes. No one listened except to say that I would have a "big distracting hat for the beginning" and a "marvelous umbrella" apparently to keep the viewer's mind off my bulk.

The make-up man was consoling. "We'll start with you made up 'pretty' then gradually take everything off." "Uh, huh ... but when we get down to me, I'm only 42. How about 90? Will I be so tired I'll look 90?" "Oh, we'll shoot a little silver on your hair there at the end, and shadow under your eyes, no problem..."

He was so casual I choked off my worries, being sure we would have a chance to try it all out Sunday morning.

Now as to Red Vest, I believe they were called Floor Managers at NBC. I had done live TV in various cities, beginning in 1947. They were usually bright young men, courteous and efficient, wearing headphones, and squatting by the camera giving cues. But, like all people who are listening to voices coming from some OTHER place, they have a faintly Martian quality. They are not with YOU. They are with them; in the booth; in the soundtrack; some place where you are not.

Our Red Vest was calm. He looked like Arnie Palmer, evoking the same confidence.

We walked through the long show. We paced out the "stations" where each scene would take place. We did camera moves. Along about 1 a.m., we finished. The lucky people who lived nearby in the Valley said "See you in the morning," and trotted off. I had to Parnelli-Jones it back to Redondo Beach, check on the four kids, kiss John, my husband, then sleep fast to return to NBC in five hours.

That Sunday was 48 hours long, filmed in slow motion. The dress rehearsal seemed all right, though during its four-hour run I got the stunning news, "Oh, no, dear, we can't do your old age changes because there wouldn't be time to wash your hair and face and start over, would there?"

At four p.m. when "Air time" struck, everything began to go wrong. Doors wouldn't open. Bells wouldn't ring. Seated at the piano, I saw with horror that the hand clutching leaves off a calendar to show the passage of time, couldn't get off a single day, and finally knocked the whole thing to the floor. A fitting end for such a device.

I looked for Red Vest. Surely it was high time to get off the piano bench and run to the next station? He was nowhere in sight. I eventually got up and left with the camera eye still "on." From then on, it was gallop-a-gallop, from set to set in the dark, only occasionally glimpsing Red Vest in the distance.

A wardrobe lady would pull off clothing or throw shawls at me, as we ran. A hairdresser would unpin bangs, slap on buns, remove curls and switches. A make-up man, jogging beside me, would pull off eyelashes, and later, squirt silver spray at my temples, and even use his thumbs to put eye shadow under my eyes.

When I would arrive in a pool of light and settle down for a serious scene, I had to fight the suspicion that I looked like Mad Agnes or Bozo, the Clown.

Finally it was over. I stumbled out for a curtain call with Mrs. McDowell. She, at 94, looked fresh as a daisy, while I was Lazarus, barely able to stand. You see what I mean about "Live TV"?

CHAPTER 32
WIND 'EM UP!

Have you ever played a scene with a pigeon?
No?
Then, if possible, avoid that experience.

A few months ago I listened to Oliver Clark rehearsing a monologue he was to have with a pigeon in *We've Got Each Other*. The lines were funny and as long as you only imagined the pigeon, it was charming.

I asked him if he had ever worked with pigeons, and when he said "No," I didn't have the heart to tell him how difficult it could be.

If everything goes well, the pigeon will get the credit and the actor will age five years. If there are problems, the actor will age 10 years and play to a stuffed pigeon who will look better than the actor.

October 1963 was the hottest weather I can remember in Los Angeles County. And how well I remember it!

Arthur O'Connell and I were doing an hour TV show at Paramount. It was part of a pseudo-psychoanalytical series called *The Eleventh Hour*, which won several prizes, none of them named "Neilsen."

My husband and I had received a prestigious appointment from the State Department to travel as "Cultural Specialists" to Pakistan. Our departure time was eight a.m. the next morning.

We had Pan Am tickets to Rome, connecting with a flight to Karachi. If this show was not finished and I left anyway, I would be in trouble with the Screen Actors Guild. If I stayed to finish on the following Monday, the tour arrangements would be wiped out.

The thermometer measured 110° in Hollywood, and had hovered there for days.

That morning the filming was interrupted by a fire in the prop department storage area under our stage. Smoke began pouring through the old flooring around our feet. We were all ordered out into the broiling sun. But hot as the stage had become, we soon drifted back inside in search of shade.

The firemen finally got the fire out and we went back to an outdoor scene where Arthur and I were to have an Auld Lang Syne rendezvous on a park bench.

The director, Arnold Lavin, loved autumn light, pigeons, trees, and flowers, as do we all; though not necessarily in that order.

The set was lovely—a big park lit with soft golden floods. The greensmen had done wonders with trees, shrubs, and fallen maple leaves. It only remained for the actors and pigeons to add the charm the script indicated.

Outside my dressing room I heard a prop man say, "Them pigeons are sure peppy."

Then another voice, obviously the bird trainer, mumbled, "They told me to have 'em ready to work hours ago. Finally had to feed 'em 'cause they were peckin' each other. Now they're not hungry."

Indeed they were very lively—interested only in escaping the lights and the crew. As there were plenty of trees and bushes to hide in, this was going to be a problem for sight and sound because they were making loud gargling noises in stereo.

Arthur and I rehearsed the scene while the bird man and assistants tried to coax the pigeons to sit on the park bench, or peck around our feet. They sprinkled us with crumbs, grain, and popcorn... but no go. The pigeons hid while the clock moved on.

Finally, about five o'clock, with a move to another set and two more scenes to do, the assistant said to the director, "I'm afraid we'll have to wind 'em up, sir."

Lavin looked nervously around at the birds and nodded "OK." The second assistant and prop man seized a pigeon and the first assistant yelled, "Places!"

Before he could answer, the sound man called, "Speed!" and the men holding the birds at arm's length, like discus throwers, whirled them 'round and 'round about 20 times. Then they set the little feathered bundles carefully on the bench, seized two more and did the same thing.

The pigeon near my shoulder looked like a sailor on the deck of a rolling ship. He also had the hiccups. Two more birds were placed at our feet, just as the director said "Action."

Arthur was making a small gurgling sound and I thought it was pigeon talk, until I saw he was shaking with laughter. The bird on his side had tripped and sprawled flat, legs up. Lavin called "Cut!" and we had to start over.

This time the birds' low cooing became a kind of rock squawk, "out of sync" and growly. The sound man cried, "Cut! I can't hear the dialogue!"

Since Arthur and I were playing a couple of frail old crocks and the scene was sentimental, it was going to be odd to shout the lines... but we had to top the birds' racket.

So... once more 'round and 'round for our reluctant friends.

Ready for "Action," surrounded by teetering birds and sprinkled with crumbs, Lavin said, with forced optimism, "Please, it's getting late. Let's concentrate and get this beautiful scene." Then he unfortunately added, "These pigeons can take only so much of this."

That did it. Arthur and I were gone again. We laughed until we wept. We choked and howled helplessly. Meanwhile, the pigeons staggered back into the shrubbery.

The director was getting starchy now. He said, "Miss DeCamp, it is you, I believe, who has to finish tonight. Try to pull yourself together. Catch the birds, wind 'em up, and we'll go right away. "

Those birds were just bright enough to know what was coming, so it took a lot of crawling, swearing, and wing-flapping to get them back for the merry-go-round.

This time was better. They were wound up firmly and clung to their spots. Though one of them fell off the bench and one threw up, Arthur and I managed to get through the scene by not looking at each other or our feathered extras.

I'm sorry I missed that show (it didn't play Karachi). The tipsy birds must have been far more entertaining than the two sedate humans. Next time you see a scene with a pigeon, watch for the whites of its eyes.

Why did we laugh so much?

Perhaps we found the pigeons funny because they were actors, too, defying authority in a wild refusal to play the director's game. We were wound up and had to perform on cue, but the birds were free. We were like a class of well-disciplined children, watching a rebel throw spitballs at the teacher. It was "Hurrah for chaos, and screw you, Boss!"

CHAPTER 33
KARACHI TO THE KHYBER TO BENGAL

Sitar music, the beat of the tablah, turbans, and bhurkas. Camels and water buffalo competing with Volkswagens and gilded rickshaws. The naked and the bearded—kohl-eyed babies—betel nut spittle—maimed children begging. And over it all the many-layered odor of Asia: woodsmoke, camel dung, curry, roasting grain, and incense. That was Karachi in October 1963 where it was 90° at one o'clock in the morning.

John and I were very proud of this assignment—determined to be absolutely correct and yet to do more than asked. Like many people at that time we were under the spell of President Kennedy's words, "Ask not what your country can do for you, but what you can do for your country!"

In our briefings the State Department tried to cushion us for the cultural shock we would be facing. While we were titled "Cultural Specialists," privately we felt a little lost because the world we were entering was both Mohammedan and politically hostile. We had spent months studying the religion, as well as the background of Pakistan unrest. However, no books, no briefings can really prepare anyone for the impact of the subcontinent.

My original assignment came from the Cultural Division of our State Department via two dear friends, Jack and Margaret Bryan, who were finishing a six-year tour in West Pakistan; he as Cultural Attaché, and she as teacher for the United States Information Service (USIS). I was told to prepare three plays for production in four cities in West Pakistan and for Dacca, the capital of what was then called East Pakistan, or Bengal. It is now known as Bangladesh.

My husband's assignment was more prestigious, but simpler. He was to speak at law schools and universities in various cities, both East and West, so he could use the same material over and over.

From March to October we studied and talked to Indians as well as Pakistanis, trying to prepare for the unknown. We knew it was important to bring from our country to theirs, the best material to which they could relate and find of value.

I memorized *Death of a Salesman*, *Time Out for Ginger*, and *There Shall Be No Night*, as those were the selections chosen by the State Department people. I must admit I had some qualms about my ability to do justice to the first, to

Visiting Pakistan in 1963

make Ginger valuable, and to make understandable *There Shall Be No Night* 20 years after the Finnish war with Russia.

Fortunately, I also took a number of Eugene O'Neill's plays, Tennessee Williams' *Glass Menagerie*, and Albee's *Zoo Story* and *Sandbox*.

I chose the works of some of the finest of American poets: Carl Sandburg, Edward Arlington Robinson, Edgar Lee Masters, Edna St. Vincent Millay, e.e. cummings, Emily Dickinson, Walt Whitman, Henry Wadsworth Longfellow, and the best loved of all, Edgar Allan Poe. They were relatively simple, and strong selections, because I had a suspicion that the claimed English literacy of eight percent was inflated. It was closer to four percent.

Two weeks before we left I was informed that plays were out and poetry was in. What luck! They also wrote something that didn't quite get through to me, or I might have been less jubilant... "We will work out a program on your arrival."

We had a day and a half in Washington, D.C. for briefings at the State Department before the flight to Rome, Beirut, and Karachi. We were treated generously as precious VIPs. Several times we were asked if we wished to see ANYONE. The term anyone was stressed with significant looks. As I had worked hard in Los Angeles County for John F. Kennedy in 1960, I was tempted to say, "The President, please." Unfortunately, I reasoned that when we returned we would have something to say and would have earned the right to say it. A month later he was assassinated, and I deeply regret my decision.

We saw Chief Justice Earl Warren instead, as he was an old fishing friend of my husband's. He was gracious and waited after hours to see us, giving John a few good words for the subcontinent where he is adored as The First American, because of his decisions for minorities.

At last the briefings were over and we were airborne to the other side of the world.

There had been a complete set of Rudyard Kipling's works in one of the company houses of my childhood. I read them all before I was 12; consequently Lahore, Peshawar, the Khyber Rifles, and the Great Bazaar were so familiar it was like visiting a land I had known in my dreams. The butterfly turbans of silver and gold tissue, the shining marble mosques, soft dark eyes, golden skin, and the saried ladies with diamond nose buttons were all a part of a fantasy I had loved and longed to be a part of.

But the reality of what I was expected to do intruded hourly on the visual circus. My first shock was the news that the Pakistan Arts Council had no theater—no pupils—and no program, and that I would have to RECRUIT my students, and then evolve a program to fit.

How? Where? And what to do?

The Cultural Attaché, Russell Harris and his associate, Bob Jones, suggested I be the second half of a Eugene O'Neill program two nights hence.

John and I worked about 18 hours, spelling each other on an old typewriter. We prepared excerpts from *Desire Under the Elms*, *Anna Christie*, *Strange Interlude*, *Mourning Becomes Electra*, and *The Emperor Jones*, in all of which I would play all the parts. John, bless him, not only typed, but rehearsed me in the whole schmeer.

The event was held after dark in the formal Arts Council Gardens in the center of Karachi. Dr. Maya Jamil, a beautiful lady in a gold sari, was the main speaker. She had received her degree in The Drama of O'Neill from Columbia University, and though she was courteous, I felt she was less than enthusiastic about the addition to her program.

The audience was "Raj." Some of the US officials were in Western dress, but there were a hundred or so jeweled turbans and saris, whose owners were seated by bearers, in winged chairs, or on silk cushions.

Dr. Jamil spoke in detail, and at length, proving her doctorate, and beclouding a subject that was already far from lucid. Like most actors, I am sensitive to the reactions of an audience, and these people seemed either asleep, or very restless. Those somber faces had closed eyes, or else were looking about for a bathroom.

My whole tour was dependent upon this evening. The embassy people would be evaluating me here for the ensuing months and cities ahead.

When at last I was introduced, I did an unprecedented and dangerous thing. I thanked Dr. Jamil and all those present for the opportunity of meeting them, and then begged for an intermission; promising them some drama, if they would "rise and walk about a bit, and return."

Our cultural staff looked grim, but the audience fairly scampered for water and facilities. The temperature was 90° and the mosquitoes were winning the battle with the ladies' fans.

It was a fortunate gamble. They all returned. Then I began doing portions of the plays John had helped me to rehearse. It was encouraging to see young people gathering at the edges of the audience. They drifted closer, attracted by the racket I was making with all those different voices and accents. The louder I got the better they liked it. Naturally, if you don't understand English very well, you want a lot of noise and action.

The final selection was from *The Emperor Jones*. Can you imagine a plump, middle-aged blonde actress screaming, "Oh, Lordy-Jesus! Save me! Lead me, Jesus! Oh, God, save me! Lead me outta here, Lord Jesus!" all in a deep black accent? Preposterous? Right!

They cheered and cried, "Wah! Wah! Wah!" the Pakistani equivalent of "Bravo." Everyone was happy. I was wringing wet. The next morning I had 34 pupils waiting to see the lady who had created the previous night's disturbance.

Looking at those dear, dark faces that first day, I trembled at the barriers between us. I prayed to be kind, and not to demand too much, because they were not like any class I had ever seen before.

In age they ranged from 15 to 60. In language they went from NO English, up through a fourth grade vocabulary, to the Phukka Sahib accent left over from the British occupation.

They were very clean. The men wore immaculately ironed white shirts, though some of their trousers were threadbare, or their shoes worn through. They were uniformly thin, almost to emaciation. Some appeared ill and feverish. Some had racking coughs. Some had badly scarred faces, pitted by acne or smallpox. But they all had beautiful big, dark eyes, were graceful, and full of longing to act; to express their dramatic heritage of race and religion, and political frustration. The Mohammedan faith is physically athletic in prayer, and melodramatic in attitude.

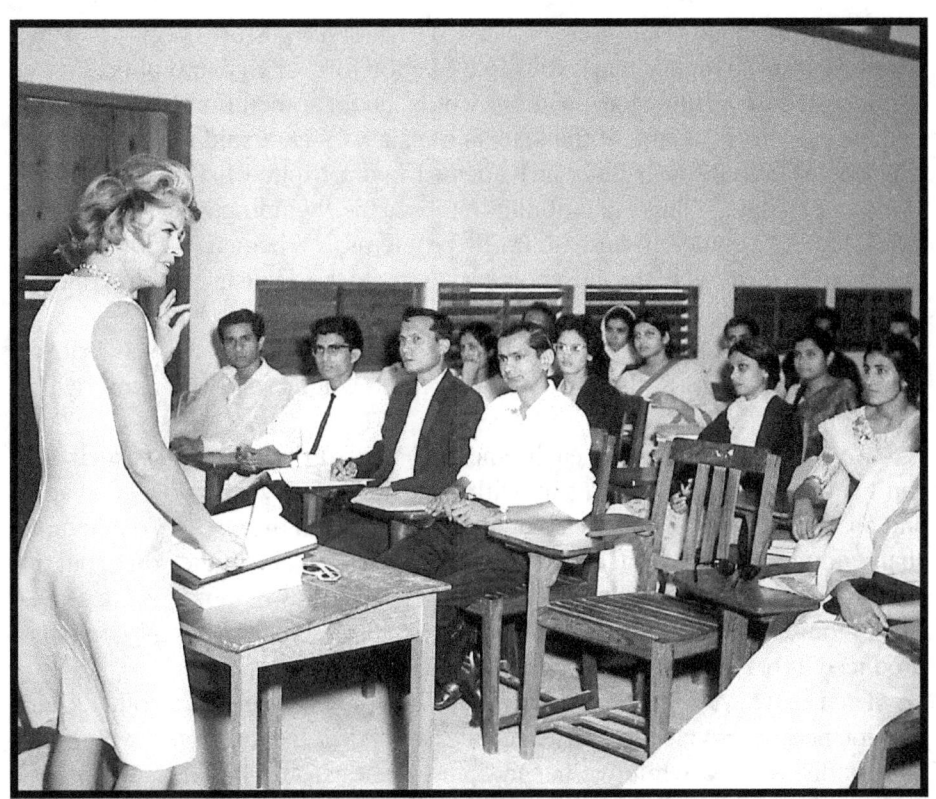

Teaching a drama class in Karachi, Pakistan for the US State Department

There were only three girls. One, from a Catholic school, wore Western dress, and the other two wore saris. I had hoped for more women, but even an educated Pakistani prefers to keep his women in purdah behind screens. Besides, the Koran, like our Old Testament, is against any form of idolatry. They believe in the commandment, "Thou shalt have none other gods but me. Make to thyself no image of anything on the earth, above it or on the seas beneath..." Of course, sculpture and drama fall into the forbidden area of representation, so I had to be grateful that any students were there at all. Those who had come were the rebels. They were going against the old ways of the Koran, as well as the political climate of their government at that time.

Pakistan was receiving enormous sums of money from the United States, and like all borrowers, resented the giver. India, their old religious enemy, was fighting China, so Pakistan was making overtures to China and Russia, to appear independent.

I thought of all this, as I looked into their dark, seeking eyes. Obviously we had for the time being only one common denominator—pantomime.

I spoke a little of the things I had seen and admired in their country—of the beauty and expressiveness of the human body, doing elementary emotional alphabet of the hand. They were persuaded to do some gestures peculiar to their society. I showed them a marvelous Red Skelton film, all in pantomime. I asked them to prepare a little story, without words, about something they saw or did in their daily lives. Some of the leaders translated what I said to those with no English. After only four days in Karachi I had a limited list of suggestions: "buying perfume," "buying clothing in a bazaar," "winding a sari," "catching a rickshaw," "a camel driver with traffic problems," "a beggar." Oddly enough, two Western ideas were the most popular: "a trip to the dentist," and slow-motion tennis, or baseball.

I won't subject you to the whole course. You can see that I was learning along with these pupils, though there were times when I felt I was not progressing as quickly as they were.

We read poetry aloud to each other. We played rhythm games, such as "*I* can't stay with you," "I *can't* stay with you, 'I can't *stay* with you," and so on and on, explaining the difference in meaning to match the stress. For a tongue-sharpening exercise we did Vachel Lindsay's lines, "Not that they died, but that they died like sheep. Not that they served, but that they had no gods to serve." This, along with "Theophilus Thistle" and "Baby's rubber buggy bumpers," produced a lot of giggles, and better diction.

Then there were the troublesome "W"s. For some reason or other, many Semitic peoples reverse W and V, and we had to drill the difference with breath and candle. After a while we began doing scenes from *The Glass Menagerie* and *Our Town*, and some simple sketches I wrote. Their pantomimes became remarkably funny and clear. The non-speakers became good stage hands, as well as mimes. After three weeks we gave a performance for the end of the course. It was strung together—or apart—by a dusty old black cloth for a curtain, and lit by two ancient spotlights. All the embassy friends came and it was quite a festive occasion.

I was both excited and apprehensive, but I needn't have been. They were wonderful. So dear, portraying a completely foreign world with such diligence, and loving the chance to perform so joyfully.

They gave me a lovely good-bye party, which they could ill afford, and little presents made of wool or feathers, with hand-painted cards. I wept, which pleased them deeply. And never will I forget my first Pakistani graduating class.

The next city was Kipling's own Lahore, several hundred miles north by plane. Lahore is a kind of San Francisco of West Pakistan, without the Bay. The Great Fort is there, a monument to Mogul might in the late 18th century. Within the fort is a huge Moorish palace covered with smoky mirrors, inside and out. There is a mosque so vast one can hardly see across the marble courtyard to its entrance on the opposite side.

Kipling's father was curator of the old museum in the center of the city. Nearby is a formal Anglican cathedral hung with flags and coats of arms of all the British regiments that served on the Western Frontier. The heroes are buried under marble or brass slabs in the floor. Their names seem wistfully British—so far from home.

We stayed in a giant structure that had once been a Shah's palace, which had come down in the world to commercial hotel status. It was called The Park Gardens and had several hundred rooms. Our suite was on the top floor and had vents in the roof where swarms of pigeons flapped and muttered.

When the bearer, in turban, lungi, and bare feet, brought the morning tea, he would flap a rag at the pigeon droppings, and place the tray ceremoniously between our beds. There was always a fat tea cozy covering the pot, but the bread, butter, and milk faced the world unsheltered. We were usually hungry, and as John said, "We've had our pigeon shots, haven't we?"

There was one scheduled program for me to appear before the assembled Pakistani Arts Council and the US consular folk. It was held in a small airless theater. I realized the atmosphere was not too friendly when a curt Pakistani introduced me as "Miss DeCamp, who is 52 years old and traveling with Judge Jawn Shah-eed-lar." Poisonous. I couldn't resist correcting him by saying, "Fifty-three, sir. Karachi gave me a beautiful birthday party a week ago." There was no use in referring to the implication that I was John's mistress. After all, in a country where lots of men still had four wives, why bother?

I read some very fine poetry, both lyrical and dramatic. But it was to little avail. With the exception of my countrymen, the audience was cold and indifferent.

Norah Troxler, wife of Paul Troxler who was engaged in a huge World Bank engineering project for West Pakistan, entertained us that night and became my dear friend and mentor during the difficult month ahead. She spoke Urdu and had a fund of inside knowledge of Lahore society and its political undercurrents. She assured me that there had been news of my successful work in Karachi, and that was the cause of my cold reception. I said that was rather thin, and wondered if she was merely trying to buck me up.

"Oh, no, my dear, these two cities are very jealous of each other. And besides, you must remember that this is a male-oriented society which does not suffer females on any podium."

She proved to be right, and I had to earn my place the hard way, when I returned to Lahore two weeks later.

John put me on a plane for Peshawar, where I was to do four days of classes with university students. He went to a formal luncheon in Lahore to meet Ayub Khan, the Sandhurst-educated Pataan, who was President of the Democracy of Pakistan, East and West.

It was that noon that President Kennedy was assassinated; I did not know about it until the following morning when the bearer brought my tea and a newspaper.

That day in Peshawar was a long, lonely shock. The USIS officer, Charles Provence, was called to Lahore for conferences. Everyone was in a flurry of anxiety and shock, trying to figure out what this meant to our country and its Foreign Service.

John arrived that night in Peshawar. We had dinner in the Provence home with all the consular personnel. It was decided we would take five days off over Thanksgiving and visit the Kingdom of Swat, after which the decision about classes and continuing lectures would be resolved. Everyone was trying to be very matter of fact—stiff upper lipped and all, though it was a sad little gathering.

That night when the lights were out and we were alone, the horror of Kennedy's death became smothering. I cried and cried. John tried to comfort me saying—"Our country is strong. Johnson will be all right. The job is so big he will become big to fit the Presidency." But there was little comfort for millions of us around the world that night.

Peshawar is for me the navel of Kipling's India. It is an ancient layered city which has known centuries of invaders ebbing and flowing through the Khyber Pass.

Its Bazaar is a dream-like wandering market. We saw it early one cold November morning in the company of a young army officer, who spoke Urdu, Arabic, Punjabi, French, and English. Looking back I am sure he was more than his oak leaves indicated.

Little charcoal braziers burned everywhere. A dentist squatted, turbaned and wrapped in shawls, on a priceless rug. A tray of extracted teeth and a chest of cobras advertised his profession. We watched as he skillfully milked a little serpent's venom to anesthetize a patient, who sat cross-legged, holding his jaw and rocking back and forth in pain. The dentist rubbed the venom on the patient's gums with one bare, dirty finger, and then motioned the man aside to show us his cobras and his collection of teeth. I doubt he did any remedial filling, or grinding. It was "pull 'em out, or nothing."

I wanted to hang around for the extraction, but our officer said there was a rare and ancient place we must see before the bazaar became crowded.

He led us to a dark aisle of booths open to the silvery sky. In each one sat a white-bearded Pataan with the straw-banded pale blue turbans of the north. They looked misty and unreal, like paintings, with shafts of sunlight touching their robes.

The Major watched our faces and then laughed, happy at our surprise. "This goes 'way back in time... long before Kipling. This is the Street of the Storytellers."

We could only marvel that even here, in this marketplace, men, women, and children with a few pennies to spare, needed stories, dreams, and fantasies to ease their lives.

Presently a boy of 11 or so came up to the first booth, put some coins beside the patriarch, and then leaned on his elbows as the old man began gesturing and talking. His eyes were closed, so I asked if he were blind.

"I don't know. Many of them are, but they close their eyes when they tell the old legends to avoid distractions."

I asked him if he had ever bought a story. "Oh, yes. They are simple tales of love, and luck, and danger, always with a happy ending... like *One Thousand and One Nights*."

We moved on to the Street of the Letter Writers, whose booths housed younger experts, far more practical than the street of dreams we had left.

In the bazaar we bought little gold embroidered caps, curved knives with inlaid ivory handles, and ruby rings. The Major said they were made from gold wire and smashed taillights, or, if you preferred sapphires and Bromo-Seltzer bottles.

The Kingdom of Swat was ruled by the Wali of Swat in 1963. The week before we had our audience with him, *Time* magazine had made a terrible gaffe by referring to him as the "Mali." Mali is an Urdu word meaning sweeper-up-of-refuse, or, a garbage man. The Wali was understandably miffed.

Swat is the poor man's Shangri-La, high in the Western Himalayas. Our corner suite in the only hotel in Swat's capital, Saidu-Sharif, had a top-of-the-world view of dozens of terraced mountains and the Hindu Kush. This mountain range looms almost as high as the Himalayas, its snow covered fangs curling over like a tidal wave.

The audience with the Wali was civilized. His bodyguards must have been imported, as they were seven feet tall, in a land where five foot 10 is tops.

The Wali was Buddha-faced, but beautifully dressed in British cashmere. He asked us for our opinion of his country. We expressed admiration for the schoolchildren we had met, who had greeted us in English. He replied that there were penalties for teachers whose pupils could not speak English. The word "penalty" reminded us of our arrival on his doorstep where the Wali's mali was mopping up bits of bone and blood. He mentioned that he had had to resolve a family feud a half-hour or so before. "Resolve" was explained by his story of a man accused of murder by the widow of the victim. The Wali had heard all evidence, deliberated, decided a guilty verdict and offered the widow a choice of blood money, or a gun to execute the murderer. She chose to execute then and there. You could not say "justice delayed is justice denied" in Swat.

After the pause engendered by this tale, we complimented the Wali on his educational program: free schooling for every child to 12 years. Total literacy, the aim.

He chuckled and said, "Yes, it is good. But before education we had more peace."

Back in Peshawar we visited a surprising hospital. It had 50 beds and 500 outpatients. Each narrow cot was piled with what appeared to be bundles of rags and old clothes. The doctor would prod the bundle and there would be grandma, and one or two others, lying with her to keep warm. It was impossible to see who was the patient. The families brought food, as the hospital was very poor. There were live chickens and goats, grain, and little fires beside the beds to roast chipattis, or meat. It was a compassionate place, where the patients would take the livestock and relatives to bed for protection, while it was hosed out twice a day.

The American doctors in Peshawar said they did frequent plastic surgery on women whose noses had been severed. The tribesmen of the North Territory near Afghanistan don't tolerate infidelity in their wives. Cutting off their noses is a strong deterrent, and presumably keeps the tribe "pure."

My last memory of Peshawar was of hundreds of people standing in line to sign with a name or an "X," the condolence message to Mrs. Kennedy, the President's widow. She had visited the hospitals and the orphanage there not long before, and was a romantic symbol of our country to the poor, and especially to the children.

The weeks in Lahore which followed were more difficult sessions than those of Karachi, though eventually more rewarding. I was alone now, except for the Troxlers, as John had to fly back to his work in California.

The first day I was surprised to see workmen in turbans building a very ugly tin tent on the lawn in front of the Arts Council. The head of that organization, Sansur Namin, was evasive. "Uh, Miss DeCamp, we feel that the theater upstairs is too small for you, and the theater downstairs is in use for rehearsals." This was deliberately insulting. We were being relegated to an outhouse, to see if we could accomplish anything on a dirt floor in the freezing fog.

However, with Pakistanis I had learned that cheerful acceptance was the only path to success. Cheerfulness made them suspicious that they might be doing you an unwitting good turn.

We had a lot of fun in the tin tent. We introduced ourselves, did hand, foot, and body pantomimes. We even got Namin to join us and show off. He was very good and we applauded him enthusiastically. Then, lo, and behold! Several days later we were told the theater upstairs was to be our new home, the tin tent was to   be torn down. Since the cost of this whole episode was borne by the USIS, I regretted it, but was secretly glad we had won out and could now perform indoors, with-out coats, sweaters, scarves, and heavy socks.

These students were more advanced than those in Karachi. They were more experienced actors, and were intensely interested in every aspect of the theater, poetry, diction, movement, and meaning. They ranged from 14 to 65 in years, and had an equally wide range of occupations.

Our final performance was packed, and favorably reviewed by two papers. In a simple, rather primitive way, it was very moving. I am sure Albee would never have recognized the excerpt from *Zoo Story*, or Tennessee Williams what we had done to *The Glass Menagerie* or Thornton Wilder the fragment of *Our Town*.

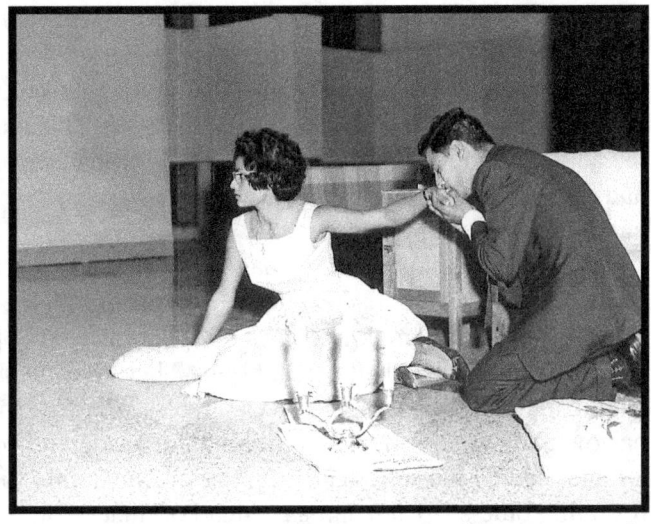

My students doing a scene from *The Glass Menagerie*, in Karachi

Perhaps Edna St. Vincent Millay would have wondered if that was really her "Elegy," and Edgar Lee Masters would have been bewildered at the treatment of *Spoon River*. But Carl Sandburg might have been pleased with "The Junk Man" and "Snatch of Sliphorn Jazz."

One of my students, Margaret Ghoury, wrote a poem about me that summed up our four weeks' work. Namin announced that he was naming a drama school in Lahore after me, and all of my students brought me gifts. Many years later, I still have the poem, and a large, brass milking stool, and a feather plaque that says, "Allah bless this house," in Arabic.

I had to fly to Dacca with that stool on my lap—900 miles across India— somewhat dismayed that I was not allowed an Indian visa to visit the Taj Mahal. Also, I was commanded to appear in Dacca before Christmas, although all the schools and universities would be closed for three weeks. This was again a symptom of the jealousy of the Eastern half of Pakistan for the West, which began in 1947, when partition gave West Pakistan the seat of government, and a great deal more land for half the population of poor, crowded Bengal.

My month in Dacca was frustrating. I visited eight different cities, one of which was Rashahi. It took an hour plane ride to a WW II landing strip and then a three-hour ride by Jeep through the jungle, to reach it. The University of Rashahi housed 400 young men.

I was introduced at their assembly in the Bengali tongue, a clue that they would understand very little of what I would say. So I had better be loud, take off my scarf and swing it around, and use all kinds of visual tricks to hold their attention. I did some Vachel Lindsay—"Fat black bucks in a wine barrel room... Boom lay, Boom lay, Boom," and some Edgar Allan Poe. I had found earlier I could always hypnotize my Pakistani audience with "Ulalume," although it was often merely substituting drowsiness for restlessness. In all Pakistani audiences the students move around like flies in a bottle. I suspected it had something to do with malnutrition and/or hyper-kinesthesia. This afternoon one boy rose in the audience and asked me about Sabu. They had seen *Jungle Book* and Sabu had come from the jungles near Rashahi. I was sad to have to tell him that Sabu had died a few years before.

It would take hundreds of pages to chronicle my return from Rashahi to Dacca. There was a six-hour train ride during which my USIS companion, Robert Barr, and I drank two cans of apple juice and opened a tin of sardines, the only food we had had for 30 hours. There was an all night boat ride on the Brahmaputra River, dodging river pirates. This was followed by transfer to a narrow gauge train ride for eight hours in a sleeping compartment, with Robert and me and three Bengalis, one of whom calmly took off his business suit revealing blue-striped pajamas instead of underwear.

When I arrived in Dacca at 7:30 a.m., I must have looked as old as I felt, and my raincoat in which I had slept looked equally bedraggled.

Fortunately time heals everything. I left for home with a lei of hibiscus around my neck, donated by a grateful law student who had met my husband a month earlier. The lei was crawling with ants, and I thought the plane would never take off, so I could snatch it away from my neck.

I arrived a few days later at Los Angeles International Airport, with one traveler's check for $10 and one dime to call home collect. Good planning? No, just luck. I had worked my way around a good share of the world and had returned fired with a new sense of patriotism, and a new respect for my countrymen abroad.

The Americans I encountered in our foreign service were doing wonderful work against almost impossible odds. They have to fight not only the press of the countries they work in, but also the effect of the airmail editions of our own controversies. They get the often bigoted and incomprehensible USIS bulletins, the CIA's machinations, and the indelible old "ugly, rich American" image. They are courageous, bright, underpaid, and fortunately for all of us they have a great ability to laugh at themselves, our mistakes, and the misunderstandings of the natives. Because of their generosity and many unexpected kindnesses, I came home with a new patriotism and love for my country.

CHAPTER 34
MEMORIES OF A MULE

Not long ago I received a surprising present from Jack Kerr, Dick Miller, and the United States Borax Company. They threw in a large projector, a screen, 25 years of commercials, and a few of the half hour shows in which my daughter Valerie and I had starred. In the midst of everything else that was going on during that time in my life, I had both the security and the time-consuming responsibility of my contract with the US Borax Company.

"Play it again, Mom! I wanna see Marsie and the toucan."

"What do you think this is—*Sunset Boulevard*? I'm not Gloria Swanson, y'know."

"Come on, Mom. I wanna see Val when she was fat."

The first dozen times it was fun to see but playing them over and over became boring. Our daughters, however, find it entertaining to watch themselves grow up, and the shows brought back our debut into the world of commercial television.

In the spring of 1952 in New York City, Dorothy McCann said, "Rosemary, I'm too old to learn film production, but I'm going to try anyhow and I want your help."

I assured her I knew very little of the other side of the camera. She laughed and said she could hire people to teach her that. "I want you and your children to do the commercials for *Death Valley Days*."

I was dubious. Television was still new and I was well aware of the caste system in Hollywood. I knew that even in radio, the seller, or pitch man, no matter how fine an actor, was diminished if he spoke for the sponsor. It was a national attitude which changed very gradually. I am not sure that it has reversed even now. For instance, was Sir Laurence Olivier's image enhanced by doing a commercial?

After our fourth daughter arrived, I had gained weight. I hadn't worked for several months and wondered if I ever would. I bought a mink coat to wear to an interview, because it made me look thinner, and I felt successful inside of it. The IRS was unsympathetic, not allowing me one cent deduction for its cost. Those button-down-collar fellows have never tried out for a film, or borne four children. They understand the martini lunch write-off, but not the expense of recovering a self-image. Besides, the money the children would receive would help to pay for their college educations.

All this went through my mind as Dorothy was talking. She was a pioneer with an unlimited vision, and she was very persuasive. It was an offer I could not refuse.

The contract she achieved for us was the first long-term commercial contract for film TV. The Screen Actors Guild lawyers drew it up.

The filming of a TV commercial is one of the strangest rites performed by man in the 20th century. It makes the mating dance of the gooney bird appear sedate and rational.

My 25 years in that arena are divided into sections: Me, meaning when I worked alone, and Us when I was accompanied by four offspring, age four months to 12 years, in the beginning.

Besides "Me" and "Us" there were bleachers full of "Them," composed of studio executives advertising account executives, US Borax executives, film technicians, directors, producers, cameramen, make-up, hair and set designers—all with the card-carrying right to give orders to Me and Us.

The arrangements for each session began with work permits from the Board of Education, plus health permits from the Board of Health, and letters from principals saying "so and so may work, her grades will not suffer." These permits were obtained by many hours of driving, medical examinations, and some perjury here and there.

Each shooting day dawned around 4:30 a.m., ready for eight o'clock, with curlers, dryers, the packing of double wardrobe (before and after laundry), and packing of lunches. Goldie, our nurse, was an integral part of the entourage, so it meant breakfast for six and then everyone in the bus for a 25-mile drive.

From then on it was, "Say your lines..." "Run my lines for me..." "Don't kick your sister!" "You may go to the bathroom now..." or "Not now..." "Go with the teacher." "Wipe your chin and smile!" "Don't eat your lunch now!" and over and over, "Be quiet! And LISTEN!"

Sometimes the scripts called for rough ballgames, spilling jam, or mud fights, which they did with such vigor it was difficult to calm them down for the "after laundry" phase—all ladylike and clean. Frequently our pets were involved and these were dogs, cats, a toucan, and a kinkajou. The latter was a mean little beast, who would "con" you lovingly, and then draw blood. It's fun to see all that now on film, but it was hell during the shooting.

The Me alone phase of this contract ran concurrently and continued for many more years, because the children grew up, and after Dorothy's death in '61, the commercials were less innovative but more "hard sell."

One I call "On a Ladder in Limbo." It was a dandy. It was a rainy day—two days—an eternity, at Producers Studio, a termite haven at the corner of Melrose and Marathon. The stuffing was sticking out of the walls of the soundstage and rain was coming through the roof.

The makers of Guess What had built a replica box of their product 20 feet high, standing stark and imposing in the middle of a limbo cyclorama; that is, all white, curving nowhere. So far, great... stunning!

But the cameraman was young and arty. He had installed himself on a platform half a football field away, just under the roof. When they called, "Ready," I tiptoed over the snow expanse, climbed the ladder to the top of the box, where there was a three-by-three platform. The wardrobe lady followed with my blue silk blouse. Then a hairdresser, clinging to a strut, ran a comb through my hair and we were ready.

Whoops! No! Now there are footprints on the white limbo which have to be repainted. Oh, oh! The wrong paint. It could take two days to dry. Well, why can't we shoot wet? The cameraman director shouts at me over his microphone.

Death Valley Days **with Robert Cornthwaite, Gilbert Green, me, and Peggy Rea in "Canary Harris vs. the Almighty" (1969)**

He sounds like God, amplified. His voice is bouncing around the rafters. I am not wired to speak. I can only swear, impotently. I have to go to the ladies' room, half a block away. Can't they get me off in a breeches buoy? Why don't we shoot?

God rumbles again, "We have to get a microphone up to you and the paint is not dry." The rain is pattering on the roof.

The wardrobe lady becomes threatening, "Don't you dare perspire on your blouse!"

And so on and on. Two days later when they looked at the film, the sound man had picked up the rain which sounded like tap dancers on the roof, and the cameraman had included the hairdresser in the shot, so we had to do it all over.

Then there was one I called "The Tank Caper." It took two days to get the right towel to "sink" on a set that harbored 50 technicians, executives, and research chemists, as well as FCC monitors, all instructing Old Me, who presided over two big glass tanks of water, and piles of Right Towels and Wrong Towels. The concept was valid. I've washed hundreds of towels and a towel washed in Borax is much more absorbent than an ordinary one. It is just difficult to prove, in the center of an arena, in 54 seconds. We all grew older on that one.

During the 1960s, while I was working on *That Girl*, I began my traveling period in which I thought of myself as the "Twenty-First Mule"—at least

Posing with Robert Taylor of *Death Valley Days*

I was working like a mule. By then *Death Valley Days* was in syndication, so Neil Reagan at McCann Erickson, with Joe Santley, evolved a practical and unusual program of salesmanship and public relations in the 80 cities where that program was shown.

The stations eventually numbered over a hundred, in the United States and Canada. The stations got some very good half-hour shows in exchange for commercial time and "promo" spots for Twenty Mule Team products. Added to this trade, they also got Joe Santley and me, jabbing them at least twice a year with a personal visit. As you can imagine, the success of this depended wholly on the stamina of the Mule (me) and Joe's amazing knowledge of every TV station and entertainment editor from Vancouver to Toronto, to Miami, to Phoenix, to Chicago, to San Francisco, and all points in between.

Those years are a blur of planes, hotels, room service, packing, filming, talk shows, phoning home to see if I had one; and calling my agent to see if I still had a part in *That Girl*.

The daily grind of a traveling saleswoman was rougher than four-a-day in vaudeville. A sample day went like this:

Land at airport at 7:30 a.m., taxi to TV station, appear on *Romper Room* or its equivalent, tape a "promo," hang around for *Dialing for Dollars*, or a local gourmet cookout, where I'd have to whomp up some economy snack. Grab a cab to lunch with an editor, drama, to talk of *Death Valley Days*, or *That Girl* or home economics, to talk product. Then off to another station, or visit a shopping center to do a stand-up personal appearance for a broker, salesman, or grocery chain. Hurry to hotel for cocktail party for wives of either or both of the above. Then dinner with the US Borax representatives and spouses, followed by plane trip to the next city. In the morning, start all over again.

This went on intermittently for five years. Sometimes it meant 40 or 50 visits a year to whatever cities were indicated by sales or Neilsen reports. It was a remarkable program, and I doubt if it could be duplicated, because the times and the situations were unique. No wonder my part in *That Girl* became smaller and smaller. Marlo was considerate to allow so many absences.

Sometimes I look at those re-runs and wonder why I look so inert. Then there pass before my eyes the crazy mishaps. I've lost one of my eyelashes... my false fingernails seem to have come off in my pantyhose... I am landing a half-hour late for a cocktail party in Rock Island, only to discover my clothes have gone to Miami... waking up in the morning and trying to find a match book, or a menu, or anything that will tell me what city I am in... running through O'Hare Airport in my stocking feet because my heels were too high for the sprint to catch the next plane.

All these traumatic experiences are balanced by my memories of the wonderful friends I made during that period—their warm hospitality and generous support.

The one person who made all these trips possible was my darling husband. He kept four daughters well and happy, and, as he says, "Out of custody." We talked on the phone every night and paid the resultant bills without complaint, because it was that tenuous line to home that kept me going.

CHAPTER 35
THE FACES OF MARLO

Marlo's faces overlay all my memories of the four years I was her mother in *That Girl*.

I could say that was because her close-ups comprised a large part of the film on that series... or that she had the best make-up artist and the finest cameramen available. But it would not be really true because my clearest memory of her is the first time we met, without camera, soft lighting, or make-up.

Her dark hair was pulled back into an inch-long ponytail held by a rubber band. She was a skinny little "bicycle thief" who could have been scrounging scraps in the Rome of World War II. Her eyes were big and black, and aware. They would glint with mischief or become opaque as an Arab's. Her mouth was delicate... cruel or merry...a twist of fun or contempt. A willful child, not to be crossed, and starving for something... love?

Then there was the designed face of *That Girl*, a fragile blending of Nefertiti and Marie Laurencin's child-women. Her hair was almost Egyptian. I'm not sure whether it matched the period or she created the style. Her image is still an influence in advertising fashions. A few years ago all high school girls tried to achieve her Snow White mask. They knew the enlarged hairdo made their arms and legs and waists seem slender. She was the perfect brunette doll, elegant and brittle. That face was shadowed by the midnight hair, pearly skin, and childlike smile which occasionally reached her eyes. That was the last "close-up face"— the ultimate in youthful glamour for women from 12 to 40 in 1968.

The underneath face, the one I thought I knew, was that of the cross little kid who came into make-up at six in the morning, wanted breakfast fast, read the "trades" with growly chuckles or snorts of disdain. With her hair in big rollers, she would phone imperiously for assistants, directors, or writers to "get down here now!" Under that dryer she would learn lines with deadly concentration that brooked no conversation. There was a real face: intense, lean, and utterly aware.

There was another face. The Party Face. When she was giving a party and having a lovely time she would laugh, pat, introduce all to all, wave, tell "one-liners," and generously see to the crew, guests, relatives, and bit players—miraculously remembering their names. It was also the Christmas face. She gave us lovely gifts and wished us well with sweetness and fervor.

Dream Wife **with Ted Bessell in 1965, a year or so away from co-starring on** ***That Girl***

Before beginning the *That Girl* series, I had only the average fan's knowledge of Danny Thomas' family. Daddy Danny's slick manner frightened me even while my mind applauded his skill and assurance. Marlo's mother was rumored to be a quiet, pretty lady who remained in the background but had obviously done a good job of raising three talented and interesting children while living with Daddy Tiger Thomas.

My agent took me on an interview to meet the producer of Marlo's new series, who had indicated I might play her mother. I read a few lines for him and the writers.

Any competitive reading is traumatic, and the writers are usually there to see how you mangle their golden words. I remember one phrase that stuck in my throat. The mother said something about everyone staying for dinner and she would "make turkey." That is a kind of Brooklyn way of talking about preparing food. It didn't fit the woman's character as the wife of a fine restaurant owner. You can "make dinner" if you must, but who "makes turkey?" However, for once in my life I read the line as written and made no comment.

This new attitude of submission probably had nothing to do with my being signed for the series. I found out later I had more likely been chosen because

Marlo's own mother was named Rosemary. She, too, was blonde and we were physically similar.

The regular cast was small: Marlo; her boyfriend, played by the late Ted Bessell; her father, the late Lew Parker; and me, as her mother.

When we gathered around the table for the first reading, we were considerably outnumbered by writers, producers, directors, wardrobe people, make-up, and set designers and assistants.

There is a rigid etiquette, a kind of caste system, at these meetings. The star's opinions are usually law. All arguments to the contrary are expressed with great delicacy and tact. In *That Girl* rehearsals this pattern was doubly reinforced because Marlo was in an unusually powerful position.

From the beginning we marveled at her expertise. She was financing the show—to what degree I do not know, but she signed all checks and kept a cool eye on expenses. She saw all the "dailies," that is the film from the previous day's shooting, and/or the rough cut of the last week's show. To do this, she often sacrificed her lunch, sometimes squeezing interviews into the projection room time. She was actually the producer, and selected sets, furniture, wardrobe, and music. She also read the submitted scripts and was in on the casting and choices of directors, in addition to being in almost every shot, looking divine. She seldom got to the studio later than six a.m., and that was every working day. If she left earlier than seven p.m., it was for wardrobe fittings or magazine layouts.

This routine she continued for five years, with a three- or four-month hiatus during which she did an occasional feature picture, guest shots, or, as in *Free to be You and Me*, designed and produced documentaries.

I doubt there is any woman in films, past or present (with the exception of Carol Burnett), brave or talented enough to attempt such an operation, or any who could perform this routine with the success Marlo Thomas achieved.

The production schedule was elastic because Marlo wanted quality first, and she has impeccable taste. Some of the shows took eight days. Most of them were read on Monday and shot Tuesday through Friday.

There were arguments, denunciations, firings, re-castings, and long delays in lighting Marlo's close-ups. Her hair and her hairdresser became a costly problem, and she eventually settled for wigs. There were days when Lew Parker, a dear, talented man, and I would sit in our dressing rooms wondering if we'd ever finish the week's work. There was also a lot of fun and laughter and admiration of one another.

When, like all stars, Marlo had a "spell" or a grouch, we tiptoed around till it was over. We once had a rough confrontation during which she told me I "wasn't real." She may have been right, but I was so angry I sat down and counted to 50 before screaming the cutting words I longed to let fly. Mainly I had to sit down because my knees get weak with anger. But, if there is anything

That Girl with Lew Parker and Marlo Thomas

that scares producers, it's a lull. So, by the time I got to "49," both Marlo and the director looked as if they were thinking, "Come on! All is forgiven. Let's go on."

Just counting was a good out. My mother had been fond of saying, "Words are like rocks. They hang around a long time after you've gone down the road."

There was one episode in *That Girl* I particularly enjoyed. Ethel Merman was the guest star. The plot was rife with seriocomic mishaps, in which I assume my husband, Marlo's father, is enamored of Ethel. It had some funny scenes and was well written.

Knowing Merman even briefly was a privilege. In 1930 on my way to Europe with the Mills College group, I had seen her in the elegant Central Park Casino. She was slim and dark, and when she belted out Cole Porter's "You're the Top," she brought all those white tie diners to their feet. Now she was a tradition. She had known a lot of pain, and even a few defeats, but she was always warm, affirmative, and STRONG.

The lot where Marlo's company, Daisy Productions, filmed was swarming with talent in the mid 1960s. The beloved casts of *Gomer Pyle*, *The Andy Griffith Show*, and *Mayberry R.F.D.* came through the gates and visited around on all the stages when they had time.

Danny Arnold, who occasionally directed *That Girl*, started his *My World and Welcome to It* then. That was the innovative James Thurber show with William Windom. It was ahead of its time, witty and unusual with its use of Thurber cartoons framing live actors. Danny went on to create many beautifully constructed television series that were not simply comedies, but wry and loving stories of the human condition. *Barney Miller* and *Fish* are two of this inventive man's successes.

That Girl went on to high ratings and many re-runs. Lew Parker was a popular part of its format, lovable and funny with his big eyes and sad, comic face.

Ted Bessell was both a delight and a relief for everyone. He understood Marlo's moods and her awesome work load. He could almost always make her laugh or talk her out of her sulks and angers. How he went the full five years no one could guess, because the program tightened down into the story of their involvement with each other almost exclusively. This meant that Marlo and Ted were playing "duo" with fewer additions to the cast. I don't think they had a romantic relationship beyond the studio, but they may have. And, if they did, he must have been a miracle of humor and tact to carry on when it was over.

It's probable that Marlo's private life is a mystery, even to Marlo. Perhaps there was so much room for "Daddy" that there was no place for anyone else.

CHAPTER 36
THE KIDNAPPED ROLLS ROYCE

Snowball was my darling. She cost me a year's salary but she was a gleaming ivory, with a voluptuously rounded rear and a beautiful long hood, ending in the winged lady and the famous Rolls Royce radiator. Inside she was all natural leather, burled walnut panels, and tea trays, silver knobs, and handles. She smelled like a fine saddle, and her seats were cozy divans.

I didn't mind how many kids piled into her, but no sand, wet suits, or animals with sharp claws.

We had eight happy years together. She got 13 miles to the gallon on good days and had a quiet purring power that made noisy fast-backs slow down in awe. She also saved my life one winter night when a car sped through a stop light and sliced off her front end, without even turning us sideways. She was a tough old girl, my Silver Cloud Snowball.

Our relationship was seldom marred before the final tragedy, except by the rising cost of her upkeep. I finally realized I was working to support her. There were minor annoyances such as friends who asked us to dine and then hinted slyly we should "come early and park right out in front." Or the hassle with parking lot attendants when I insisted on parking and locking her myself—two yards from the nearest car. Or the suspicion that, when we arrived in Snowball, the price of everything went up.

But they were jolly years. I remember when I first got her, I drove into Hancock Park (a kind of millionaires' section of Los Angeles) with a Kennedy sticker on her front bumper. Suddenly there was a swarm of 10-year-olds dancing around us in a rage, screaming, "Democrat, Go Home!"

Snowball made it fun to ignore signs such as "Executive Parking Lot" or "Reserved for Press." I could park anywhere and her shining dignity made us immune to the customary traffic tickets. Instead of "Getoutta here!" it was "Would you mind pulling up a little, we're expecting the Chief any moment."

The last day I saw her, there was a bill for a new muffler assembly (chrome pipes from London); the lighter no longer worked, and she had a bad cough in her ignition.

This particular morning I parked in front of the *That Girl* stage and emptied the trunk of my wardrobe for the day's shooting. As I started Snowball to return her to the parking lot, she wheezed and sputtered into a low roar.

Just then a grip from our company strolled out of the stage and said, "I'll park the Rolls for you, Miss DeCamp, if you like."

It seemed a good idea, as I was late. Then I said, "By the way, the lighter doesn't work. Do you know anyone who can fix it?" Why I said that I don't know. Maybe I thought he was an electrician. Anyway, he took the car and later that afternoon brought me back the keys, saying, "It's all OK." I reached for my checkbook, but he said, "Oh, no. I was glad to do it... but... I wonder... could I just take my wife out to dinner in it? She's never even seen a Rolls Royce."

I said I was sorry but I would have no way to get back to Redondo Beach that night.

He looked very sad, then said, "Maybe you could take my Lincoln Continental. It's out in the parking lot."

I hesitated... but not long enough. The assistant yelled, "Places!" and I went into the scene, nodding to the grip, "I guess so, we'll talk later."

After the scene, he was so exuberantly grateful I didn't seem to have the energy or guts to say "No." He handed me his keys and disappeared.

About seven o'clock I found the Continental in an empty parking lot. No sign of Snowball. On my way home it occurred to me it was Friday night and that this heavy old car and I were to spend the weekend together. The trunk rattled and it steered like a truck.

The next evening the grip called with these grim words, "Uh, Miss DeCamp... I don't know how to tell you this... but... uh... your car was sideswiped last night. It was just parked... outside the restaurant. I have no way of knowing who did it, but don't worry. I know a good body man and I'll have it ready in two or three days... as good as new."

What to say? I mumbled something, and he said, "How's the Continental doing? OK?"

It wasn't OK. It was old and had been mistreated, and it slurped up gas like a thirsty rhino at a water hole. I grudgingly admitted that it was adequate for transportation. Then he asked about insurance and I told him I assumed we had the same coverage we had always had, and hung up to think over the week ahead.

I was not in the next show so apparently was stuck with the "truck" for domestic errands. Some sad facts began to trickle in on Monday. My husband remembered he had not renewed insurance for the Rolls except for public liability. "Oh well," I thought, "that grip is liable for the repairs."

But Monday evening I got a disturbing phone call. The voice was that of a young woman telling me she was the owner of the Continental, that she was the divorced wife of our friendly grip, that she needed her car as she was working eight-to-five and driving a friend's Volkswagen.

I felt like a fly in a giant web.

My suggestion that she get hold of the grip brought sobs and recriminations. I finally said, "Your Continental is the only grip I've got on YOUR grip... and my Rolls... and I'm going to keep it till I get my car back!"

Then her mother got into this soap opera. She read me off bitterly until I finally convinced her we had a common enemy—Mr. Grip. That, it seemed, was familiar ground and she promised to wait.

The next call from El Grippo was worse. Now he has what he classified as "bad news." The Rolls had been "creamed" while awaiting repairs outside the body shop.

Ah ha! Then I began to suspect that all was not chance. All was not accident. There seemed to be a plan.

Since I lacked insurance for the now enormous cost of repairs, he proposed that I appear at the "hospital" (or maybe even "mortuary") where Snowball was resting. There Mr. Grip indicated that they would purchase her remains and he would "work the rest of his life to pay it off."

I did not break into sobs at this prophecy because the pattern of his involvement was beginning to look very suspect.

My husband and I made the trip to Santa Monica where the "body shop-foreign car-used car" sales office was located.

The agate-eyed owner of the establishment gave a Nixonian display of regret at our bereavement and ended with an offer of a few hundred dollars for Snowball's remains.

We asked to see the body.

The salesman-owner turned on the violins and throbbed, "Ah, Miss DeCamp, we had to farm it out for structural repairs. Your car is now in Van Nuys being put back together."

My husband looked at me knowingly and said, "Well, that's a long way, but we can go right over now and see it if you'll give us the address."

As I expected, old marble-eyes looked at his watch, pursed his lips, and said sadly, "Ahhh, I'm afraid they are closed. It's six o'clock."

I thought of that ugly rape quote, "... relax and enjoy it" and got mad enough to look that bandit in the eye and say, "You will pay us $5,000.00 right now, or we will take you to court for... for kidnapping my car! And remember, my husband's a judge... so we have a built-in lawyer....and we'll see that you spend lots of days sitting around waiting for... for an adverse judgment!"

This was not only highly unethical, it was pure fiction. I could see John squirm; his philosophy being "Happiness is not suing or being sued by anyone... ever."

Now the bandit-owner was equally uncomfortable. He moaned and fussed and played both organ and violins decrying our cynical attitude. Finally he wrote out a check and we left. I couldn't resist a backward look at the used car lot behind the office where I could see a half-dozen foreign cars being dismantled or refinished.

I wondered if Snowball had been painted pink or zebra, or if they knew about her chronic ailments. Certainly they knew her charms, or they would not have gone to so much trouble to sneak her away.

It was "Good-bye and God Bless," but it was also a freedom from expenses that could only proliferate beyond reason.

Two days later I faced returning to the show. My husband was sensible about the whole thing saying, "Now when you get there, don't mention what happened. Take your loss and forget it."

Of course, he was right. There was nothing I could do anyway, and whining about it would simply reveal how stupid and naïve I had been. Besides, no one connected with Marlo's company had any knowledge of the car-napping operation, save the grip, who was around as usual. He would salute me, assuming an instant look of melancholy to preserve the myth that he was working out the car's cost. Anyway, I had not a shred of evidence to prove his conspiracy.

Perhaps if I had protested, it would have warned the next victim. But, without tangible proof, anything I said would have been construed as either libel or publicity seeking. The result was that I bought a nice anonymous coupe and resolved to forget Snowball.

But I still have friends who say, "Where's your Rolls?" They may not remember any of my ROLES, but they can't forget old Snowball.

CHAPTER 37
THE PLEASURE
OF YOUR COMPANY

"The pleasure of your company" is a quaint and charming phrase that I feel belongs especially to actors. We are often lonely, seeking souls; homeless in the psychological sense, with a need for a family, a coven. The big studios, in the old days, created that company. They became substitute families and gave actors a feeling of belonging.

When television first took over, it created the same neo-family. The great comedy shows were companies using continuous casts. The series did the same thing, and some still do—like the old stock companies in the theater. The director, assistants, and crew remained constant week after week. But gradually the pressure of rising production costs made speed the factor of success. The broadcasting cronies became giant stores with bits of stories stocked here and there on the shelves.

The framework remained recognizable. A star was continuous, with a few surrounding faces appearing regularly, telling a different story every week. But directors found the preparation, editing, and shooting schedules too grueling to stay with a show steadily, so they were hired by the week, or the show.

Director-plus-star more than any other formula makes a company. When you have only a star with a different cast of principals every few days, the company does not exist. The star has too much on his mind to be the paterfamilias, or even to become acquainted with the other actors. It all goes too fast for any satisfying relationship.

The exceptions were the great continuing shows like *Barney Miller*, *All in the Family*, *The Waltons*, and a few others where the characters were so strong and beloved that rotating directors, writers, and even producers could not erode the company.

I had lucky experiences in several series, and then my career became a long "do-si-do of guest shots, as they are aptly called, for it is "shoot and fall back."

Death Valley Days was an example. I was doing the commercials for the show, although I starred in only four episodes. The stories were valid, even documented, having been collected by Ruth Woodman Knight for years throughout

The Rockford Files in 1974 as Mary Ramsey with James Garner

the Southwest. The shooting schedules were cheap and fast, three days to a segment, all done on location. The cast and director were different for each episode. The final cut had a host—Robert Taylor, Ronald Reagan, John Payne, or Cliff Robertson (the original Old Ranger was played by Stanley Andrews)—who filmed their lines from a TelePrompTer in a studio far from the action. There was no sense of belonging, or even responsibility for quality. We did them as quickly as possible, packed up and went home, often unacquainted with more than the first name of the director or hairdresser.

The hour shows had a little more stability. Mike Connors of *Mannix* had the warmth and good manners of a real host. He talked to his casts, was concerned and available. Jim Garner of *Rockford Files* made everyone on his shows feel a part of them. He is one of the nicest men who ever put on greasepaint.

The number of parts I've played in the past 20 years is too long to enumerate. I will try to give you an idea of why I eventually felt like a marble in a pinball machine, utterly manipulated without any joy or creativity.

My visual image had now reached a vague plateau of "young grandma," but too old for "Mom"; my face showed the erosion of time, though my hair was not yet white. So the roles I was assigned were not stereotypes. In TV there is so little time. The viewer's eye must know instantly by the face and body what is its relationship to the story. There is no time for discovery. Consequently, not looking like any recognizable category, I became a floater, guesting here and there in all kinds of comedies and dramas.

There is a jumping-off-the-cliff time seldom discussed in acting for the camera. That is probably because those who work in front of "the eye" regularly are so accustomed to the practice it would not occur to them to point it out. As for those who come to the edge of the cliff unprepared, they must be too terrified to talk.

This nadir usually confronts a TV film actor at eight a.m. when he has not yet met the cast, director, or cameraman. The set is lit only by work lights. The crew, fellow actors, and assistants stand around watching. It's a colder audience than the corner pool room. The director says, "All right, you," pointing to the newcomer. "You come through that door and start the scene." Then the actor begins to talk, or walk, or whatever his script says to do, which he knew so well at home. The cameraman watches, everyone watches, while the whole scene is played. And believe me how it is played will determine whether that actor gets good attention from the camera—close-ups or even two-shots. If the actor stumbles, mumbles, or bores the watchers, he will get short shrift on the lighting and set-ups covering the scene. This practice is necessary because the cameraman has to know where to put his camera during the entire scene, though it seems to the newcomer like deliberate torture.

I doubt if any other experience in the world of acting is this rough. In the theater, for example, an actor is led quietly from a sit-down reading, through rehearsals, holding his script, up to a complete dress rehearsal, by which time he should know all the moves, his fellow actors, the props, and "business."

So when theater people make fun of the film techniques doing a few lines at a time for a camera shot, I always wonder how they would get through that first confrontation.

As TV costs mounted, less and less rehearsal time was allotted. Playing a guest shot on a continuing show means many little discomfitures. A day or so before shooting you bring in your own "wardrobe" to the wardrobe mistress assigned to you. Five or six alternatives for two or three changes are minimal. She will look at them and select what you will wear, dismissing the rejects with, "This is too bright," "This cameraman hates yellow," "No checks," "You can't wear this because So-and-So is already wearing pink," "Red is out!" "Of course, I'll buy you something for Change One when I shop today." These last words are scary because you suspect it will not fit and that it will be a horrid puce color and not your own taste; still, you have to be agreeable. You are only a guest in one segment. You are not running the show.

The first morning is usually an early call: 6:30 a.m. or 8:00 a.m. if you don't have "hair" before "make-up"—otherwise it will be 6:00 a.m. No one else is around. The coffee is not made. The stage is a vast, dark cavern. When the make-up man arrives, he has had a fight with his wife, or boyfriend. You tact-

Reunited with Ray Bolger in *The Partridge Family* in "The Forty Year Itch"

fully suggest a shadow for your jowls which he usually ignores, though some of them are friendly wizards who make you look far better than you deserve. He gives you a final swat with a powder puff and sends you to the hairdresser who tells you she will find you later. You wander off in search of your trailer, or dressing room, in which is hung the new dress you will wear. It is usually adequate because the wardrobe lady is the "good witch of the West," knows her business, and will not knowingly do you in, unless you have been ugly to her.

You now wait hours, sometimes falling asleep and wrecking your make-up. Eventually you are called for your scenes and go through the jumping-off-the-cliff period I have just described. The rest of the day is a long series of waits, alternating with short moments of concentration when the camera is rolling.

The guest shot usually runs three or four days, after which you go home and forget it until six or eight weeks later when someone says, "Oh, I saw you last night on *Love Boat*, *Rockford Files*, *Police Story*, *Night Gallery*, *Love American Style*, and so on into re-runs and re-runs of re-runs.

A TV series I especially enjoyed being involved with was *The Partridge Family*. It holds memories of lovely Shirley Jones, whose mother I played, and her brood of talented and appealing children.

Shirley is the loveliest, calmest movie star I have ever encountered. She helped create a world of fame for David Cassidy, her stepson, and went on for over five years with that series. She did not need those long hours or all the confusion inherent in her five days a week production schedule. But she did it

Gordon Jump, Danny Bonaduce, Ray Bolger, me, Susan Dey, David Cassidy, Suzanne Crough, and Shirley Jones in *The Partridge Family* **"The Mod Father" (Courtesy Photofest)**

graciously, in at six o'clock every morning, never demanding special consideration, even putting her own star status second to the show, and always pushing the youngsters forward for more recognition.

David Cassidy became such a star the last few years of that show that it was difficult to get through the gate at Columbia Ranch because of the fans, three deep, at all hours.

During this time I was privileged to enjoy Ray Bolger as my husband and fellow grandparent. He was delightful and quixotic. It was especially fun to play a grandmother since I had recently become one. But it was Shirley Jones who made it a true family.

The list of shows, over the past 20 years, in which I've taken part is only interesting because the names are familiar. I had no involvement in their success or mediocrity. They were all segments, and I was only a fragment within a segment.

As Aunt Helen in *Petticoat Junction* with Edgar Buchanan as Uncle Joe

For me the days of the sheltering company—the great old studios, as well as the togetherness of series such as *The Bob Cummings Show*, *The Beverly Hillbillies*, *Petticoat Junction*, and *That Girl* make the present method of television seem a jigsaw clutter of bits and pieces with no sense of continuity and very little pride in the creation of character.

Several years ago, I worked on a small part in *Blind Ambition* with some fine actors and one of film's great directors, George Schaeffer. He had prepared the little scenes with exquisite care and imagination to reveal a few moments of human pain and joy. But Schaeffer's art merely pointed up the bleakness of most TV experiences and left me longing for the pleasure of "the company."

CHAPTER 38
HOW DO YOU LIKE THE MOVIES NOW?

"What do you think of today's movies... hmmmm?"

This is an opening line I often get from certain sleeve-plucking acquaintances who, I suspect, are hoping for a diatribe or at least a few expletives comparing the old days with the now days. I consistently answer with one word.

"Fascinating!"

This allows them to express their views, which is probably what they wanted in the first place. As they vilify violence, sex, and vulgarity, half of my mind muses on the wonderful films I have seen in recent years. Some memorable ones are *Rocky*, *Turning Point*, *Julia*, *A Special Day*, *Star Wars*, *Small Change*, *Annie Hall*, *Interiors*, *Coming Home*, *Jesus of Nazareth*, and on and on. I refrain from saying, "You choose what you want to see. You pay your money. If you want sex and violence, go on in. But don't blame the filmmaker. He panders to your taste and gives you what you are willing to pay for."

As my 10-year-old friend, Heidi, says, "I'm taking only beautiful pictures with my eyes." We keep the film vaults. What we put in them is what we are, and we can play anything again whenever we wish. Call the Projectionist! "Roll it!"

The camera has become a searching, subjective analyst. In the hands of some very creative people it enriches the viewer and deepens our understanding of ourselves and of mankind.

But the material is not always as good as the instrument. I long for more joy, more celebration of human courage. Consequently, I skip pictures which dwell on cruelty, perversions, or satanic plots and practices. Our family believed that old saying, "Don't mess wit de devil, cuz he'll rub off on you."

The actual technique of filming a story has changed a good deal since the stationary camera of pre-Griffith days. After D.W. invented the close-up it took only a decade or two for directors to overdo it. Close-ups were punched in like stereopticon slides long before films achieved the flowing grace we see today in the style of Fred Zinneman.

There was a rough period, before live TV's use of two and three cameras helped create that modern flow. The director would shoot a master shot of a scene—with the camera back—to catch everyone involved. Then he would shoot everyone on one side of the room, or set—two-shots, over shoulders, close-ups, and all, because that side of the room was "lit." The lighting takes time, and time is expensive. When one side was done, he would reverse camera and shoot the other side of the set and everybody over there.

This is still the simplest way to "cover" a scene and not leave out any action or reaction. But it doesn't have any flow. The tempo will be determined in the cutting room with shears, and that tends to create a staccato effect. Also, this method is tough on the actor.

Imagine that you are playing a romantic scene and you say, "I love you!" on one side of a room. Then maybe two hours later the object of your affections on the other side says, "You do?" Well, you can see there is a lot of lag, and maybe sag, in there. It's been a long time. By this time "You-do?" is tired and out of the mood. And maybe it's six o'clock and "I love you" has gone home.

This period produced some flat, dull pictures with predictable editing. Fortunately this cut-and-dried shooting is seldom done now. The camera moves and catches the action as it takes place.

Today nothing is sacred. The camera invades our minds and our emotions, even our bowels, and is said to be working on the soul. Television technique, directors, and cameramen, modern lenses, and mobile cameras all share responsibility for much of this skill and beauty perception.

But commercial television is going to present a bill to this generation that may bankrupt us, and from which we may never recover. I am not referring to the CONTENT of TV. I mean the TIME CONDITIONING.

For instance, if you empty your bladder every 10 minutes, it won't be long before that old bladder is going to demand relief every 10 minutes. If you are allowed to pay attention to only five minutes of a story, and then your eyes and ears receive three to six 30-second separate messages, then your mind is taken back to the story for another five minutes—then into the same cycle repeated over and over—your mind, like your bladder, will be emptied at increasingly shorter intervals.

How can a child think an idea through to a conclusion when subjected to this kind of conditioning? A child indeed! How can any of us survive this rapidly scheduled "interruptus" for even an hour or so a day? We are Pavlov's dog salivating on cues that seem to come faster and faster.

Talk shows have contrived instant help for every householder with time to listen. Sometimes they tell us more than we wish to know, but they have provided an antidote for "cabin fever" by giving their audiences an astounding awareness of contemporary opinion, gossip, and merchandise.

Originally, I suspect, the format was a device for filling time economically with one salaried wit asking provocative, or even insulting, questions of any victim who could be persuaded to submit. Jack Paar, I believe, was the popular pioneer and possessed a delightfully inventive and original mind.

When I was on the Screen Actors Guild Board, I remember that we censured the practice of appearing on talk and game shows because "we would be competing with our own theater or TV assignments." Besides, these "talk" appearances build a show for the network with a big name cast for minimum pay. Cheap!

Now, however, talk shows have become a useful tool for actors, as well as politicians, and publicity seekers of all kinds, who use them for personal promotion, or for a movie, or for a book. As entertainment, these programs are chancy—a thousand monkeys at a thousand typewriters who will eventually produce a book. Combine enough well-known faces and one ringmaster and maybe you'll get a circus.

Merv Griffin was one of the thoughtful and witty interviewers, but some of the others seem to have a very high "I" index and appear to be fretting about their next victim, instead of listening to the one they have snared. (These remarks will surely be censored. But I've said it and I'm glad.)

Television has become everyone's target, but the tube itself is innocent. Its masters are the whoremongers. The miracle of transmission so outshines its use that it is a temptation to damn the whole thing.

But without TV we would have missed Steve Allen's *Meeting of the Minds*, Sir Kenneth Clark's *Civilization*, and a lot of great British acting which for me is the best in the world. We would not have been able to see the great Shakespeare series, the fine Edwardian biographies, and might not have been able to see the entire Zefferelli *Jesus of Nazareth* (in my opinion the ultimate in film art).

Television is potentially a One World-maker and I think that is only philosophically desirable. It communicates too much. Too much is said. Every idea is picked over and stale before it is fully understood. Besides, TV is dangerously instructive. There are many crimes and violent acts we would like to be spared. I don't want to know how to give myself a heroin fix, or what it is like to be raped, or what Idi Amin is doing, or vow to shoot to kill, and so on ad nauseam.

Inevitably, television will rule our minds—level our speech patterns—and clone all culture. I enjoy the certainty of missing that, but it was exciting to be in at the beginning.

CHAPTER 39
GOOD-BYE AND DON'T CRY

As each of our four daughters reached adolescence I made the painful discovery that "Mom" seemed often in the way. I became the No No Lady, The Fun Chopper, The Pits, frequent victim of such dialogue as:

"So I was late. So I was having fun. So what?"

"Nobody wears that stuff anymore. That's yuuuhkk!"

"I don't talk because I've got nothing to say. OK?"

"Please, just leave me alone!"

From Child Psychology courses I knew this was normal, but it hurt anyway. Now it was John saying, "Don't cry, Mom. They'll outgrow it."

Maybe guilt was mingled with my self-pity because I had not been with them constantly. I had never really had enough of them. They are wonderfully bright and pretty, so their reaching this turning point bewildered me.

I would literally run after them and beg, even bribe for their attention and affection. Nothing worked. They were just contemptuous of a mother who clung. I tried to remember whether I had acted that way toward my mother. Probably—but I had been on a much tighter leash, and rebellion then had been unthinkable.

It must be much worse for mothers who have no husbands to assuage those rejections. That would be very lonely. John was a kind and protective partner during those years. But he was secure in his work and became more and more important to the public he served, where-as I began to have ambivalent feelings about my career. I worked steadily but without any real delight. There were many guest spots and I traveled thousands of miles for the U.S. Borax company but it began to seem repetitive and purposeless—as if I were playing the same scene over and over.

Our daughters serenade us at our 50th anniversary party.

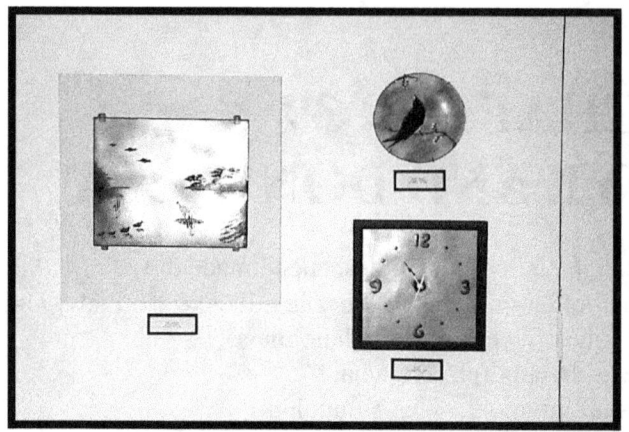

Some of my prize-winning copper enamels

Then a surprising thing happened. I fell in love with the ancient Oriental art of copper enameling. It had such magnetic appeal that I spent all my free daylight hours working with two fine enamelists, Mel and Fran Harrison, then I'd dream in copper at night.

I worked at their studio for five years before getting my own. It was an old tool shed in some pine trees near our swimming pool. The big kiln was wired in next to a wide table covered with marble (to hold the hot pieces while they cool). I covered the stone floor with old rug scraps, whitewashed the walls, nailed a big copper dragon on the door and lo! here was my fairy tale "hut in the forest." Here I could hammer and heat and glaze beautiful bowls and plaques that would outlive anything I had ever done before.

The years of study and the love of the craft paid off in some modest prizes and several exhibitions—a beautiful, big show at the Los Angeles Museum of Science and Industry, a show at CBS, one at the Joslyn Center in Torrance, another at The Cloisters in Georgia for the International Ceramics Institute, and many lecture exhibits in Hollywood, Palm Springs, and one at the Beverly Hills Hotel for Bob Coleman's A.I.D. convention.

The CBS Building, which displayed my art in 1970

Creating something that will last, with your own hands, is emotionally very satisfying. Everything else I have ever done seems as ephemeral as the wind, but a piece of enameled copper, barring a direct hit, or a "melt-down," will be around for thousands of years. That may be only the blink of a bird's eye in eternity, but possibly more durable than 40 years of shadows on film.

I was lucky to have found a satisfying escape from clinging. Mom in "the studio" was more respected than Mom at our children's heels begging to be a part of everything they did. Now they have grown up to be John's and my best friends. They barely remember the Rejection Period and love to come back to the old house for all the recurring birthdays and anniversaries. The things they remember about their early years are amazing to John and me—they are so different and so dear.

One day Margaret, the eldest, brought her son and my grandson, Vahid Zambrano, home. A macho little boy with shy eyes and a sweet, secret smile, he spoke with the voice of Jimmy Durante, shocking all grown ups. He acquired the name "John" after his grandfather, but at that time we called him "Va."

While he was here, we discovered a mutual interest in nursery rhymes. He recited "Jack and Jill" very well. Although he would rather have read about trucks and spaceships, we discussed "Little Red Riding Hood" (probably nearsighted), and "Goldilocks" (a trespasser deserving of a good fright) and *Aesop's Fables*. He loved Chicken Little, Turkey Lurkey, Foxy Loxy, and Ducky Lucky. He looked askance when the little Red Hen found no one to help bake her bread and thus became a shrew, laboring alone.

However, interest perked with "The Three Little Pigs!" There was a tale! I have great affinity for that one although it may be responsible for my worst habits.

If the Smart Little Pig hadn't been so successful, if the other two pigs had been more cautious and had built sturdier houses, then, it is comforting for me to believe, I would not be so compulsive.

Since the First and Second Little Pigs each planned and failed to secure their Houses against the Big Bad Wolf, the message is clear: You have to do it *exactly* right.

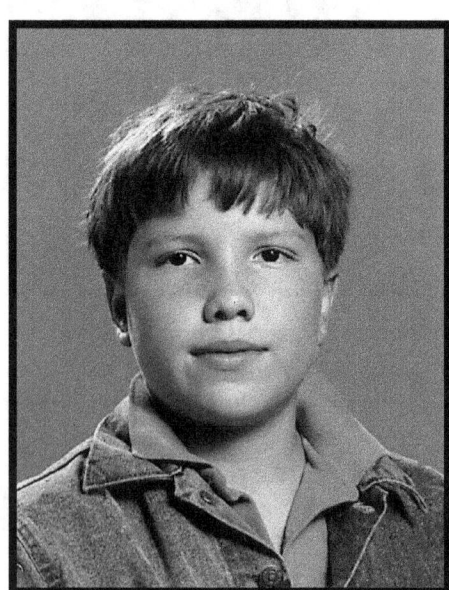

My grandson John

And being on time is not enough. You have to arrive *early*. The two unlucky pigs were on time, weren't they? Did it help them? No. Moral: If the wolf says, "Meetcha at eight a.m.," then you get up at six a. m. and outwit him.

The Third Little Pig was smart and knew what a great huffer and puffer the wolf was, so his house had to be really solid. Yes, sir! Bricks! But that was *still not enough*. After all the huffing and puffing, the wolf would discover he couldn't blow the house down. Now, what would he do?

Ahhh hah! The next step. Plan ahead. Put yourself in the head of the wolf. What would he *do*? Why, he'd try to climb down the chimney, of course! So, place a pot of boiling water under

With my daughters at my 86th birthday party, Thanksgiving 1996

the chimney. It works! Wolf climbs down chimney and lands in the soup! Success!

The Smart Little Pig syndrome has made me a clock-watcher, a restless and overzealous planner, a hostess who gets dinner on too soon, too hot. A chauffeur who is outside honking 10 minutes early. An actress who arrives for the interview before the office is open. All this I blame on the Smart Little Pig.

After Vahid and I acted out the whole story (he played the wolf, of course), I asked him, "Don't you think I'm kind of like the Smart Little Pig? You know, kind of overdoing things... too much of this... too much of that... ?"

He patted my arm lovingly and croaked, "Oh, no, Gramma. You're the Little Red Hen."

Before he returned home, he said, "Grandma, the gardener wrecked my garage with his mower."

I made appropriate sounds of regret, remembering my ranch ruined so long ago and feeling a surge of anger at the damage.

"Just tell him to be careful, Grandma. I can get another truck, but he oughta watch where he's going."

Indeed. I was lost in admiration of his calm reasoning.

He looked at the door of my hut with its copper emblem.

"Grandma, what's behind the dragon?"

"It's dark and hot in there and the dragon hates strangers. When you come to visit me next time, you will be bigger. I will take you safely past the dragon and into my other kingdom."

He looked off at the sky. "I don't want to go away."
I put my arms around his solid little body, "And I don't want you to go."
His mother called from the driveway.
With a small square hand he patted my cheek, "Don't cry, Grandma."
He ran toward the gate and looked around, "Bye—I'll be back."
He looked off at the sky. "I don't want to go away."
I put my arms around his solid little body, "And I don't want you to go."
His mother called from the driveway.
With a small square hand he patted my cheek, "Don't cry, Grandma."
He ran toward the gate and looked around, "Bye—I'll be back."
He looked off at the sky. "I don't want to go away."
I put my arms around his solid little body, "And I don't want you to go."
His mother called from the driveway.
With a small square hand he patted my cheek, "Don't cry, Grandma."
He ran toward the gate and looked around. "Bye—I'll be back."

CHAPTER 40
GHOSTS AT WARNER BROS.

My last day in front of a movie camera was so fair, there was no place for regrets. It was a lovely gazebo in *Murder, She Wrote*. The little scene went well. The cameraman gave me an "A-Okay" sign, I thanked beloved Angela Lansbury and signaled the company driver I was ready to ride back to Universal for my car. He was young and movie struck, and said, "Miss DeCamp, you used to be at Warners, didn't you?" "Oh, yes. Sometimes in two or three films at a time." He said, "The lot's closed down now, but we could drive around through there if you like."

We entered a kind of Ray Bradbury scene of great soundstages lining empty streets. The boy pointed to the gym and he said, "There's where Burt Lancaster practiced his circus stunts for *Trapeze*." Next to it was the big musical stage. I thought I could hear Irving Berlin's reedy voice singing, "This is the Army, Mr. Jones! No private rooms or telephones." And then, behind him in memory, was luscious Frances Langford belting out, "It's the Last Time," for the last time.

Behind the huge stage was a recording studio where Oscar Levant was furiously impersonating George Gershwin playing "Rhapsody in Blue." We turned a corner and there was the make-up building, Perc Westmore's Petite Trianon. I remembered him showing me the six blond wigs that Marion Davies wore. He rotated them carefully by order of William Randolph Hearst, two going, two coming, and two shampooing. We all spent a lot of hours in that building, but now it looked so shabby, windows barred and dirty.

My driver said, "Right there is the stage where they made those *Moon* pictures with Doris Day and Gordon MacRae." Ah, if I could only hear those beautiful voices blending in "Shine On, Harvest Moon." As we moved on, the streets seemed shockingly empty. No trucks, bicycles, crews. No Bogie, no Bacall, Bette Davis, or Joan Leslie. Just vacant alleys like wind tunnels. When we neared the big gate, the boy said, "Hey, there's the big stage where they made *Yankee Doodle Dandy*. Remember that?" Oh, yes, indeed. He went on. "Sometimes when we work at night, you know, I drive by here and I can hear a band playing, "It's a Grand Old Flag," and then, you know, if it's quiet, I can hear Cagney's feet tapping out that rhythm, 'It's a grand old flag, it's a high-flying flag.' Spooky, huh?"

I thanked him for the tour, thinking it was a fine end to all those years in the dream factory. Now I can say good-bye with nostalgia and no regrets. And thank you, for staying with me through those crazy years.

Publisher's Note

Rosemary DeCamp passed away February 20, 2001 from complications from pneumonia. She did get to see her biography published by Midnight Marquee Press, Inc. in October 2000.

She is survived by her four daughters and grandchildren.

Michael G. Fitzgerald, film historian and writer, who helped Rosemary with the book passed away February 14, 2006.

FILMOGRAPHY

FEATURE FILMS

Cheers for Miss Bishop (United Artists, 1941)
Hold Back the Dawn (Paramount, 1941)
Commandos Strike at Dawn (Columbia, 1942)
Smith of Minnesota (Columbia, 1942)
Jungle Book (United Artists, 1942)
Yankee Doodle Dandy (Warner Bros., 1942)
Eyes in the Night (MGM, 1942)
This is the Army (Warner Bros., 1943)
City Without Men (Columbia, 1943)
Practically Yours (Paramount, 1944)
The Merry Monahans (Universal, 1944)
Bowery to Broadway (Universal, 1944)
Pride of the Marines (Warner Bros., 1945)
Weekend at the Waldorf (MGM, 1945)
Danger Signal (Warner Bros., 1945)
Rhapsody in Blue (Warner Bros., 1945)
Blood on the Sun (United Artists, 1945)
To Young to Know (Warner Bros., 1945)
From This Day Forward (RKO-Radio, 1946)
Two Guys from Milwaukee (Warner Bros., 1946)
Nora Prentiss (Warner Bros., 1947)
Night Unto Night (Warner Bros. filmed in 1947, released in 1949)
The Story of Seabiscuit (Warner Bros., 1949)
Look for the Silver Lining (Warner Bros., 1949)
The Life of Riley (Universal-International, 1949)
The Big Hangover (MGM, 1950)
Night into Morning (MGM, 1951)
Treasure of Lost Canyon (Universal-International, 1951)
On Moonlight Bay (Warner Bros., 1951)
Scandal Sheet (Columbia, 1952)
By the Light of the Silvery Moon (Warner Bros., 1953)
Main Street to Broadway (MGM, 1953)
So This is Love (Warner Bros., 1953)
Many Rivers to Cross (MGM, 1954)
Strategic Air Command (Paramount, 1955)

13 Ghosts (Columbia, 1960)
Tora! Tora! Tora! (20th Century-Fox, 1970; scenes deleted)
Saturday the 14th (New World Pictures, 1981)

TV MOVIES
The Time Machine (1978)
Blind Ambition (1979)

RADIO
Dr. Christian (1937--1954)

TV (as a regular)
The Life of Riley" (1949-1950)
Death Valley Days (commercial spokeswoman, 1952-1977)
The Bob Cummings Show (aka Love That Bob) 1955-1959
The Baileys of Balboa (1964)
Petticoat Junction (1966)
That Girl (1966-1969)

TV (appearances)
Ford Theatre:
Madame .44 (1953)
Alias Nora Hale (1953)
Good of His Soul (1954)
Segment (1954)

Cavalcade Theatre
Nobody's Fool (1955)

TV Readers Digest
The Sad Death of a Hero (1955)
The Old, Old Story (1956)

Climax!
The 78th Floor (1956)

Studio One
Trial by Slander (1958)
No Place to Run (1958)

G.E. Theatre
Night Club (1959)

The Red Skeleton Show
Clem's Other Clem (1961)

87th Precinct
Killer's Payoff (1962)

Follow the Sun
Chalk One Up for Johnny (1962)

Rawhide
The House of the Hunter (1962)

Hazel
Hazel's Cousin (1962)

Ensign O'Toole
Operation Swindle (1962)

The Beverly Hillibillies
The Family Tree (1963)
Jed Cuts the Family Tree (1963)

The Breaking Point
A Little Anger is a Good Thing (1964)

The Littlest Hobo
You Can't Buy a Friend (1965)

Dr. Kildare
Music Hath Charms (1965)
Amos Burke, Secret Agent
Operation Long Shadow (1965)

Death Valley Days
Canary Harris vs. the Almighty (1967)

Love American Style
Love and the Other Love (1969)
Love and the Anniversary (1973)

The Partridge Family
Whatever Happened to the Old Songs? (1970)
The Forty-Year Itch (1971)
The Mod Father (1972)
Made in San Pueblo (1973)

Mannix
The Crime that Wasn't (1971)
Little Girl Lost (1973)

Night Gallery
The Painted Mirror (1971)

Longstreet
Long Way Home (1971)

Marcus Welby, M.D.
Dark corridors (1975)

The Rockford Files
Gearjammers (1975)

B.J. and the Bear
For Adults Only (1981)

Quincy
Whatever Happened to Morris Perlmutter (1983)

St. Elsewhere
A Room with a View (1986)

INDEX

13 Ghosts (1960) 163
Abel, Walter 139
Ace, Goodman 68, 70
Ace, Jane 70
Adventures of Ozzie and Harriett, The 186
Aesop 252
Albee, Edward 214, 223
Alda, Robert 11, 164-165
All Brides Are Beautiful (Working Title) 156
All in the Family 240
All Shook Up (Song) 192
Allen, Dusty 112
Allen, Gracie 70
Allen, Steve 248
Allen, Woody 32
Allgood, Sara 170
Allyson, June 169
Ames, Leon 140, 164, 174-176
Amoco 54
Andrews, Stanley 241
Andy Griffith Show 235
Anna Christie 215
Annie Hall 246
Arch Obeler's Theater 83
Arms, Russell 174
Arnaz, Desi 144
Arness, James 163
Arnold, Danny 235
Arnold, Edward 112, 135, 163-164
Ashe, Warren 158
Astor, Mary 63
Atlantic Family, The 70, 71, 74
Ayres, N.W. 70
Bacall, Lauren 255
Ball, Lucille 141, 144-145
Barney Miller 235, 240
Barr, Robert 224
Barstow, Dorothy 71, 80-83
Bau, George and Gordon 98-99
Baylis, Madge 50
Beefeater (Dog) 22-24
Bell, Galt 56
Bell, James 169
Benchley, Robert 131
Bendix, William 177-179, 181-183,
Bennett, Bruce 167-168
Benny, Jack 190
Berg, Gertrude Molly 75

Berlin, Irving 165, 255
Berry, John 157-158
Bessell, Ted 232-233, 235
Beverly Hillbillies 195, 245
Bey, Turhan 128-12
Big Hangover (1950) 140, 164
Bixby, Bob 56
Blind Ambition 245
Blondell, Joan 85
Blood on the Sun (1945) 160
Blyth, Ann 11, 125-126, 128, 153, 167
Bob Cummings Show 11, 186-197, 245-246
Body and Soul (1946) 141, 144
Bogart, Humphrey 109, 255
Bolger, Ray 159, 243, 244
Bolton, Whitney 73
Bonaduce, Danny 244
Booth, Shirley 59
Bowery to Broadway (1944) 128-131, 159
Boyer, Charles 139-140
Boyle, Johnny 107
Bradbury, Ray 255
Brady Bunch 195
Brecher, Irving 177-178, 182-185
Bryan, Jack and Margaret 213
Brynner, Yul 88
Buchanan, Edgar 245
Burnett, Carol 233
Burns and Allen 186
Burns, George 186, 190
Burr, Ann 172
Bushman, Francis X. 174
Butler, David 173-176
By the Light of the Silvery Moon (1953) 174, 176, 186
Byington, Spring 131-132
Cagney, James 11, 104-107, 110, 153, 160, 255
Cagney, Jeanne 104-107
Calleia, Joseph 99-100
Calling All Cars 83
Cameo Theater 207
Cannon, Joan 91-92
Carey, Sr., Harry 39-40
Carney, Art 185
Carnovsky, Morris 164-165

Cash, Don 87
Cassidy, David 243-244
Castle, William 162
Cat on a Hot Tin Roof 141
Chaney, Sr., Lon 130
Cheers for Miss Bishop (1941) 86, 87, 95, 186
City Without Men (1943) 170
Civilization 248
Claire, Ina 60
Clark, Dane 142
Clark, Oliver 210
Clark, Sir Kenneth 248
Clurman, Harold 60
Cohan, George M. 65
Colbert, Claudette 139-140
Coleman, Bob 251
Colman, Ronald 146
Coming Home 246
Commandoes Strike at Dawn (1942) 113, 114, 115, 156, 170-171
Conchita 40
Connors, Mike 241
Cook, Donald 128
Cornthwaite, Robert 228
Cowan, Jerome 98-100
Cowan, Lester 113
Crawford, Broderick 160-161, 172
Crosby, Bing 43
Crough, Suzanne 244
Crump, Oliver 171
Cugat, Xavier 135
Cummings, E.E. 214
Cummings, Mary (Elliott) 188, 194
Cummings, Robert 186-195
Cunningham, Imogene 45
Curtiz, Michael 105, 109-110, 165
Da Pron, Louis 126-127
Dana, Viola 25
Danger Signal (1945) 167, 168, 171
Dante 40-41
Darnell, Linda 170
Daves, Delmar 143
Davies, Marion 85, 255
Davis, Ann B. 186, 189, 191-193, 195
Davis, Bette 255
Davis, Nancy (Reagan) 162

Day, Doris 8-9, 11, 153, 174-176, 255
De Camp, Elizabeth 49
De Camp, Jerry 41-42, 48-49, 52, 78-79, 93, 135, 147
De Camp, Mary Elizabeth JoJo Hinman 11, 16-17, 19, 21-25, 28, 31, 33, 36, 78-79, 82, 85, 90, 101, 103, 116-117, 120, 125, 132, 139, 146-149
De Camp, William Val 11, 16-17, 19, 21-24, 33-34, 36-40, 42, 45, 48-49, 52-53, 60, 73, 78-79, 90, 131, 132
De Havilland, Olivia 139-140
Death of a Salesman 213
Death Valley Days 71, 72, 84, 225, 228, 229-230, 240-241
DeGrafenreid, Tom 56
Deidre of the Sorrows 54
Denny, Reginald 164
dePew, Joe 186, 195
Desire Under the Elms 215
Devil and Daniel Webster (1941) 108
Dey, Susan 244
Dickinson, Angie 192
Dickinson, Emily 214
Dionne Quintuplets 80
Dobie Gillis 195
Dodsworth (1936) 108
Douglas, Helen Gahagan 113
Douglas, Mike 248
Dove, Billie 85
Doyle, Sir Arthur Conan 34
Dozier, William 157
Dr. Christian 55, 81, 82, 83, 84, 86, 88, 136, 155, 167, 177, 184
Durant, Will and Ariel 156
Durante, Jimmy 252
East is East 39
Easy Aces 70
Eddy, Nelson 146
Elephant Boy (1937) 98
Eleventh Hour 210
Elliott, Mary (Cummings) 188, 194
Emerson, Faye 167, 169
Emery, John 164
Emperor Jones 215-216
Eno's Crime Clues 70

Eyes in the Night (1942) 112, 163
Farrow, John 113-114
Farrow, Mia 114
Fennessy, Ruth 50
Ferber, Edna 60
Ferguson, Frank 56
Fielder, Ann 97-98
Fish 235
Fitzgerald, Barry 173
Fitzgerald, Michael 156
Fitzpatrick, Kathleen 56
Flannery, Walter 176
Florey, Robert 168
Fontaine, Joan 156-157
Ford Theater, 'Segment' 182
Forrest, William 173
Foster, Susanna 128-129
Four Daughters (1939) 141
Free to Be You and Me 233
Freeman, Mona 167
Frings, Ketti and Kurt 140
From This Day Forward (1946) 156, 157
Gagswell, Lionel 196-203
Garbo, Greta 90, 163
Gardner, Ava 138
Garfield, John 138, 141-144,
Garland, Judy 156
Garner, James 241
Garnett, Tay 86
Geer, Will 195
Gershwin, George 165, 255
Ghoury, Margaret 223
Gilmore, Art 82
Ginsberg, Col. George 148
Gish, Lillian 114
Glass Menagerie 214, 218, 223
Gleason, Jackie 182-185
Goddard, Paulette 139-140
Goldbergs 75
Golden Boy 141
Gomery Pyle, USMC 235
Goodman, Benny 71
Goodwin, Bill 179-182
Gordon, Max 60
Gordon, Shirley 193-194
Grand Hotel (1932) 80, 135
Grant, Cary 85
Gray, Billy 175,-176
Grayson, Kathryn 169
Greed 80
Green, Gilbert 228

Griffin, Merv 174, 248
Griffith, D.W. 246
Guilbert, Yvette 45
Guillaroff, Sidney 136
Gunsmoke 163
Hamilton, Margaret 163
Harding, Ann 164
Harris, Phil 44
Harris, Russell 215
Harris, Sam 59-61, 64-69, 73
Haver, June 11, 153, 159
Hays, Helen 70
Hearst, William Randolph 255
Hedda Hopper's Show 83
Heindorf, Ray 107, 108
Hendrix, Wanda 167
Henning, Paul 186, 192-195
Hepburn, Katharine 137
Herbert, Charles 163
Hersholt, Jean 80-82, 84, 86, 89, 155
Heydt, Louis Jean 114, 117
Hickman, Dwayne 11, 153, 186, 191, 192, 193, 195
Hitler 78
Hochscheild, Maurice 78
Hold Back the Dawn (1941) 95, 139, 140
Holden, Fay 140
Hollywood Hotel 83
Honeychile (Patricia Wilder) 71
Honeymooners 185
Hope, Bob 70-71
Hope, Dolores 71
Hornblow, Arthur 139
Horne, Victoria (Mrs. Jack Oakie) 127, 179
Howe, James Wong 168
Hughes, Howard 47-49
Humoresque (1946) 144
Huston, John 109
Huston, Walter 104-109
Hutton, Robert 153, 158-159, 167
I Love a Mystery 83
Interiors 246
"It's the Last Time" 251
Ivo, Tommy 133
Jack Benny Program 83
James, Allen 85
Jamil, Dr. Maya 215-216
Jean, Gloria 97
Jeffers, Robinson 47
Jefferson, Thomas 87
Jenkins, Allen 164
Jesus of Nazarath 246,

Johnson, Van 135, 137, 140-141, 164
Jones, Shirley 11, 163, 243-244
Julia 246
Jungle Book (1942) 11, 94-102, 113, 186, 224
Junk Man, The 223
Kaufman, George 60, 62-63
Kennedy, Jackie 222
Kennedy, John F. 113, 213, 215, 220, 222, 236
Kerr, Jack 225
Kipling, Rudyard 34-35, 94, 215, 218-221
Knickerbocker Holiday 108
Knight, Ruth Woodman 240
Koche, Frederick 40
Korda, Alexander 94, 100-102
Korda, Vincent 94, 100-101
Korda, Zoltan 94-95, 99-101
Krasna, Norman 141
Kulp, Nancy 189, 195
Kuster, Robert 47
Lamont, Charles 132
Lancaster, Burt 255
Landis, Jessie Royce 63
Langford, Frances 255
Lansbury, Angela 255
Lavin, Arnold 211, 212
Leisen, Mitchell 139-140
Leonard, Robert 136-137
Leslie, Joan 104-106, 158-159, 255
Let's Dance 71, 81
Levant, Oscar 165, 255
Liebling, Bill 60
Life of Riley (1949) 177-182
Life of Riley 183-185
Lindford, Viveca 160, 171-172
Lindsay, Vachel 218, 224
Lloyd, Harold 83
Lockhart, Gene 140
Long, Richard 178
Longfellow, Henry Wadsworth 214
Longstreet, Stephen 71
Look for the Silver Lining (1949) 159
Lorre, Peter 164
Love Boat 243
Love That Bob see: *The Bob Cummings Show*
Love, American Style 243
Lovett, Dorothy 84, 86
Lux Radio Theater 83
Mac Arthur, Douglas 110
Mac Bride, Donald 173
Mac Cleery, Albert 207-208

Mac Murray, Fred 139
MacRae, Gordon 9, 159, 174, 176, 255
Mallinson, Rory 141
Manhoff, Bill 193
Mannix 241
Maria Elena 139
Marion, Frances 109
Martin, Dean 156
Masters, Edgar Lee 214
Mayberry, RFD 235
Mayer, Louis B. 135
Mayor of the Town 185
Mc Cann, Dorothy 88, 225-226
Mc Cann, Harry K. 71-72, 83, 88
Mc Carthy, Joseph 144-145
Mc Dowell, Edward 207
Mc Dowell, Marion 207, 209
Mc Hugh, Frank 128-129, 132
Mc Kenna, Kenneth 63
McCallister, Lon 173
Meadows, Audrey 185
Meeting of the Minds 248
Melcher, Marty 174
Merman, Ethel 234
Merrily We Roll Along 60-63
Merry Monahans, The (1944) 125-127, 153
Milland, Ray 162
Millay, Edna St. Vincent 214, 223
Miller, Dick 225
Miller, Marilyn 63, 159
Millet, Bea 103
Millet, Bill 103
Milner, Martin 163
Minter, Mary Miles 17
Mix, Tom 39
Montez, Maria 128-129
Montgomery, George 194
Moore, Grace 169
Moore, Victor 83
Moorehead, Agnes 70
Moreland, Dean Helen 42
Morgan, Dennis 255
Morgan, Henry Harry 156
Morris, Phillip 145
Morrow, Jo 163
Morse, Carlton 53-54
Mourning Becomes Electra 215
Much Ado About Nothing 45
Muni, Paul 113-116, 156
Murder, She Wrote 255
Murphy, George 165-166
My World and Welcome to It 235
Neiulan, Mickey 46
Nelson, Barry 164

Night Gallery 85, 243
Night Into Morning (1951) 162
Night Unto Night (1949) 160, 171, 172
Nora Prentiss (1947) 159, 166, 167
O'Connell, Arthur 210-212
O'Connor, Donald 125-126, 128
O'Neill, Eugene 214-215
O'Sullivan, Maureen 113
Oakie, Jack 125-128, 130
Odetts, Clifford 156, 158
Odor of Violets, The 163,
Olivier, Sir Lawrence 225
Olsen, Moroni 142
On Moonlight Bay (1951) 8, 174, 175
Once in a Lifetime 60
One Man's Family 53, 54
One Thousand and One Nights 221
Our Town 86, 218, 223
Paar, Jack 248
Palmer, Maria 174
Parker, Eleanor 138
Parker, Lew 233-235
Partridge Family 243-245
Partridge, Roy 45
Payne, John 241
Petrified Forest 60
Petticoat Junction 195, 245
Phantom of the Opera (1925) 130
Phillips, Bill 207
Phillips, Edie 128
Pidgeon, Walter 135
Poe, Edgar Allan 214, 224
Police Story 243
Porter, Cole 234
Postman Always Rings Twice (1946) 141
Powell Dick 83, 85
Powell, William 133-134
Practically Yours (1944) 139, 140
Presley, Elvis 192
Pride of the Marines (1945) 138, 141, 142, 143, 144, 148
Private Secretary (aka *Susie*) 186
Provence, Charles 220
Puglia, Frank 99
Qualen, John 99
Raffetto, Mike 53
Rainer, Luise 158
Randall, Meg 177-178, 180
Rapper, Irving 165
Rea, Peggy 228
Reagan, Neil 152, 229

Reagan, Ronald 11, 153, 160, 166, 171-173, 241
Reed, Donna 164
Rees, Lanny 177-178, 181, 184
Rhapsody in Blue (1945) 164, 165
Rhythm Boys 43
Rice, Elmer 47
Robertson, Cliff 241
Robin Hood (1922) 98
Robinson, Edward Arlington 214
Rockford Files 241, 243
Rocky 246
Rogers, Ginger 135-138
Romer, Gene 191
Roosevelt, Elliott 168-169
Roosevelt, Franklin Delano 63, 105, 168-169
Rubin, Eddie 188
Rudley, Herbert 164-165
Ruggles, Charles 159
Ryan, Peggy 125, 126
Sabu 11, 96-101, 153, 224
Sally of the Star 83
Sandbox 214
Sandburg, Carl 214, 223
Santley, Joe 229-230
Sarg, Tony 59
Sarnoff 68
Scandal Sheet (1952) 160-161
Schaffer, George 245
Schuberts 60
Schultz, Dutch 65
Scott, Martha 86-87
Scott, Zachary 167
See Naples and Die 47
September Song 108
Serling, Rod 85
Shadow, The 70
Shakespeare, William 248
Sheridan, Ann 166
Shidler, Judge John 90-93, 96, 103, 111-114, 116-117, 120-121, 125, 135, 147-150, 154-155, 170, 184, 205-208, 210, 213, 215, 219-221, 249
Shidler, Fred 91
Shidler, Margaret Nana 116, 119-123, 135, 146, 150, 154, 205-206, 225, 249, 252-253
Shidler, Martha 120-123 154, 205,
Shidler, Mina Shy 103
Shidler, Nita 122, 123, 154, 155, 205-206, 225
Shidler, Valerie 121-123, 154, 205-206, 225

Shields, Arthur 159
Siegel, Bugsy 146
Siegel, Max 60
Small Change 248
Smith of Minnesota (1942) 158
Smith, Bruce 158
Smith, Kent 166
Smith, Mark 70
Snatch of Sliphorn Jazz 223
Snowden, Leigh 189
So Big 60
So This is Love (1953) 169
Special Day, A 246
Spoon River 223
Stallings, Lawrence 94
Stanislavsky 55
Star Wars 246
Stauffer, Dorothy 43
Steffens, Lincoln 53
Steiger, Rod 195
Stephens, Louise 51
Stevens, Connie 192
Stevens, Mark 156, 157
Stevenson, Adlai 176
Stewart, James 169
Stewart, Paul 68, 70
Story of Seabiscuit (1949) 173
Strange Interlude 215
Strategic Air Command (1955) 169
Sturgess, Olive 193
Sunday Morning Funnies 70
Sunny 63
Sunset Boulevard (1950) 225
Swanson, Gloria 225
Tarkington, Booth 174
Tattelman, Harry 113
Taylor, Elizabeth 141, 149, 164
Taylor, Robert 163, 241
Taylor, Terry 163
Taylor, Tessie 163
Temple, Shirley 173
Tetley, Walter 70
Tetzlaff, Ted 133
That Girl 229-235, 237, 245
Thaxter, Phyllis 135
The Drunkard 56-58
The Rose and the Ring 59
Theiss, Ursula 163
There Shall Be No Light 213-214
Thief of Bagdad (1940) 94

This is the Army (1943) 11, 166
This is the Army Mr. Jones 165, 255
Thomas, Danny 232
Thomas, John Charles 89

Thomas, Marlo 11, 153, 231-235, 239
Thomas, Rosemarie 233
Time Out for Ginger 213-214
Tojo 78
Too Young to Know (1945) 158-159, 167
Trapeze (1956) 255
Treasure of Lost Canyon (1951) 133, 134
Treasure of the Sierra Madre (1948) 109
Trilling, Steve 151-152
Troxler, Nora and Paul 219
Truman Tapes 195
Tucker, Sophie 63
Turner, Lana 135, 138
Turning Point 246
Tuttle, Bill 207
Twilight Zone, The 85
Universal Pictures 156
Urcan, Eleanor 155
Ustinov, Peter 195
Victoria Regina 60
Wagner, Jack 56
Wall, Geraldine 176
Waltons, The 240
Ward, Doris 79
Ward, Jack 79
Warner, Jack 169, 175
Warren, Earl 215
Washington, George 84
Watkin, Pierre 173
We've Got Each Other 210
Weekend at the Waldorf (1945) 135-137
Weissmuller, Johnny 85
Welles, Orson 70
Wendell, Howard 176
Wesson, Dick 193-194
Westmore, Ernie 16, 117
Westmore, Perc 207, 255
Westmores, The 117
"When I Take My Sugar to Tea" 44
Whitman, Walt 214
Wickes, Mary 9, 174-176
Wilde, Harry 190
Wilde, Lee 159
Wilde, Lyn 159
Wilder, Patricia 71
Wilder, Thornton 86, 223
Williams, Tennessee 214, 223

**If you enjoyed this book
call or e-mail for a free a catalog.
Midnight Marquee Press, Inc.,
9721 Britinay Lane,
Baltimore, MD 21234
410-665-1198
MMarquee@aol.com
visit our website at www.midmar.com**

www.ingramcontent.com/pod-product-compliance
Lightning Source LLC
Chambersburg PA
CBHW071227080526
44587CB00013BA/1520